THE COMPETITIVE ETHOS
AND DEMOCRATIC EDUCATION

The Competitive Ethos
and Democratic Education

John G. Nicholls

Harvard University Press
Cambridge, Massachusetts
London, England
1989

Library of Congress Cataloging-in-Publication Data

Nicholls, John G., 1940–
   The competitive ethos and democratic education.

   Bibliography: p.
   Includes index.
   1. Motivation in education. 2. Child development.
   3. Performance. 4. Achievement motivation in
   children. I. Title.
LB1065.N53   1988   370.15′4   88-16303
ISBN 0-674-15417-7 (alk. paper)

For Esther and Gordon, who bear some responsibility

Acknowledgments

To what can one attribute a book? In the case of this one, a study leave from Purdue University in 1986 provided the time for me to complete a first draft. The first version was improved as a result of comments by Thomas Berndt, Paul Cobb, John Keller, Martin Maehr, Arden Miller, and Theresa Thorkildsen. The publisher's reviewers stimulated further reading, reflection, and writing, and the editors at Harvard University Press offered valuable suggestions. Throughout it all, Jill Brady patiently kept track of the accumulations and transformations in her word processor.

To take someone's ideas seriously enough to question them is a significant form of respect. It builds communities where controversy stimulates thought instead of enmity; where the clash of ideas leads not to victory for one party but to new questions and new answers for everyone. For this reason, and because their suggestions helped me improve the manuscript, I am grateful to those who commented on drafts of this book. Thanks also to the many students, colleagues, and friends who have, over the years, taken me seriously enough to argue with me and to keep at it even when I was frothing at the mouth. These discussions make it all worthwhile. My hope is that this book will promote more such dialogue. If it does, the questions posed and the answers suggested here will themselves be changed.

Contents

Introduction

"It would be wrong to say that 'need for competence' is the simple and sovereign motive of life. It does, however," claimed Gordon Allport, "come as close as any" (1961, p. 214). According to Robert White (1973) and Brewster Smith (1974), counselors should discard "mental health" as a goal for their clients and pay more attention to the problem of how their clients might find ways of developing their interests and competencies. For John Rawls (1971), a just society would recognize the most important primary good as self-respect. And to achieve self-respect, individuals must be able to lead their lives so as to satisfy a principle that Rawls attributes to Aristotle: "human beings enjoy the exercise of their realized capacities (their innate or trained abilities), and this enjoyment increases the more the capacity is realized, or the greater its complexity" (p. 426).

The activities wherein people seek competence are many. Diversity also characterizes the wider purposes served by our strivings for competence and the criteria we use to judge ourselves and our accomplishments. Consider James D. Watson (1968), worrying that Linus Pauling would discover the structure of DNA before he and Francis Crick could and concerned that this structure "might turn out to be . . . dull, suggesting nothing about either its replication or its function" (p. 188). Eventually, he gained satisfaction on all points. "It seemed almost unbelievable that the DNA structure was solved, that the answer was incredibly exciting, and that our names would be associated with the double helix" (p. 198).

Sir Cyril Burt, a psychologist of eminence, exceptional gifts, and outstanding accomplishments gained less excitement from his work. While maintaining "a polite exterior and apparent reasonableness" (Hearnshaw, 1979, p. 206), Burt became, toward the end of his career, "extremely sensitive to those who in any way seemed to challenge his authority in his own areas of competence" (pp. 204–205). He grew "increasingly obsessed with questions of priority—increasingly touchy and egotistical" (p. 287). He showed "a steely determination . . . to humiliate his opponents" (p. 206). He "had to win" (p. 270). To this end he made false claims about his role in the development of factor analysis and even faked evidence to support his views on the inheritance of intelligence.

A sense of accomplishment is not the sole preserve of the eminent. Nor are feelings of competence or accomplishment always based on the egotistical desire for superiority over others. Consider John Holt's (1964) observations of a mathematics lesson given by Dr. Gattegno. The students were retarded fourteen- and fifteen-year-olds.

> One who caught my eye . . . was tall, pale, with black hair. I have rarely seen on a human face such anxiety and tension as showed on his. He kept darting looks around the room as if enemies might come from any quarter . . . His tongue worked continuously in his mouth . . . he scratched—or rather clawed—at his leg with one hand. He was a terrifying and pitiful sight . . . Gattegno . . . took two blue [9 cm. long Cuisenaire] rods and between [and parallel to] them put a dark green [6 cm. long rod], so that between the two blue rods and above the dark green there was an empty space 3 cm. long. He said to the group [all of whom had a set of rods], "Make one like this." They did. Then he said, "Now find the rod that will just fill up that space." . . . After several trials [the dark haired boy] and the others found that a light green [3 cm.] rod would fill the space.
>
> Then Gattegno, holding his blue rods at the upper end, shook them so that . . . the dark green rod fell out [leaving] a 6 cm. space . . . He asked the class to do the same. They did. Then he asked them to find the rod that would fill that space. Did they pick out the rod that had just come out of that space? Not one did. Instead, more trial and error. [After they succeeded] Gattegno shook the rods so the light green fell out, leaving the 3 cm. space . . . Again he asked the children to fill the space, and again, by trial and error

they found the needed rod . . . Gattegno went through this cycle at least four or five times . . . Then . . . the dark-haired boy saw! . . . for the first time, his hand visibly shaking with excitement, he reached without trial and error for the right rod. He could hardly stuff it into the empty space. It worked! The tongue going round in the mouth, and the hand clawing away at the leg under the table doubled their pace. When the time came to turn the rods over and fill the other empty space, he was almost too excited to pick up the rod he wanted; but he got it in. "It fits! It fits!" he said and held up the rods for all of us to see.   (pp. 122–125)

As all parents must know, pleasure in competence or accomplishment is evident in very young children too. The accompanying picture shows a boy just after he pulled himself into a standing position for the first time. His smile seems to show both his own sense of accomplishment and his reaction to the sounds of parental pride and encouragement that were coming from behind the camera.

Freud presented the ability to love and to work as a human ideal. This book is concerned with the second half of this formula. This is the domain covered by terms such as competence motivation, mastery motivation, intrinsic motivation, and—perhaps most inclusive—achievement motivation. I want to include the different shades of meaning conveyed by these terms and the range of experiences hinted at by the examples in the preceeding paragraphs. I also want to include the slightly different shades of meaning that can be associated with the terms ability and competence. And I want to keep in mind the problem of finding a mode of accomplishment that "affirms the individuality of the self and at the same time . . . unites the self with man and nature" (Fromm, 1941, p. 287).

My thinking about this topic has been shaped by two centers of interest—the nature of developmental change and the problems of education in Western societies. In each case I looked to general theories of achievement motivation for a framework. Useful though these frameworks are, they were not fully adequate for my particular purposes.

With regard to education, one of the questions I sought to answer was: What light can theories of achievement motivation cast on the problem of sustaining optimum motivation for intel-

lectual development in children of all levels of ability? How can we arrange things so that everyone gets a fair share of the sort of meaningful, competence-affirming learning experience Holt observed in that retarded teenager (Nicholls, 1979b)?

Some people think such ethical concerns should not intrude so brazenly on psychological research. Is not "real" science devoid of, even above such ethical and practical concerns? But the view that the mantle of science endows one with the power to see nature without bias, objectively, as it "really is," is difficult to sustain. Scientists do not and cannot start simply with observed facts and deduce the structure of nature. They always approach their work with specific problems in mind and hope that the phenomena or processes that they study will shed light on those problems (Toulmin, 1983).

Psychology encompasses many forms of legitimate problems or questions. For example, students of personality can ask about environmental influences on behavior, the personality variables that mediate environmental effects on behavior, or subjective experiences of the environment (Mischel, 1977). Aristotle distinguished "at a minimum, nineteen distinct kinds of things to be said about a human being at any given time" (Toulmin, 1983, p. 104). This means that the questions researchers want to address can become a source of disagreement among them. Very often this is not acknowledged, and debate about what question should be addressed takes the form of a blood feud over what is and what is not good scientific method (Mischel, 1977). Any question can be answered with a degree of adequacy; it makes no sense, however, to argue that only one type of question (or answer) is objective or scientific.

These issues can be restated in terms of thinking of science as an attempt to find languages with which to speak of nature. The scientific successes of Galileo and his followers seemed to demonstrate the value of the rejection of teleology and anthropomorphism in favor of the language of mathematics. But it does not follow that mathematics is the language in which all of nature "wants" to be described or that the language of science should always be devoid of teleology, metaphysical comfort and moral significance (Rorty, 1983, p. 157). Galileo's success is better interpreted as indicating that "a given vocabulary works better than another for a given purpose" (p. 157).

If we wish to speak of human affairs, we should seek languages that will help us reflect on what we should want to accomplish and how we should live. Rather than being "value-neutral" or more "objective," approaches to psychology that seek to expunge anything of political relevance and moral significance reduce their value for answering questions about what we should want and how we should live. This is at best; at the worst, they make it easier to assume that the way we should live and relate to others can be worked out on a technical rather than an ethical basis. Nothing that diminishes our ethical concerns for our fellows can be construed as value-neutral. It is this bias on the part of those who would be objective, in the sense of value-neutral, that leads Rorty to observe: "The only sort of policy makers who would be receptive to most of what presently passes for 'behavioral science' would be the rulers of the Gulag, or of Huxley's Brave New World." (1983, pp. 161–162).

The notion that approaches to science are inextricably intertwined with ethics gained specific meaning for me when I attempted to use existing theories of achievement motivation to address the problem of sustaining optimum motivation for intellectual development in all children. Some theories of motivation (Weiner, 1979) seemed designed to explain and—presumably inadvertently—even to sustain inequality rather than to create equality of optimum motivation. Diagnosis does not always lead to cure, and the prescriptions that follow from some diagnoses sustain the illness. The problem of achieving optimum motivation in all students (and workers) seemed thus to demand new thinking about motivation (Nicholls, 1979b).

My second focus of interest, developmental change in concepts of competence and in achievement motivation, also sent me looking to established theories for a framework. I took note of John W. Atkinson's (1969) criticism of researchers who "dart in and out of the conceptual scheme evolved studying older subjects but never seem to make full and systematic use of it" when studying children (pp. 201–202). On the other side, research on children can contribute to our understanding of adults. In my own work it was surprising indeed to recognize that, although it evolved in the study of adults, Atkinson's conceptual scheme and some other schemes incorporated conceptions of task difficulty and ability that were characteristic of five-year-old children rather than adults (Nicholls and Miller, 1983). How could a theory of adult achievement motivation "work" if—without any acknowledgment or rationale—its key concepts were those of young children? Other theories incorporated adult-like conceptions (Nicholls, 1984b). Surely these must come closer to the "truth" about adults? This tension was resolved by the hypothesis that at some times adults are like little children and at other times they are not. The different schemes that have been used to describe adults might each be "right" at different times. This is a key to the framework advanced in the second part of this book.

My concerns with equality in Western education and with motivational development happened to converge. We have it on good authority that "except ye be converted and become as little children, ye shall not enter the kingdom of heaven." The proposal I advance is less grand. It might be slightly easier to argue for, but probably is no easier to carry out. It is that equality of optimum motivation for intellectual development, substantial accomplishment, satisfaction in work, and more productive relationships with our fellows will all be more likely if we become more like little children. So let us start with them.

I

Development and
Its Discontents

1

Early Development

In the beginning, according to Freud, is id. Functioning on the basis of the pleasure principle, Freudian infants seek at first to satisfy their basic impulses without concern for the harsh world beyond their wishes. But this cannot continue: unresponsiveness to dangers in the environment and to the distinction between real and imagined gratifications would lead to death and an end to pleasure. Thus Freud posited the ego and endowed it with the administrative ability to direct id energy according to the reality principle. Freud and later drive theorists did not embrace the notion that a tendency to seek understanding of the world was a fundamental human impulse. For them the ego functions of understanding and mastery depended on id energy. But, as others soon pointed out, Freud had not dealt satisfactorily with the source of the ego's energy. The Freudian ego held an administrative position. But administrative decisions could not be made, let alone imposed, on the unruly id, if the ego had to derive all its energy from the id. If the Freudian child was to survive, its ego needed some energy of its own.

To other observers (White, 1959), young children's curiosity and interest in the effects of their own actions appeared at least as basic and omnipresent as those impulses that fascinated Freud. Piaget, for example, recorded that his daughter Lucienne, at three months of age, "shakes her bassinet by moving her legs violently which makes the cloth dolls swing from the hood. Lucienne looks at them, smiling, and recommences at once. The movements are simply the concomitants of joy." However, "The next day I present the dolls: Lucienne immediately moves, shakes her legs, but this time without smiling. Her interest is intense and sustained." Two days later, "a chance movement disturbs the dolls: Lucienne again looks at them and this time shakes herself with regularity. She stares at the dolls, barely smiles and moves her legs vigorously and thoroughly. At each movement she is distracted by her hands . . . she examines them for a moment then returns to the dolls." Eight days later, "as soon as I suspend the dolls she shakes them, without smiling, with precise and rhythmical movements with quite an interval between shakes, as though she were studying the phenomenon. Success gradually causes her to smile" (Piaget, 1952, pp. 157–158).

Lucienne is not the child that Freud had in mind. She seems drawn to transact with the environment rather than being forced forward by id instincts. Her growing ability to influence events seems to make these events more interesting and to increase the attention and effort she applies to produce them. Is she merely "learning" how to shake the dolls on her bassinet? It may not be too much to propose that, in addition, she is gaining a sense that things can be made to happen; a primitive sense of competence. Passivity, apathy, and profound retardation are, for infants, the consequences of extremely unresponsive environments such as were once found in some hospitals and orphanages (Casler, 1961). When, as in these extreme environments, infants cannot make anything happen, they stop trying. On the other hand, when infants have the experience of creating events in their environment, they become more active and more competent learners of new skills than infants who have merely observed the same events (Finkelstein and Ramey, 1977).

Given a responsive world of objects and people, infants go on seeking to create new effects. As many writers have observed, such behavior appears as inherently satisfying for the infant as it is adaptive for our species (Hunt, 1963; Stott, 1961; White, 1959). Although far from equipped to survive alone, infants do not need to be taught "a flexible, knowledgeable power of transaction with the environment" (Bruner, 1972).

The dolls hanging on the bassinet eventually lose their allure. Children are soon crawling, standing, walking, joining games their parents start, taking over these games themselves, and so on. Each new achievement brings obvious satisfaction and opens the gate to new challenges. As children grow, the goals they set become more long-term and their activities are sustained for longer periods. But more is involved than increases in the complexity of the tasks children select, the remoteness of their goals, and the persistence and vigor of their striving. Conceptions of competence also change. These changes are, I argue, the key to the understanding of the development of achievement motivation.

Early Changes in Conceptions of Competence

A change in conceptions of competence occurs toward the end of the second year. At about this time children become better able to construe themselves as separate individuals who can be categorized as, among other things, competent or incompetent (Lewis and Brooks-Gunn, 1979). The development of a separate identity appears to be accompanied by an increased desire to establish one's independent role as an achiever. The child will now more often resist adult assistance with tasks she is working on and assert "I can do it myself." (Geppert and Kuster, 1983).

This more distinct conception of one's role in bringing about a particular achievement is a two-edged sword. As well as allowing a heightened sense of one's competence, it permits a sharper awareness of personal incompetence. What earlier would have been not much more than a feeling of frustration at not getting the thing done may now be more clearly a feeling of personal incompetence. Thus in the second year we observe not only increased smiling after task mastery, but also more obvious displeasure after failure (Kagan, 1981).

Furthermore, the standard for judging one's competence can now be derived from the observed behavior of others. Piaget would have been hard-pressed to have made his three-month-old daughter feel incompetent because she could not fasten and unfasten the dolls on her bassinet as he could. But increasingly over the second year children show an apparently self-imposed desire to figure out what is "right" and to do things "properly." This is evident in their reactions to an adult's modeling of novel activities with toys. Younger children will play happily with the toys in their own way. But as they approach two years, children are more likely to react by crying or clinging to a parent. In short, they display signs of concern and doubt about their ability to display the level of competence implicit in the model's actions (Kagan, 1981).

Although these standards seem self-imposed, they are not self-referenced in the same sense as the performance standards of younger children. At about two, children may adopt standards that exceed their capacities. These standards are extrinsic in the sense that they bear no relationship to the children's own competencies, and also in the sense that children would not have adopted them if they had not observed the accomplishment of another. In a romantic idealization of infancy, this may be the point in development at which William Wordsworth first sensed that although "Heaven lies about us in our infancy, shades of the prison-house begin to close upon the growing boy" (1904, p. 354).

A little later, children aged between about two-and-a-half and three-and-a-half are able to note not merely whether an adult does something they cannot do, but who does something more quickly (Heckhausen, 1982, 1984). At this point children can gain a sense of competence from a solitary achievement like building a tower with blocks. But if an adult says "Let's see who can build it first," signs of shame are evident if the child comes in second. Younger children are unresponsive to such calls to competition and proceed with their own agendas. Again, as children grow, it becomes easier to transform activities that they find inherently satisfying into a source of shame.

A similar pattern was observed when pairs of children working with a large collection of blocks were asked who could make the better construction (Greenberg, 1932). Two-year-olds appeared unresponsive to this call to demonstrate superiority. Around age three, children almost always claimed their work was better than the work of others. However, it was usually not until four or later that this answer was accompanied by systematic comparisons of the two buildings and by directly competitive behavior like grabbing blocks from the competitor, self-praise, denigration of the competitor and his work, and sustained attempts to win.

Leuba (1933) reported a similar trend with pairs of children who were each presented a peg-board and asked to put in all the pegs. Rivalry was almost nonexistent in two-year-olds. Three- and four-year-olds talked of "beating" each other but this talk was not accompanied by systematic attempts to do better than the other. For example, after the experimental session (Leuba, 1933, p. 373), three-year-old Kenny and Teddy go back to their incomplete peg-boards.

"I'm going to beat Kenny."
"I'm going to beat."
(*Teddy finishes first.*) "I beat. I beat."
"I'm going to beat myself. I'm going to beat Miss H."
"You can beat Miss H . . . See, see, Kenny." (*Teddy points at his completed board.*)
"I beat." (*Kenny on finishing second.*)
"Oh, Kenny beat."
"Teddy beat me."
"Yes and you beat me."

Though they value winning, these three-year-olds give new meaning to the notion that winning is everything. By age five most children understand that only one person can win in such situations. Five-year-olds also show more of the focused and sustained attention their Little League coaches and school teachers will soon demand.

The Social Context of Self-Evaluation

The studies just reviewed convey something approaching half the truth. They indicate the nature of young children's developing conceptions of competence. They do not, however, indicate the extent to which children use these conceptions to evaluate their own accomplishments in their daily lives. When, as in the above studies, an adult models activities in front of a child, asks a child who is faster, or asks which child can build better, children's concerns about their competence are likely to be aroused and expressed. If, on the other hand, there is no implication of evaluation, if the situation is play-like and comparative standards of performance are not emphasized, we may see few self-evaluations based on the performance of others. Although five-year-olds can be made to feel incompetent when they observe the superior performance of a peer or adult, it does not follow that they are always preoccupied with comparing their performance with that of others.

Morrison and Kuhn (1983), for example, had four- to six-year-olds working with construction sets, all seated so they could easily observe the constructions of other children. The sets could be used at many levels of sophistication, but the researchers did nothing to alert children to these different levels or to the work of the other children and referred to the activity as play. Sixty percent of the time children were engrossed in their own constructions. Eleven percent of the time was spent observing the "play" of others. Children selectively observed those who were making more sophisticated constructions than their own. But these observations appear to have been made less for the purposes of explicit self-evaluative comparisons with others than to learn from the others: children who observed more showed greater advances in sophistication and those who selectively observed constructions that were more complex than their own advanced farther. A few children who observed constructions that proved too complex for them to learn from showed frustration and gave up. The children described by Morrison and Kuhn were clearly old enough to become upset by the display of a superior construction, but they looked at the work of others mainly in order to learn. The actions of these children resemble those of Piaget's daughter with her dolls rather than those of Kagan's two-year-olds confronted by an adult demonstrating activities with toys, but their conceptions of competence are more advanced.

Like adults, young children sometimes look to others to discover truth and beauty so that they may themselves produce more of it. At other times they look to others to evaluate their own competence. Most of us can recall occasions when another's superior knowledge made us feel stupid and embarrassed. But surely we can also recall times when another's superior knowledge provided a gratifying source of insight or aesthetic pleasure. Research with adults (reviewed in Part II) reveals that evaluative conditions and interpersonal competition increase our level of ego involvement—our tendency to evaluate our ability relative to that of others. Our involvement in the task for its own sake, and the tendency to feel competent simply when (like Lucienne) we gain insight or competence, are thereby diminished. No comparable studies appear to have been done with young children, but the studies reviewed above are consistent with the notion that when we draw a young child's attention to the standards of competence implicit in the work of others, the quality of the child's involvement is likely to change from a focus on the requirements of the task, or her relationship to it, to a state of ego involvement wherein the child evaluates herself in terms of another's performance.

We have seen that at an early age children are largely unresponsive to pressures of social comparison. At about two, they can take an adult's action as a criterion of competence and judge themselves accordingly. They progressively gain a fuller understanding that such things as finishing faster or building taller than another indicate greater competence, and become better able to judge who is faster and who builds taller. Correspondingly, they show increased competitiveness and greater responsiveness to questions about who is faster or who can do something better. It becomes more likely that pleasure in mastery will be undermined when children cannot, or think they cannot, match the performance of another. However, the young child does not always use the capacity to evaluate himself or herself in terms of another's performance. The superior accomplishment of another can be an object of admiration, a source of knowledge, or an insult to self-esteem.

We should not confuse what we are capable of doing or construing with what we actually do, or the way we construe things in the diverse situations of our daily lives. We all have more cognitive competencies than we can use at any one time, and the conceptions we employ depend on our current concerns. For the remainder of Part I, my objective is to present a clear description of the conceptions of comptence of children and adolescents. The data I discuss in this section show nothing about the origins of these conceptions or when they will be used. Their use will be my concern in Part II.

2

Luck and Skill

The evidence that five-year-olds become upset if others complete a task faster than they do might be taken to indicate that their notions about ability closely resemble those of adults. Like adults, they seem to realize that social comparisons of accomplishments are important for judging ability. Even infants show signs akin to depression when their actions produce no effects. This suggests that, like adults, infants recognize at some level that competencies have limits and that the lower those limits the more helpless one is. In short, it is conceivable that by about age five children construe ability in essentially the same way as adults. This hypothesis is consistent with a currently popular view "that very young children may have the capacity to represent knowledge in a format quite like that of the adult" (Flavell and Markman, 1983, p. ix). Specifically, a number of researchers claim that young children understand much more than Piaget thought they did (Gelman and Baillargeon, 1983; Wellman, 1985).

One reason for the dramatic impact of Piaget's work on the study of child development was his claim that young children did not understand many things that were axiomatic to adults. It seemed inconceivable to many that young children could be as "misinformed" about the "givens" of nature and logic as Piaget claimed. Among quite a few parents, teachers, and researchers, resistance to Piaget's claims was strong from the beginning. This resistance has recently reappeared as a revisionist position and is even described as a new discovery. There are, nevertheless, significant new notes in this old refrain. For example, whereas Piaget's early work often neglected the things young children *could* do, neo-Piagetian researchers have often highlighted these competencies (Gelman and Baillargeon, 1983; Wellman, 1985).

The fact remains that, like parents and teachers, researchers can be misled by young children's apparent competence. For example, a popular revisionist claim is that, contrary to Piaget's thesis, three- and four-year-olds understand number conservation; understand that the number of a group of objects remains unchanged when the arrangement of these objects (the appearance of the group) is altered. But as Halford and Boyle (1985) demonstrated, number conservation is beyond the grasp of children in this age group. A crucial difference between their studies and those of the revisionists is that Halford and Boyle started with a clear theoretical definition of the concept at issue (Larsen, 1977). They defined number conservation as the understanding that the number of a group of objects remains unchanged despite transformations of the layout of these objects. Although this may not appear to be an especially significant point, it becomes one when it is noted that the tests used by the revisionists did not embody this definition. Their tests enabled children to make superficially adult-like judgments of number without such an understanding. For example, stimuli were used that permitted children to ignore transformations and to determine the number of objects by counting. But anyone who has to count to tell whether rearranging an array of objects alters its number is not employing the concept of number conservation. Studies that employ such methods can tell us something interesting and important about children's understanding of number, but they fail to test Piaget's ingenious and counterintuitive hypothesis that young children do not understand number conservation.

The danger of overlooking young children's competencies is equal to the danger of overestimating them. Five-year-olds' behavior indicates sufficient understanding of the nature of ability to make us suspect that they are much like adults. The similarities are clear. But until we have formulated a clear definition of the concept of ability and devised stringent tests of this concept, we cannot be sure. The definition of ability I propose has three aspects requiring three separate tests. The first, to be considered in this chapter, is perhaps the most fundamental in that it is completely taken for granted in most adult discourse on the nature of ability. This is the assumption that ability is a concept that pertains to skill and not to luck or guessing. For adults this point is too obvious to merit mention, but we cannot assume that children see luck and skill as distinctly different domains or types of causality.

The second and third aspects of the definition of ability are considered in the subsequent two chapters. These concern, respectively, the role of social comparison in judging ability and task difficulty, and the notion of capacity as distinct from effort. I have included a table summarizing these three aspects of the concept of ability (Table 2.1). Even in its abbreviated form it may be of some help as a sketch map of the territory immediately ahead.

Distinguishing Between Luck and Skill

Johnson and Wellman (1980) found that an understanding of the difference between luck and skill is limited among four- and five-year-olds. The problem was choosing which of two boxes had a block hidden under it. The children did not see the block being hidden; in adult terms, they had to guess where it was. When they guessed correctly, four- and five-year-olds answered all the following questions affirmatively: "Did you know it was there? Did you remember it was there? Did you guess it was there?" Eight-year-old students, on the other hand, said "No" to the first two questions and "Yes" to the third one. This shows considerable changes in the understanding of "guess" between four and eight years. However, we should be wary about leaping to the conclusion that eight-year-olds distinguish the concepts know and guess in the manner that adults do. As Johnson and Wellman note, "young children can selectively use mental verbs quite appropriately, even while having ill-defined notions of their meanings" (1980, p. 1102). This caveat can also apply to eight-year-olds.

We employed a test of the concepts of luck and skill that was not dependent on the child's ability to use or respond to words like "guess" (Nicholls and Miller, 1985). This task embodied what

Table 2.1 Levels of Differentiation of the Concept of Ability from Difficulty, Luck, and Effort

Difficulty and ability	Luck and skill	Effort and ability
	At ages up to 7	
(1) Children's own expectations of success are the basis for judging task difficulty and ability.	(1) Tasks are not distinguished in terms of the dependence of outcomes on luck versus skill. Children focus on the apparent difficulty of mastering a task.	(1) Accomplishment with higher effort means higher ability. Effort and outcomes are imperfectly distinguished as cause and effect.
(2) Concrete properties of tasks (such as complexity) are the basis for judging task difficulty and the ability indicated by outcomes.		
	At ages 7 to 11	
	(2) Effort is expected to improve performance on luck and skill tasks, but skill tasks are seen as more affected by effort.	(2) Effort is the cause of outcomes. Equal effort by different students is expected to lead to equal outcomes.
(3) Task difficulty and ability are judged in relation to the performance of others. Tasks that few can do are seen as hard and success on these is viewed as indicating high ability.	(3) It is recognized that luck tasks do not offer a means of using one's senses to influence outcomes. Yet some faith remains that outcomes can be influenced.	(3) Ability (as a cause of outcomes) is partially differentiated from effort.

Table 2.1   (continued)

Difficulty and ability	Luck and skill	Effort and ability
	At ages 11 and older	
	(4) Luck and skill are clearly differentiated. Effort is expected to have no impact on outcomes dependent on luck.	(4) Ability is conceived as capacity; the effect of effort on performance relative to others is limited by capacity.

we construed as an adult definition of a "luck" or guessing task: one on which no level of effort or skill can influence outcomes.

To assess students' understanding of this concept of luck, we used luck and skill versions of a visual matching task. In the skill version, a standard line drawing (a ship, for example) was displayed on a card. Another six cards had six additional drawings: one identical to the standard and the others differing very slightly. In the luck version, equivalent cards were used, but only the figure on the standard was visible; the other cards were placed with the figures face down. The problem was to identify the figure that matched the standard. From an adult perspective, guessing is the only available strategy for the second task. No amount of effort or ability can influence the outcome, whereas they can influence performance on the skill task. These two tasks provided what seemed to us the simplest possible test to assess the understanding that skill and luck outcomes are quite different in nature. Note that children need not use terms like "guess" or "luck" to convince us they understand the concept. They simply have to maintain that there is no way to influence the outcome on the luck task, in contrast to the skill task.

Students from age five to fourteen were made thoroughly familiar with both tasks. They were then shown incorrect responses on each task that were said to have been made by some other students. We then presented the standard set of questions, here answered by a thirteen-year-old:

"Do you think they both could have got their one right?"
"No. This one [luck task] couldn't."
"What if they both tried harder or were more careful?"
"This one [skill task] could have done it right 'cause you can look at them. On this one [luck task] you can't."
"If they both try again, which girl will most likely get it right?"
"This one [skill task] 'cause you can look at the pictures."

Other students of about the same age started by saying that respondents could improve on both tasks, but reversed themselves on the second question and thereafter maintained this position.[1] One student said, "Well, on this [skill task] she could have looked more closely but on this one you'd just have to make a wild guess." Another said the student couldn't improve on the luck task "because you really can't tell. On that [skill task] she could study it more closely. This one [luck task] she'd have no idea—just guessing." Although the first of these three students did not use the word "guess" and the two others did, the logic of their positions was the same and justified for us the conclusion that these children's concepts of luck and skill were not confounded.

The same could not be said for the responses of younger children. They certainly did see the two tasks as different, and most of them saw the luck task as easier. But the difference did not hinge on the effect that one's effort or ability could have on the skill task as against the luck one. For the younger children, the concepts of luck and skill were relatively undifferentiated: despite their recognition of differences between the tasks, they did not show evidence of understanding the two different forms of causality and the fact that only the skill task offered a chance to control outcomes. For example,

"Do you think they both could have got their one right?"
"Yes."
"What if they both tried harder or were more careful?"
"They'd get it right."
"So could George [luck task] have got this one right if he tried?"
"Yes."

"So could Fred [skill task] have got this right if he tried?"
"Yes."
"How can you tell they'd both do better?"
"'Cause they'd look them over more, one thing at a time."
"If they both try again which boy will most likely get it right?"
"Him [luck task]."
"How can you tell?"
"That one [skill task] has more stuff." (*Student points at the pictures on the cards of the skill task.*)

Responses of this type were common among five-year-olds. Two other children, for example, explained that students could improve on both tasks because "If they don't hurry and don't try to find them too fast they'll get them right," and because "They could have compared more." These two children explained that it would be easier to do better on the luck task because "This one [skill task] looks a lot harder," and "'cause it [luck task] is easier. This one [skill task] has more details." It could be argued that a few interviews like these are not compelling, and one could easily conclude that the children must have misunderstood the questions. But when such responses keep occurring, and when children stick to their positions after questions are reworded and repeated, we have to wonder if the young child's concepts of luck and skill do not differ dramatically from ours. As I will shortly show, associated evidence of persistence on luck and skill tasks supports the hypothesis that younger children's responses indicate a real confusion of luck and skill.

In between these two extremes we detected two intermediate levels. These four levels are described in the list below. Level 1 predominates in five-year-olds. At second grade children are approximately equally spread over levels 1, 2, and 3. Sixth graders are spread between levels 3 and 4 and by grade 8 almost all students are at level 4.

Levels of Differentiation of Luck and Skill

1. Luck and skill per se are undifferentiated and are not the basis for distinguishing luck and skill tasks. Tasks are distinguished in terms of apparent difficulty. Effort is expected to improve outcomes on both tasks, but the skill task is seen as re-

quiring more effort or as more difficult because of the complexity of its visual stimuli. The luck task, having no such stimuli, is seen as easier or as requiring less effort.

2. Skill and luck outcomes are partially differentiated, but the basis for the distinction is not articulated. Effort is expected to improve performance on both tasks, but the skill task is seen as offering more chance to do well through effort. This distinction is not, however, established by explaining that the luck task offers no chance to compare stimuli, whereas the skill tasks does.

3. Skill and luck outcomes are partially differentiated, and the basis for the distinction is made explicit. The skill task is seen as offering more chance to do well through effort because it is possible to compare stimuli on it but not on the luck task. Effort is, nevertheless, expected to improve performance on the luck task.

4. Skill and luck outcomes are clearly distinguished. It is seen that there is no way for effort to affect outcomes on the luck task, whereas effort is presumed to affect outcomes on the skill task.

Qualitative Change

The different conceptions of luck and skill involve qualitative differences: that is, differences in the meaning or intensive content of these concepts. Shortly before his death, Piaget judged his work on the logic of operations as "too closely linked to the traditional model of extensional logic and truth tables." "A better way," he believed, "of capturing the natural growth of logical thinking is to pursue a kind of logic of meanings . . . a meaning is never isolated but always inserted into a system of meanings, with reciprocal implications" (Furth, 1981, p. xv). Thus Piaget aligns himself with Dewey, Wittgenstein, and Heidegger, who "hammer away at the holistic point that words take their meanings from other words rather than by virtue of their representative character, and the corollary that vocabularies acquire their privileges from the men who use them rather than from their transparency to the real" (Rorty, 1979, p. 368).

The development of meanings can be characterized as a process of differentiation and hierarchic integration. In this case, only at level 4 are the concepts of luck and skill fully differentiated from one another. But the meaning of each concept still depends on that of the other. The concept of luck is made clear by virtue of its distinction from skill; conversely, without a notion of luck the concept of skill would be ill-defined.

On the basis of our interviews we judged that these concepts are imperfectly differentiated in most five-year-olds and that four levels of differentiation could be isolated. Our making such judgments could cause some researchers to characterize this sort of work as lacking in objectivity. But judgments—explicit or implicit—about the meaning of responses are inevitable, even when a method of studying this topic appears to be more objective. For instance, rather than considering the entire interview for each child and trying to judge how the child construes luck and skill, we could have simply recorded students' responses to discrete questions, such as: "Marty got this one [either luck or skill task] right. Was it probably because he was just lucky or because he tried hard?" Responses to this type of question show that with age children are more likely to attribute skill outcomes to skill and luck outcomes to luck (Nicholls and Miller, 1985). Similarly, kindergarten children expect ability, effort, and practice to increase performance on both luck and skill tasks to about the same degree, whereas by the eighth grade they expect clear effects only on skill tasks (Weisz et al., 1982). It would be easy to conclude simply that young children are more prone than older ones to expect effort and ability to play a role on chance tasks. But this conclusion also involves an implicit judgment: namely, that luck and skill have the same meanings for children as they do for researchers. Adults, including researchers, can differ among themselves in the extent to which they think luck and effort play a role in tasks such as IQ tests without differing in what they mean by luck and effort. That is, statements about the importance of effort and luck in outcomes need not imply different meanings of effort and luck. Likewise, the statement that young children are more likely than adults to believe that skill can affect chance outcomes does not rule out the possibility that skill and chance have similar meanings for children and adults. This type of attempt to be "objective" in fact involves an imposition of adult meanings on children's responses.

To reduce the tendency to impose our adult meanings on children, stimuli and questions can be designed to provide as much of a conceptual context as possible. This increases the chance that we will discern the unique features of the child's world (Damon, 1977; Inhelder, Sinclair, and Bovet, 1974; Turiel, 1983). Adequate assessment, in this view, is not etablished by avoiding interpretation. Instead, one plans stimuli and questions to check systematically on the adequacy of possible interpretations. This is done most directly in the planning of the interviews by designing questions to check on various possible interpretations and, during interviews, by seeking clarification of ambiguous answers. It is also done by checking whether independent researchers see the same meanings in protocols. In the case of the concepts of luck and skill, we found 90 percent agreement between independent categorizations of interview protocols.

Confidence in our categorization is also strengthened (though less directly) by significant convergent trends in data that did not require these judgments of meaning. For example, respective percentages of children at levels 1 through 4 who chose low effort or ability over bad luck, or having to guess, as an explanation for another child's failure at a luck task were 67, 59, 44, and 0 (Nicholls and Miller, 1985). Weisz and his coauthors (1982) had earlier obtained age trends in a considerable range of quantitative judgments that appear to parallel these results. Weisz (1984) even found similar evidence outside the laboratory. Younger (but not older) children made similar judgments about chance and skill-determined games at a state fair.

Finally, the validity of our assessment of levels of conception of luck and skill is also suggested by evidence that persistence on luck and skill tasks is a function of these conceptions. After students had been interviewed to determine their conceptions of luck and skill, they went to a second researcher who (with no knowledge of their previous responses) presented them with a series of either luck or skill tasks, the initial six of which had no correct answers. On the skill version, students at level 4 (where skill and luck are fully differentiated) persisted significantly longer on these impossible tasks than students at the lower levels (see Table 2.2). On the luck task, however, this trend was reversed: the most differentiated level was associated with the least persistence on the impossible luck tasks (significantly less than levels

2 and 3). Not only are luck and skill concepts most clearly differentiated at level 4, but so is persistence on luck and skill tasks (when right answers are not forthcoming).

The Pros and Cons of Maturity

At first glance, the consequences of the differentiation of the concepts of luck and skill for the child's emotional well-being and achievement behavior might appear positive. When the concepts are differentiated, children are unlikely to waste effort on chance tasks and are more likely to try hard on tasks where this can pay off. Furthermore, as an excuse for failure, "bad luck" would be of little use to young children for whom the notion "bad luck" would not be sharply different from "low ability" or "lack of effort." But "bad luck" could be a more effective excuse for older students.

On the other hand, the differentiation of the concepts of skill and luck might serve to make the emotional highs of success and the lows of failure more extreme on skill tasks and less extreme on luck tasks. When playing games of chance, even adults tend to get emotionally involved and act as if outcomes could be influenced (Langer, 1975). But the evidence we have reviewed indicates that young children are more likely to do so. I certainly recall observing frequent instances of what looked like pride over winning and shame over losing at games of chance when my children were young. But I found no formal evidence that this is the case. It is also possible that when luck and skill are less differentiated, success on skill tasks does not occasion sharp pride nor failure sharp shame. This might help explain young children's often

Table 2.2   Total Time (in Seconds) on Six Luck and Six Skill Tasks as a Function of Level of Differentiation of Luck and Skill

Task	Level of differentiation		
	(1)	(2) and (3)	(4)
Luck	40.09	63.51	31.98
Skill	139.02	165.04	245.75

relatively playful approach to achievement activities (Harter, 1975) and less negative effects of decisive failure in skill tasks on the performance of younger students (Miller, 1985; Rholes et al., 1980). When young children think they are about to be shown up as incompetent, this expectation includes elements of an adult's feelings at being dealt a bad hand of cards. But adolescents' expectations of appearing incompetent would be more starkly an expectation of being incompetent: feeling that something is wrong with them personally. Feelings of incompetence would thus have more negative effects on self-esteem, learning, and performance for adolescents than for young children.

3

Difficulty and Ability

Adult conceptions of ability and task difficulty are formulated on the basis of comparing the accomplishments of different people. Intelligence test scores thus set individuals against their peers in order to judge them as high or low in intelligence. What does it mean for someone to have answered correctly 15 out of 20 test questions? We can decide the degree of difficulty of gaining this score and what the score reveals about a person's competence only if we know the scores obtained by others. Why is climbing Mount Everest judged an impressive accomplishment? Because few have been able to do it. As more teams reach the summit, its significance as a mark of mountaineering competence declines. Those who seek to demonstrate exceptional competence then seek new and more difficult routes.

From about two years of age, children's self-evaluations can be influenced by their observation of another's performance (see chapter 1). Two-year-olds get upset if presented with accomplishments they judge as beyond them. By about three they become upset if another finishes a task faster than they do. Furthermore, preschool children will attempt to surpass others, especially if rivalry is encouraged. There should, then, be no question that young children resemble adults in their ability to evaluate their own competence with reference to that of others. But this resemblance could be misleading. A more direct test is needed to see if young children have what we call *normative conceptions of ability and task difficulty*: understanding that tasks are more difficult and demand more ability if fewer members of a reference group can do them. A desire to do as well as others is not sufficient, because it could be a simple urge to follow the crowd in the belief that it is the "correct" way or the "right" thing to do. That is, another's performance might have more or less the same meaning as a parent's saying "that's what you should do."

The Normative Conception of Ability

The test we developed for this concept was based on a method devised by Veroff (1969). We presented children with four small covered boxes, each containing a puzzle (Nicholls and Miller, 1983). On each box, schematic faces represented different numbers of students, said to be of the child's age, who could and could not do each puzzle. We asked first: "Which one could only very smart children do—which one would you have to be really smart to do?" When they had answered, we asked: "How can you tell you'd have to be really smart to do that one?" Children who chose the task fewest others could do (and did not give an inconsistent rationale for the choice) were judged to have the normative conception of ability. Twenty-nine percent of first graders (about six years) and 52 percent of second graders (about seven years) satisfied this criterion. With a different sample and basically the same method Nicholls (1978) found the normative conception of ability in 31 percent of five- and six-year-olds, 72 percent of seven- and eight-year-olds, and 97 percent of nine- and ten-year-olds. Recognition of the task fewest children could do as the hardest and the one most children could do as the easiest showed a similar trend across age and was quite strongly associated with the normative conception of ability (Nicholls, 1978). The question "Which one would you have to be very smart to do?" was also asked about unseen puzzles (in closed boxes) which were simply described as "easy," "in between," and "hard." (Nicholls, 1980b). Age trends and overall distributions of responses remained close to the results described above. These findings suggest that we have tapped a major change in the way children construe ability and difficulty.

In the light of these data, young children's responsiveness to the performance of others can be quite misleading if taken to indicate that their conceptions are the same as adults'. But if young children do not have normative conceptions of difficulty and ability, what is the nature of their concepts? We need a clearer picture of what they *do* understand and how is it that their actions and statements can often appear adult-like even though they are not based on adult conceptions. Even two-year-olds will say things like "Too hard!" and "I can do it" in a way that indicates they have some understanding of these terms (Bird, 1984; Bretherton and Beeghly, 1982). What, then, is the nature of this understanding?

The Differentiation of Ability and Difficulty

Three levels of differentiation of the concepts of ability and difficulty can be distinguished, with the normative being the most differentiated (and integrated). These levels are summarized in the following list.

Levels of Differentiation of Difficulty and Ability

1. Egocentric: Tasks are distinguished in terms of one's own subjective probability of success. "Hard" is equivalent to "hard for me," which is equivalent to "I'm not smart at it."

2. Objective: A continuum of levels of difficulty is recognized as demanding corresponding levels of ability. Difficulty is recognized independently of one's own expectations of success. Nevertheless, the child cannot distinguish whether failure at a given task is a result of low ability or high difficulty. The statement "It's hard" is still not distinguishable from "It's too hard for me," which is not distinguishable from "I'm not smart enough for it."

3. Normative: Ability and difficulty are completely differentiated. Difficulty and ability are understood in terms of the success rates of others. Tasks that only a few peers can carry out are judged as being harder and as needing higher ability. This means that "hard for me" can be distinguished from "hard."

At the lowest level, termed egocentric, the child judges her ability and the difficulty of tasks in a self-referenced fashion. Both are understood in terms of her subjective probabilities of success. This means that the concepts of difficulty and ability are not differentiated from one another. At this level, "hard" means the same as "hard for me" and this cannot be distinguished from "I'm not smart enough to do it." (Other evidence [Schneider, 1984, 1987] makes it clear that three- to five-year-olds' subjective anticipations of success on tasks they are familiar with can reflect their actual probabilities of success.) We identified children at the egocentric level by questioning them about a series of jigsaw puzzles with different numbers of pieces (Nicholls and Miller, 1983). A significant proportion of five-year-olds did not indicate that the puzzle with the most pieces would require most ability. We classified these children as having egocentric conceptions of ability and difficulty.

The intermediate, objective conception of ability and difficulty represents a slight advance on the egocentric view in that the children explicitly state that the most complex puzzle of a series requires the most ability. In other words, children at this level recognize variations in concrete or objective difficulty levels and in the corresponding levels of ability these tasks demand, independently of their own subjective probabilities of success. Difficulty and ability are partially differentiated from the subjective expectation of success. But ability and difficulty themselves remain imperfectly differentiated. From an adult perspective, the objective (and egocentric) conceptions do not enable one to decide whether completion of a task indicates high ability or an easy task. We can only decide this with the normative conceptions of "easy" applying to something that most people can do and "smart" applying to people who are able to do tasks most people cannot.

As one might expect, given that each of these levels incorporates and advances on the understandings of the previous ones, longitudinal and cross-sectional data indicate that these three levels form a developmental sequence (Nicholls and Miller, 1983).

Children at the egocentric level failed to identify the most complex puzzles as those demanding the most ability. Nevertheless, they did respond systematically to concrete or objective difficulty cues such as the number of pieces in a jigsaw puzzle. The children were consistent in the levels of difficulty they preferred to attempt from two different arrays of jigsaw puzzles (Table 3.1): those choosing to attempt the harder tasks from one array were also more likely to choose harder tasks from the second array.

Young children's responsiveness to chances of success is stable enough to maintain consistency in the difficulty of the tasks they attempt when difficulty cues are objective; it is also sufficient to enable them to use words like "hard" appropriately much of the time. Even for adults, "hard" often means "I can't do it." Even this undifferentiated conception would be sufficient for children to maintain their place in social hierarchies. To keep their place in a "pecking order" children need only have a sense of whether or not they are superior to each individual in the group as they encounter them. Finally, the egocentric conception of ability has the potential to promote the negative self-evaluations that can occur when young children observe another's superior performance. If someone's performance indicates the right or competent way of doing something, a young child's belief that he or she cannot match it is likely to occasion feelings of incompetence. The child can thus look remarkably like an adult despite a markedly less differentiated understanding of ability and difficulty.

When young children face specific concrete tasks they can comprehend, their task choices resemble those of adults. But the picture changes when they are told only how many other children their age can do the tasks (Veroff, 1969). Because little children lack a normative conception of ability, they do not evaluate success on tasks that few students are said to be able to do as more impressive than success on tasks that many are said to be able to accomplish. It is not surprising, therefore, that children without the normative conception generally choose (when given the option) to attempt tasks that many others are said to be able to do; they have no reason to attempt tasks at which many others have failed. Children who have normative conceptions do see success on tasks that few can do as more impressive (Nicholls, 1978, 1980b), and for them the information that many fail on a task also conveys the counterbalancing notion that success would be all the more valued. These children, therefore, have less reason to choose the easiest task and, indeed, they are less likely to do so (Nicholls and Miller, 1983). (In earlier studies I did not examine this specific relationship. Instead, I computed the associations between task choice and the understanding that success was most impressive on the most difficult task. In the 1978 study this association was quite high: students who saw success as most impressive on more difficult tasks were more likely to choose such tasks. The association was significant in one of two samples in a later study: Nicholls, 1980b.)

Children at the objective and egocentric levels generally chose tasks that most children were said to be able to do, and their normative difficulty choices were not correlated with their choices of objective difficulty levels. Preference for normatively easy tasks did not predict preference for objectively easy tasks (Nicholls and Miller, 1983). This supports the claim that the two types of difficulty cue are interpreted differently by younger children. Students at the egocentric and objective levels contrast clearly with those at the normative level, whose choices of the two types of difficulty cue are correlated: those choosing normatively difficult tasks also tend to choose objectively difficult tasks (Table 3.1). This evidence gives further support to the hypothesis that the normative conceptions of ability and difficulty mark a significant change in the meaning of social comparison.

Studies of age-related changes in behavior that do not assess the normative conception are also of interest in that they show age-related changes that are consistent with my thesis. Because the age when the normative conception (or any conception) is attained varies from sample to sample, there is little profit in arguing about the precise age at which changes occur. But we should expect changes at about six- to seven-years of age. Two studies show increases between kindergarten and first grade in the frequency with which students check on the progress of peers doing similar work (Frey and Ruble, 1985; Ruble, Feldman, and Boggiano, 1976). This increase could be accounted for by the emergence of the normative conception of ability, which gives social comparison a more important place in judgments of competence. Another study shows an increase from preschool to the early grades in students' references to performance comparisons to explain their ratings of others' abilities (Stipek and Tannatt, 1984). Older students, with the normative conceptions of ability, should be more responsive than younger ones to information about how peers have done on tasks they are working at. In line

Table 3.1   Correlations of Difficulty Level Choice with Normative and Objective Cues for Different Conceptions of Difficulty and Ability

Difficulty cues	Normative conceptions		Objective conceptions		Egocentric conceptions	
	Objective cues		Objective cues		Objective cues	
	1	2	1	2	1	2
	(N=34)		(N=62)		(N=20)	
Grade 1						
Normative cues	39[a]	38[a]	.03	.09	.04	.00
Objective cues 1	—	.70[b]	—	.60[b]	—	.69[b]
	(N=49)		(N=31)		(N=2)	
Grade 2						
Normative cues	58[b]	.44[b]	.00	−.10	—	—
Objective cues 1	—	.54[b]	—	.42[a]	—	—

Note: "Normative cues" refers to an array of four puzzles (hidden from the subjects inside four boxes) which different numbers of children were shown as able to do. "Objective Cues 1" refers to an array of four jigsaw puzzles (which children could see and touch) of varying complexity and "Objective Cues 2" to a similar array of three puzzles.

a. $p < .05$.   b. $p < .01$.

with this prediction, Boggiano and Ruble (1979) found that nine- to eleven-year-olds but not three- to five-year-olds showed greater interest in tasks when they were told their initial performance exceeded that of others. Although the studies noted in this paragraph cannot directly support the thesis that the normative conception, as we have assessed it, marks an important transition in motivational development, they are certainly consistent with it.

Learning Our Place

Teachers and parents quite often assert that young children know their academic standing in their classes. "They know what group they are in"; "they know what book they are on"; and "you can't fool them" are the sort of comments one hears. I admit to an early readiness to question the accuracy and robustness of young children's judgments of their standing. This derives from my surprise in discovering, during adolescence, that at five years of age I had been the second tallest boy in my class. This was very obvious in my class photo, where the students are ordered according to size. Although I must have seen the photo at the time, I distinctly recalled having felt smaller than my contemporaries. But such anecdotes are always suspect.

Even preschool children can have a working knowledge of their place in a hierarchy of power or dominance. Strayer and Strayer (1976) found that three- to five-year-olds who were accustomed to playing together at preschool had relatively stable dominance relationships that conformed closely to a linear model: if Jill submitted to Jack and Jack submitted to Rosemary, Jill also submitted to Rosemary in interactions involving attacks or threats. These children knew their place in a social hierarchy where personal attacks and threats were involved.

Such knowledge need not, however, imply an abstract representation of the social hierarchy and one's place in it. All it requires is the ability to recognize whether each individual a child encounters is more or less dominant than she. What do we find when we use clear and carefully presented response scales to assess students' perceptions of their standing relative to others? A number of studies show that, with age, children's rankings of their own academic ability or of their attainment relative to that of their classmates become on average lower and more highly correlated with the teachers' ratings (Nicholls, 1978, 1979a, 1980a). In these studies, students at various ages were shown a line of schematic faces representing all the children in their class, lined up from highest to lowest attainment at reading, and asked "Which one is you?" Table 3.2 shows illustrative data from Nicholls (1978). Apparently, it gets lonelier at the top as we get older.

For young children physical "toughness" may be a more salient, concrete characteristic than academic competence. When children are presented pairs of photos or names of their peers and asked to nominate the tougher of each pair, they show quite high levels of accuracy of ranking by age six. Four- and five-year-olds are less accurate. When asked to rank themselves, however, four- to seven-year-olds are much inclined to claim their own superiority (Edelman and Omark, 1973; Freedman, 1975). Young children's accuracy declines when self-evaluation is involved—an effect that seems to reflect a tendency to self-enhancement combined with intellectual immaturity (Stipek, 1984).

Even greater accuracy of self-rating among four-, five-, and six-year-olds was obtained by Morris and Nemcek (1982). In this case children compared their own running ability with only four peers (with whom they had interacted frequently) by ranking photos of themselves and the others. Mean rank-order correlations between students' rankings and independent assessments of their running ability were: .09 at three years, .35 at four years, .65 at five years, and .56 at six years. Thus the trend across age is similar to that shown in Table 3.2 except that accuracy is evident much earlier. This task does not appear to require an abstract notion of one's place in a hierarchy. Rather, recognition of who is the faster of successive pairs of children might be sufficient to produce accurate arrangements of photos. Furthermore, running ability is probably easier to discriminate than academic competence. In any case, the data converge in indicating that, with age, we get better at recognizing our place.

Similar trends are observed when children rate their ability on scales where they simply rate themselves as high or low or good or bad at an activity, rather than making direct comparisons with others (Eshel and Klein, 1981; Stipek, 1981; 1984; Stipek and Tannant, 1984). Again, estimates of the competence of other students can be more accurate than estimates of one's own competence in young children (Stipek, 1984).

As noted here and in Chapter 1, children's self-evaluations can reflect their recognition of how they perform relative to others even when they are too young to have developed the normative conception of ability. Presumably, experiences of performing better or worse than others are involved in differentiating the concepts of ability and task difficulty. This differentiation involves a clearer realization that to be smart means to be smarter than others. This realization could, in turn, make a child pay more attention to his standing relative to that of others, meaning that judgments of his own competence would increasingly reflect this standing. And because we cannot all be at the top of the class and half of us must be below average, mean levels of perceived ability should decline as the concepts of ability and difficulty become differentiated.

Table 3.2 Age Trend of Mean Self-Perception of Reading Achievement and Correlations between Child and Teacher Rating of Achievement

	Age (years)								
	5	6	7	8	9	10	11	12	13
X	3.06	5.12	9.06	9.00	11.18	13.81	11.63	12.88	15.06
SD	3.82	3.88	5.16	4.76	6.32	5.76	5.94	3.91	7.16
r	—	—	.21	.27	.58[a]	.71[b]	.57[a]	.80[b]	.78[b]

Note: The response scale was 30 schematic faces (lined up vertically on a page) said to represent the children in the student's class. (There were about 30 students per class.) The face at the top of the page represented the child who did best reading in class; scores could run from 1 (top) to 30 (bottom). N = 16 at each age.

a. $p < .05$.   b. $p < .01$.

A caveat, however, is in order. It is possible to obtain a close match between children's attainment and their ratings of their own ability even if these children are unaware of the attainment of their peers. All it would take in school, for example, is for teacher feedback to be correlated with attainment and for students' self-evaluations to reflect this feedback. Associations between students' accomplishments and their self-ratings need not depend on social comparison by students or on their having acquired the normative conception of ability. Stated another way, a good case cannot be made for the claim that greater accuracy in self-ranking of ability indicates a more differentiated conception of ability or difficulty. Quantitative change in self-ranking is not the same as qualitative change in the meaning of ability, and the one does not have to depend on the other.

Any lingering tendency to confuse accuracy of self-assessments with knowledge of the nature of ability should be dispelled by evidence that adults can be as unrealistic as young children about their likely accomplishments. This point is illustrated by a study of 2,994 entrepreneurs who had recently become business owners (Cooper, Dunkelberg, and Woo, 1988). On the average, fewer than 50 percent of businesses survive more than five years with a given owner or manager. Yet 95 percent of this sample gave themselves at least a 50 percent chance of success, 81 percent gave themselves a 70 percent chance, and 33 percent rated themselves as having a 100 percent chance of survival. New business owners and young children starting school are both venturing into the unknown on missions that they value highly. Unrealistic optimism in such contexts is no mere expression of an undifferentiated conception of competence.

No doubt, as a study by Stipek and Daniels (1987) indicates, classrooms where social comparison is emphasized hasten the trend toward lower means in self-ranking. (The data in Table 3.2 are from a school where the early grades appeared task-oriented, socially supportive, and unusually free of emphasis on social comparison.) Nevertheless, the normative conception of ability and difficulty should, once it emerges, also contribute to greater accuracy and lower means of perceived ability or attainment. In the only direct test of this hypothesis, Miller (1988) did not find the expected difference in associations between perceived and actual attainment. What he found was that remarkably fewer first-grade students who did have the normative conception of ability ranked themselves top of the class, even though the reading attainment of the students with the normative conception was significantly higher: a trend that would, on its own, lead to higher perceived rank.

Conclusion

Children as young as one-and-half years make a form of social comparison by using one another's performance as a basis of self-evaluation. And when they do, they may find themselves wanting on tasks that would otherwise have provided feelings of competence and accomplishment. Nevertheless, the normative conception of difficulty and ability that is acquired at about six years involves a significant change in the meaning of social comparison information. In the light of this conception, information about the performance of absent others can affect task evaluations, self-evaluations, and action in essentially the same way that adults are affected. The understanding that to be smart means to be smarter than others is likely to reduce the tendency for self-referenced judgments to be the basis of feelings of accomplishment. When being smart means being smarter than others, we can't all be smart—so the chances that everyone will feel smart should decline. Presumably this development also makes it harder for teachers to comment favorably on one student's performance without undermining a bystander's confidence (Miller, Brickman, and Bolen, 1975). Presumably it means that students become more inclined to interpret their grades in terms of their standing relative to their peers, and their reaction to their grades tends to depend on how others score. In short, when children want to know how smart they are, they will be more likely to reflect on how they compare with others and less likely to focus on whether what they are learning makes intrinsic sense or on whether their skills are developing.

   A competitive, meritocratic society depends for its smooth functioning upon individuals' readiness to accept positions of varying status, power, and wealth without directly confronting all the others in combat or competition for those places. The normative conception of ability seems important for the functioning of such a society. Yet there is a price to pay for the individuals who discover that they are below average on valued skills. If one guiding principle of our society is that everyone be able to attain a sense of competence from developing and exercising his or her powers, the emergence of the normative conception of ability seems likely to make just classrooms and a just society a little harder to attain. Children might escape some of the negative consequences of unfavorable comparisons of academic accomplishments by devaluing academic skills and seeking accomplishment and satisfaction in other activities. But then they would maintain a sense of competence at the expense of their academic development.

4

Ability and Effort

I have argued that an adequate definition of ability depends on a clear distinction between luck and skill and on the notion that task difficulty and ability are best judged as high or low with reference to the performance of members of a normative reference group. The third aspect of the definition of ability concerns the notion of capacity. This notion is embodied in the conventional wisdom on ability testing. Two aspects of testing are salient. First, capacity is judged with reference to the performance of others. The indices of mental age and IQ are indices of standing relative to others. In this sense, inability to do some task does not indicate a lack of capacity. Would my failure, despite maximum effort, to jump across the Mississippi River at New Orleans indicate that my capacity for jumping is low? Obviously not, because no one else can make such a jump. It is only when one cannot do what others can that one is revealed as lacking in ability. That is, one's capacity is judged as high or low relative to that of others.

The second relevant aspect of testing practice is that, whether the ability to be assessed is intellectual, musical, physical, or of some other type, we assume that to assess what people are currently capable of we must induce them to try hard. Implicit in this practice is the assumption that effort increases performance, but only up to the limit of one's present capacity. We judge intelligence test scores to be invalid if motivation during the test was inadequate, but there is no fear that individuals could be so favorably motivated as to perform beyond their current capacity.

This is logically impossible. It is often possible to improve one's capacity through practice. But this is not relevant to the topic of this chapter. The point here is that our present capacity limits the extent to which effort will increase our performance relative to that of others.

Here again we see the interdependent nature of concepts. In defining ability as capacity we imply something about the nature of effort: namely, that the effect of effort on performance is limited by one's capacity. Although effort and ability are distinct and qualitatively different concepts, their meanings are interdependent. The definition of one inevitably involves a definition of the other.

Infants will give up striving if their efforts produce no effects. In extreme cases (Casler, 1961) they will become completely passive. But their ability to recognize situations where their efforts will be fruitless does not show that they construe ability as capacity. To establish when and whether children construe ability as capacity we need a test that will show whether they recognize that when other things are equal, individuals who have to try harder than others for a given accomplishment have less capacity and would perform worse than the others if they applied equal effort.

For this purpose we used film, videotape, or a series of photographs to depict two elementary school children seated side by side working at paper and pencil problems (Miller, 1985; Nicholls, 1978b; Nicholls and Miller, 1984b; Nicholls, Patashnick and Mettetal, 1986). One child was shown working diligently while the other worked only intermittently over the same period of time, and the two children were shown as earning the same scores.[1] We judged our respondents' understanding of ability as capacity by their recognition that the lazier child performed as well as the other because of superior ability and could perform better than the other if the two applied equal effort.

Note that the scene depicts a performance or test situation rather than a long-term learning situation. Here the conception of ability as capacity refers to present capacity—to the notion that there is always a limit on how well one can perform relative to others, even if one's capacity is increasing in time. An ideal intelligence test will indicate a person's present capacity, but the question of how much that might be improved by a different education cannot be answered in such a session. The development of understanding of the nature and long-term acquisition of intellectual abilities is the subject of the following chapter, not of this one.

A student needs few words to convince us that she construes ability as capacity. For example, in the following interview, only our standard interview questions were used and the student is logically consistent in her responses.

> "Is one [of these two students who scored the same but differed in effort] smarter at these puzzles or are they the same?"
> "This [lazier] one is smarter."
> "How can you tell?"
> "She looked around [was inattentive] but got the same number right."
> "How come they both got the same score when one worked hard and one didn't work hard?"
> "This [lazier] one was smarter."
> "What would happen if they both worked hard? Would one get more or would they both get the same?"
> "This [lazier] one would get more."
> "How can you tell?"
> "The other one already tried hard."
> "So do you think one of them is smarter:"
> "Her [the lazier one]."

This is a clear example of complete differentiation of the concepts of effort and ability (see list, level 4).[2] Other students, who initially give the impression that they lack the insights illustrated in the above interview, "wake up" after being asked, "How come they got the same . . ." (Nicholls and Miller, 1984b):

> "Is one smarter at these puzzles or are they the same?"
> "The same."
> "How can you tell?"
> "Since they got the same score."
> "How come they both got the same score when one worked hard and one didn't work hard?"
> "He [the lazier one] didn't have to think as hard to get the answers."
> "What would happen if they both worked really hard? Would one get more or would they both get the same?"

"He'd [the lazier one] do more."
"How can you tell?"
"Because he got them quick."
"So do you think one of them is smarter?"
"They're the same. Well, he [the lazier] is probably a little smarter 'cause he figures out the problems easier."

Levels of Differentiation of Ability and Effort

1. Effort or outcome is ability. Effort, ability, and performance outcomes are imperfectly differentiated as cause and effect. Explanations of outcomes are tautological. Children center on effort (people who try harder than others are seen as smarter even if they get a lower score) or on outcome (people who get a higher score are said to work harder—even if they do not—and are seen as smarter).

2. Effort is the cause of outcomes. Effort and outcome are differentiated as cause and effect. Effort is the prime cause of outcomes: equal effort is expected to lead to equal outcomes. When attainment is equal but effort varies, this is seen as either inexplicable, or due to compensatory effort (the apparently lazier student must have worked really hard for a while), or to misapplied effort (the one who worked harder went too quickly and made mistakes).

3. Effort and ability are partially differentiated. Effort is not the only cause of outcomes. Explanations of equal outcomes following different effort involve suggestions that imply the conception of ability as capacity (the person working less hard is faster or brighter). These implications are not, however, systematically followed through; children may still assert that individuals would achieve equally if they applied equal effort.

4. Ability is capacity. Ability and effort are clearly differentiated. Ability is conceived as capacity, which (if low) may limit or (if high) may increase the effect of effort on performance. Conversely, the effect of effort is constrained by ability. When achievement is equal, lower effort implies higher ability.

Other respondents seem about to come to the same conclusion (and thereby be categorized as level 4) but do not do so, even when the interview is repeated with film or photos of different children.

"Is one smarter"?
"They're the same."
"How can you tell?"
" 'Cause they both got 10."
"How come they both got the same score when one worked hard and one didn't?"
"Maybe he [the lazier] is smart but playing around."
"What would happen if they both worked really hard? Would one get more or would they get the same?"
"Same."
"How can you tell?"
"If the one playing around would have tried, he would get the same. He wouldn't get worse."
"So do you think one of them is smarter?"
"They're the same."

Although this student gave a hint of differentiation of effort and ability, where the lazier actor is seen as "smart but playing around," he did not develop the idea. This illustrates level 3— which can be seen as a state of transition between levels 2 and 4—in that the student showed a glimmer of understanding that the effect of effort on performance depends on individual differences in ability. In many cases even such glimmers are absent. For example:

"Is one of them smarter . . ."
"This one [the hard worker] is."
"How can you tell?"
"He's doing his work."
"How come they both got the same score when this one worked hard and this one didn't work hard?"
"He [the lazy one] copied."[3]
"Well, yes, that sometimes happens, but we didn't want to show you anyone who copies and this boy doesn't do that."
"He [the lazy one] must have thought about it."
"What would happen if they both worked really hard? Would one get more or would they both get the same?"
"The same."

"How can you tell?"

"If they both work hard and they are good workers they can get it done."

"So do you think one of them is smarter?"

"They are the same."

"How can you tell?"

"Both are smart because they both got their work done and they both got eight right."

It is hard to determine whether this interview illustrates level 1 or level 2. It seems that the student expects equal effort to lead to equal results, despite the difference in effort that he acknowledged at the outset of the interview. He tries to account for equal scores in terms of equal effort—by suggesting that the boy who was (or seemed) lazy actually thought about the work. It seems that for this child effort as a cause is differentiated from outcomes, as is typical of level 2. But it is difficult to tell whether he simply expects effort and performance to be correlated, as do level 1 students. To provide a better test of the differentiation of the concept of effort as a cause from outcomes, we changed the supposed score. The hard worker was said to have got two out of ten and the lazier student scored eight (Nicholls, 1978). Here is how the above child responded:

"Is one of them smarter?"

"He [the lazier one who scored higher] is."

"How can you tell?"

"He got eight and he got two."

"How come the one who didn't work so hard got more right?"

"This [lazier] one is smarter."

"What does that mean?"

"He knows more."

"What would happen if they both worked really hard . . . would one get more . . .?"

"They'd get the same."

"How can you tell?"

"If they both worked hard and listened they'd get the same."

"So do you think one of them is smarter?"

"Him [the lazier one]."

This boy still expected equal effort to lead to equal outcomes, despite the fact that we had just showed him a blatant violation of this rule. But he did acknowledge that the rule didn't hold in this instance. That is, effort and outcomes were not as confused as they are at the least differentiated level. This confusion is illustrated by the following exchange with a girl whose responses to the initial situation (where the actors scored equally) were almost identical to those of the previous student. But when she was faced with the harder worker scoring two and the lazier student scoring eight, she chose the harder worker as more able because "She is working and not playing."

> "How come the one who didn't work so hard got more right?"
> "She got real busy after she was playing around."
> "How come she [the one who worked less] got more than the other one?"
> "She worked harder."
> "What would happen if they both worked really hard . . . would one get more . . .?
> "Get the same."
> "How can you tell?"
> "They'd both be working."
> "So do you think one of them is smarter?"
> "She [the hard worker] is."

This response has a hint of level 2 reasoning in that the girl implies that harder work causes higher scores. But the evident difficulty with the notion that a person working hard might score less or be less able than someone who uses little effort is typical of level 1. The child appears unable to recognize that effort and outcome need not go together. It is not that level 1 children don't recognize the discrepancy. Many of them express surprise mingled with outrage when they observe (in the film or videotape) that the higher-scoring student is "goofing off." Cries of "What!" "Huh!" and the like indicate that they recognize a violation of their beliefs about the way effort and attainment are or should be related. But this recognition does not lead level 1 students to see the harder worker, who scores lower, as less able, whereas students classified at level 2 and above do see this.[4]

Not surprisingly, one always finds a few protocols that contain elements of more than one level. If meanings are constructed from earlier meanings through negotiations with others (Doise and Mugny, 1984) and through detecting and resolving contradictions among one's schemes and between these schemes and one's experience of the world (Furth, 1981), periods of confusion and inconsistency are inevitable. Despite this, it is possible to categorize protocols into the four levels with a high level of agreement among independent raters (Miller, 1985; Nicholls, 1978; Nicholls and Miller, 1984b; Nicholls, Patashnick and Mettetal, 1986). Furthermore, we found the level of children's responses to be fairly stable over two sets of stimuli. In one set both actors were said to gain high scores, and in the other both scored low. The correlation between independent ratings of the interviews about these two sets of stimuli was .84 (Nicholls and Patashnick, unpublished data on 190 fifth-grade students).

Level 1 predominates at about five years of age and level 4 at about eleven or twelve years. But variation across samples can be considerable. In a recent study of fifth-grade classes we (Nicholls and Patashnick, unpublished data) found several schools with about 25 percent of students at level 4. In others, from areas of higher socioeconomic status in the same school district, almost 80 percent were at this level.

Weiner and Handel (1985, p. 106) interpret our claims about age trends in conceptions of ability and effort as saying that young children are unable to distinguish "cannot" from "not trying" as causes of outcomes. They object to this view and cite evidence that young children do note differences between failure due to lack of effort and failure that is not due to lack of effort. But such evidence casts little light on the conception of ability as capacity. As noted at the beginning of this chapter, it is clear that even very young children are sensitive to variations in the effect of their efforts on the environment. (An infant that lacked such sensitivity would be very poorly equipped to adapt to its world. It would have no mechanism for selecting challenging rather than impossible tasks and no mechanism, other than exhaustion, for quitting totally impossible tasks.) Even the youngest students in our interview studies recognized differences between someone who tries and someone who doesn't try very hard, regardless of what these two achieve. All children responded very differently to the harder worker and the lazier student. What they made of such differences, however, was what interested us. The fact that young children can distinguish people who fail in their attempts to do something from those who make no attempt does not tell us how they construe effort or ability. Indeed, our interviews start rather than finish with children's recognition of such differences.[5]

Reasoning About Our Own Ability

The research described above involved children's interpretations of the behavior and performance of others. One might question whether children reason in the same way when they are reasoning about their own ability. To check on this we compared interview responses from three types of situation where two students applied different effort but earned equal scores (Nicholls and Miller, 1984b). Children in one condition were interviewed about two others who were shown on a video monitor. In a second condition, children were interviewed about themselves and a videotaped student who tried harder than they did. Children in a third condition applied more effort than a videotaped student. Specific judgments of who was more able were affected by the setup. There was, however, no significant variation across these three in level of differentiation. Thus it seems that the meanings of ability and effort are the same whether children are thinking about their own ability or the ability of others.

The different levels of meaning should, under certain circumstances, be expressed as different patterns of quantitative judgments about one's own ability and effort. After an experience of failure on a task, for example, students' judgments of their own effort and ability on that task might be positively correlated among those at the lower levels of differentiation but negatively correlated at the higher level. Indeed, Rholes and his colleagues (1980) found positive associations among children of grade 3 and earlier but negative correlations at grade 5. Analogous age trends were obtained for students' causal attributions for their own successes in reading (Nicholls, 1979a). Of particular interest are the associations of ability and effort with perceptions of reading attainment (Table 4.1). Among twelve- but not six-year-olds, high perceived attainment is associated with greater attribution of success to high ability rather than to high effort. As will be noted later in this chapter, judgments of ability and effort will not always parallel conceptions of ability and effort. Nevertheless, some age-related changes in students' judgments of their own effort and ability parallel the changes in conceptions of ability and effort.

Evaluations of Ability and Effort

If the meanings of ability and effort change in the fashion that I have argued they do, evaluations of ability and effort should change likewise. Two methods have been used to test this proposition. In the first, students were asked (by someone with no knowledge of their conceptions of ability and effort) to predict a teacher's reaction to children who were described as having succeeded (1) with high effort and low ability, and (2) with low effort and high ability. Students at levels 1 and 2 of the concepts of effort and ability expected teachers to give high approval in each case. Less approval was predicted in the low effort/high ability case by level 3, and still less at level 4. Like the less mature

Table 4.1   Correlations of Perception of Own Reading Attainment with Causal Attribution of Success in Reading

Age and sex	N	Ability	Effort	Difficulty	Luck
		\multicolumn{4}{c}{Attribution of success to:}			
6 years					
F	63	.09	.01	−.12	.02
M	84	.03	.24[a]	−.03	−.26[a]
8 years					
F	54	.19	−.16	.10	−.15
M	71	.28[b]	−.12	−.09	−.08
10 years					
F	58	.17	.10	−.07	−.16
M	76	.40[c]	−.35[b]	−.04	−.07
12 years					
F	57	.59[c]	−.28[a]	−.12	−.49[c]
M	77	.57[c]	−.37[b]	−.05	−.49[c]

Note: A positive correlation indicates that perception of high attainment is associated with perception of a particular factor as an important cause of success.
    a. $p < .05$.   b. $p < .01$.   c. $p < .001$.

children, those at levels 3 and 4 predicted high approval for success with high effort and low ability (Nicholls, 1978). The expectation of high approval for high effort (on the part of all students) parallels adult responses to similar stimuli (for example, Weiner and Kukla, 1970). The younger (levels 1 and 2) children's expectation of reward for high ability does not, however, conform to the adult pattern. Children at these lower levels do not clearly distinguish the concepts of effort and ability. Therefore, for them, the description of someone as high in ability presumably creates an impression resembling an adult's conception of effortful accomplishment. Only when the concepts of effort and ability are differentiated from each other (partially at level 3 and completely at 4) would students interpret the statement that a child does well with high ability and low effort as clearly implying that the child applied little effort and would, therefore, face the teacher's disapproval.

Results were different when children were asked whether they would wish to be like the two students described. In this case children at all levels of maturity indicated a strong desire to be like both: the student described as succeeding with high effort and low ability, and the student with low effort and high ability (Nicholls, 1978). Thus, although students with the conception of ability as capacity do not expect teachers to approve of someone described as having done well because of ability rather than effort, they find the prospect of being such a person very attractive. A similar finding was reported by Harari and Covington (1981). (Related studies are reviewed by Nicholls and Miller, 1984a.)

A second study extended the above line of inquiry. At the end of interviews (of the type described above) about two children who scored the same despite unequal effort, we asked students which of the two they would rather be like (Nicholls, Patashnick, and Mettetal, 1986). Among the students at levels 1 and 2, 97 percent preferred to be like the harder working student. At level 3, 57 percent preferred to be like the harder worker, and at level 4 only 29 percent did. The advantages of being able to do well without trying were largely lost on children at the lower levels. They either emphasized that "It's smart to work" and "That's the way to learn," or "Goofing off is naughty" and could "get you into trouble." Of course students with the conception of ability as capacity (level 4) also recognized the unpleasant consequences of not working in school. Like younger students, almost all of them expected teachers to show more approval of the diligent student. For most of those at level 4, however, it seemed obvious that there were advantages in being like the lazier student because, for example, "I could do my homework quick and then watch TV." Some were ambivalent: "I'd be like him [the lazier one] then I'd work hard and do even better." This ambivalence was absent in those at the lower levels for whom the harder worker presumably embodied both competence and virtue.

These findings seem to confirm the wisdom of Erik Erikson's (1963) characterization of middle childhood as a time when the establishment of a sense of industry as opposed to a sense of inferiority is a major concern. The confounding of effort with ability and the valuing of effortful accomplishment as both good and smart that characterizes students at levels one and two (but not those who construe ability as capacity) is nicely captured by the term "industry."

Performance

After the emergence of the concept of ability as capacity, feelings of incompetence (when they occur) are likely to be more aversive and make future failure seem more inevitable. This is because a lack of ability more clearly means a deficiency of the person than when this concept is imperfectly differentiated from effort. Furthermore, when the concepts of ability and effort become differentiated, effort does not seem to make up for a lack of competence. Because the need to use more effort to accomplish a goal is more clearly an indication of incompetence when effort and ability are differentiated, effort is likely to have higher psychological costs. Low perceived ability (or the expectation that one is about to perform incompetently) is therefore likely to lead to more severely impaired performance in children with more differentiated conceptions (Nicholls and Miller, 1984a).

This prediction is supported indirectly by Rholes and coauthors (1980) in a study of the effects of failure on students' performance from kindergarten through fifth grade. Diminished persistence after failure (relative to success) was found only in fifth graders.

What is especially significant is that fifth graders' performance impairment cannot be explained in terms of lower perceived ability. After failure fifth graders did not rate their ability lower than did first or third graders. The explanation may be found in terms of the more negative implications of low self-evaluation when ability is conceived as capacity. The additional finding that, after failure, students' judgments of their own ability correlated positively with performance only in fifth graders supports this position. This interpretation is also consistent with the evidence that only at fifth grade were students' judgments of their own effort and ability negatively correlated. This is consistent with the notion that the conception of ability as capacity (where higher perceived effort leads to inferences of lower ability) predominated only among the fifth graders of this study.

The link between age, the development of the concept of capacity, and impairment of performance after failure was more directly established by Arden Miller (1985). He found impaired performance on anagrams after a series of failures among sixth graders, but not among second graders. More notably, persistence and performance was significantly impaired only in those sixth graders who (according to an independent assessment) had partially or completely mastered the conception of ability as capacity (levels 3 and 4). These two groups did not differ in ratings of their own general ability, their spelling ability, or in teachers' ratings of their ability.[6] Thus the conception of ability as capacity does appear to have the expected negative consequences for action when students face the prospect of a failure that would indicate their incompetence.

A Digression on Method

The interviews about effort and ability revealed several sources of possible confusion or misinterpretation. Detection and resolution of ambiguity and confusion are a normal part of interviews based on the method of critical exploration. These points of possible misinterpretation merit attention because they may help explain how apparently different trends were obtained with quantitative judgment methods that are not designed to deal with these potential sources of confusion.

The age trends in conceptions of ability and effort I have described are not always consistent with trends in quantitative judgments of ability found in other studies. For example, Surber (1980) and Wimmer, Wachter, and Perner (1982) found that a considerable proportion of kindergarten children inferred lower ability from evidence of harder work. This might appear to indicate that the concept of ability as capacity emerges much earlier than one would expect on the basis of the data summarized in this chapter. At the opposite extreme, Harari and Covington (1981) found a preponderance of judgments that students who employed more effort had lower ability only after the eighth grade—later than one would expect if such judgments indicate the conception of ability as capacity. How, then, could such apparently divergent findings occur?

From the perspective of the method of critical exploration, interviews should include an element of validation. That is, interviewers should come out of each session with a sense that they have checked, in several ways, their impressions of the students' conceptions. In this respect, interviews are designed in advance as experiments in which data are gathered to enable one to choose between competing interpretations of the meaning of responses. The researcher would proceed to formal studies of reliability and validity of measurement (such as those described above) only after becoming reasonably confident that most interview protocols presented a valid picture of each child's conceptions. One gains this sense informally in conducting and scoring interviews. More formal support is achieved when good levels of agreement between independent scorings of protocols are obtained—as they consistently have been (Miller, 1985; Nicholls, 1978; Nicholls and Miller, 1984b; Nicholls, Patashnick, and Mettetal, 1986).

In the course of the interview about effort and ability students were asked, "How come the two students scored the same when one worked harder than the other?" This question embodied the essence of the problem we wanted the students to confront. (It is not part of existing quantitative judgment methods.) Among the various responses there are always some that indicate that the situation is not being construed as we intended. Probably the most common "misinterpretation" is that the lazier student cheated. Less frequently, luck is brought in. Some suggest that the lazier student must have learnt the material earlier—perhaps at home. These interpretations (especially the first) could come in support of the conclusion that the harder worker was the more able student. Such interpretations are perfectly plausible and of potential interest in their own right. Researchers studying causal attributions would find them important; they are, however, not relevant to our purpose in these interviews. This is because they preclude examination of a student's conception of ability since they imply that ability was irrelevant to the outcome we are asking them to consider. Accordingly, we clarify the situation so that it is interpreted in the intended fashion. For example, "Yes, people sometimes do cheat, but we didn't want to show you anyone like that. Can you think of any other reason why the two girls might have got the same score?" If, without our knowledge, some students suspect that cheating occurred but others assume we would not show them someone who cheats, our interpretations of their answers to the question "Is one of them smarter?" are likely to be in error. The intent of our interviews is to standardize student interpretations of stimuli. From this perspective, the concept of standardization that means doing the same thing to all students can fail by failing to control interpretations of stimuli (Turiel, 1983).

A second source of possible confusion derives from the question about whether the harder worker is smarter, which can be interpreted as a question about whether the traits of diligence and ability go together—whether harder workers are generally more able. Ability and effort do go together in this sense. It is interesting to note that second- and sixth-grade students' judgments of the levels of their own effort and ability are positively correlated—students who judge themselves as able also judge themselves as hard workers (Blumenfeld, Pintrich, and Hamilton, 1986; Pintrich and Blumenfeld, 1985). But this was not the question we were trying to pose. And our interview question, "How come the two students got the same when one worked harder?" is intended to make this clear to students. A significant proportion of students start our interviews by saying the harder worker is more able, but they "wake up" when asked, "How come they got the same . . . ?" (Nicholls and Miller, 1984b). Some of them assert then that the smart children usually work hard to get their good grades, but that if you can do well without working hard you must be smart. In other words, children's judgments indicating that effort and ability are positively correlated are ambiguous. Such judgments do not tell us whether or not children understand that smarter people are those who are able to do as well as others without trying as hard.

A third source of confusion is that, like any other word, "smart" can have several meanings. Children sometimes spontaneously note this. For example, when asked whether one of two children who gained the same score was smarter, one girl said "She [the less diligent student] is smarter 'cause she knows it better, but she [the harder worker] is smarter 'cause she does the work . . . it's not smart to goof off." It seems likely that at least some children initially choose the harder worker as more able because "it's not smart to goof off." By asking how the two students could score the same despite unequal effort and how they would score if they both worked hard, we attempt to focus attention on ability in the sense of how much people know or can do, rather than in the sense of how diligent they are, without relying on students to interpret our use of the word "smart." Methods that only require students to estimate the ability of others who vary in described or displayed effort and performance appear less likely to control for variations in interpretation of the word "ability."

Fourth, if an actor is described as having "tried very hard" (Kun, 1977; Surber, 1980), children might interpret this as "had to try very hard" or "it was hard for him to do the task." For young children, the statement that a task is very hard is likely to mean that it is too hard for the person, which means the person is incompetent rather than that the task is hard for everyone (see Chapter 3 and Nicholls and Miller, 1983). Young children might, therefore, judge someone who tries "very, very hard" as not very able. This could produce the impression that these children construed ability as capacity. Again, evidence of the associations between children's perceptions of levels of effort and ability is ambiguous if one's interest is in the meanings of effort and ability.

Interviewers may come up against the ever-present problem that young children will tell them what they expect to hear. I do not know of a good study dealing with this, but indirect evidence suggests that the problem might be more significant when quantitative judgments alone are used rather than when the interviewer seeks to clarify students' interpretations of stimuli and to check systematically the meaning of their responses. Quantitative judgments might be more susceptible to situational influences (Nicholls and Miller, 1984b, p. 1998).

The method of critical exploration was developed in an attempt to deal with problems of interpretation such as described above (and in response to problems that arise with less structured clinical interviews). It seems that there is more scope for diverse interpretations in the study of conceptions of ability and effort than of luck and skill. This might account for the appreciable divergence between our findings for the meanings of effort and ability and the results of studies of judgments of level of ability. Studies of luck and skill, in contrast, show a convergence of results.

Some methods of studying intellectual development are more objective than the critical exploration method in the sense that the experimenter does not make judgments during and after testing to the extent that she or he does in the methods that follow the Piagetian tradition. But judgments about meaning cannot be avoided. For researchers whose main concern is with the meaning of concepts, the task is not to avoid such judgments but to make them as soundly as possible. With the method of critical exploration, one designs concrete stimuli and questions to make systematic checks on the meaning of responses, checks and clarifies interpretations during the interview, and checks these meanings again by independent scoring of protocols.

The preceding argument is not, however, a claim that quantitative methods for the study of childrens' ability attributions are invalid. The study of how people judge ability is not equivalent to the study of the meaning of ability. Different methods are calculated to achieve different purposes and should be considered with those purposes in mind. For our purpose, it was essential that children confront the problem of how unequal effort could lead to equal achievement. But it would be inappropriate to confront them with this problem in a study designed to see whether children pay attention to variations in effort or how they weight these variations when judging the ability of others (for example, Surber, 1980). Conversely, methods that do not confront children with the problem of how someone can do as well as another with less effort are poorly adapted to determining whether a child has the conception of ability as capacity. The convergence of our assessments of conceptions of ability with trends in students' performance and their evaluations of the achievements of others indicates that the method achieves its purpose reasonably well, not that it is the only one or that it tells the whole story.

The Meaning of Changes in the Meaning of Ability

The development, in early adolescence, of the conception of ability as capacity seems to be a significant landmark in personal growth. The world is always full of tasks we cannot do—none of us ordinary mortals can leap tall buildings in a single bound. Yet our inability to do such things does not occasion feelings of incompetence. It is being unable to do something that others can do, or—when ability is construed as capacity—needing more effort than others for an equivalent accomplishment that makes us feel incompetent. The attainment of the conception of ability as capacity means that even tasks we are able to master might—if we expect other people to need less time or effort to complete them—offer us no prospect of a sense of accomplishment. Furthermore, the harder we try to avoid low performance, the more convincingly will failure establish incompetence. Hence if we expect failure at tasks at which others succeed, hard work will be an unattractive option. Even if we do not face failure, effort as such becomes less inherently valuable when ability is construed as capacity. Effortful accomplishment is still a good thing, but it does not connote competence as clearly as it does at less differentiated levels. And if we doubt our ability we will—when we construe ability as capacity—have less faith in the power of effort to raise our performance relative to that of others. All of this adds up to the conclusion that if we feel we lack ability, even though we might be able to learn, we will see our best as not good enough and this deficiency will be experienced as more fundamental than it was before we construed ability as capacity. This feeling would make for our devaluing activities that might reveal our incompetence and lead to attempts to avoid such activities.

Our society makes it hard for students to escape from school until late adolescence. But sports organizations are voluntary, and players leave these in droves starting in early adolescence, at about the age when the conception of ability as capacity develops (Roberts, 1984). This trend is all the more impressive when we note that adolescent males view the ability to succeed in sports as more important than in other domains of accomplishment (Coleman, 1961; Roberts, 1984). Thus when students start dropping out of sports in early adolescence, it is not likely to be because they have lost their desire for athletic competence. Youths who dropped out of U.S. Wrestling Foundation teams scored lower in perceived ability and valued wrestling less than those who continued their participation (Burton and Martens, 1986); the two groups did not, however, differ in the importance they placed on other sports. It was only wrestling, at which they felt less competent, that the dropouts valued less. The development of the conception of ability as capacity could well be one of the factors contributing to the withdrawal of adolescents from sports.

In schoolwork, withdrawal must take more subtle forms. These could include seeking a sense of accomplishment in nonacademic domains such as sport, and in membership of groups that actively resist the pressure for academic attainment (Coleman, 1961; Willis, 1977).

A large, complex, competitive society requires that individuals should be prepared to modify their aspirations on the basis of abstract information about their probable standing relative to the members of an unseen reference group. Students with the conception of ability as capacity are more likely than those without it to reduce their effort when they expect to perform worse than their peers (Miller, 1985). Society would, however, be brought to its knees by an excessive loss of motivation to learn on the part of most students before they acquired the numerical and verbal skills required for low-status jobs and for filling out tax forms. The undifferentiated conceptions of effort and ability that predominate through the grade-school years seem to help maintain the level of involvement necessary to develop skills even in students with doubts about their competence.

The fact that the conception of ability as capacity emerges at an age when most students have attained basic literary and numerical skills might look to some as evidence of a "divine plan" to maintain and reproduce the social order of modern industrial and technological societies. Once basic skills are developed, this plan would require many students to reject aspirations to the higher levels of education associated with higher-level occupations. This plan seems served by the emergence, at about age eleven, of the conception of ability as capacity.

5

Intelligence and Knowledge

The conceptions of ability I have discussed until now are general in that they apply to diverse skills. For example, when researchers assess any skill, be it intellectual, musical, or physical, they try to ensure that test performance reflects skill rather than luck. They also endeavor to induce optimum effort so that performances reflect individual differences in current capacity rather than variations in motivation during testing. Furthermore, a score or performance is normally interpreted as high or low with reference to the scores of others. It is important to emphasize that the above conceptions of ability concern the process of assessing abilities rather than giving an explanation of their nature and development. This distinction can be illustrated by research on intelligence. Psychometric researchers generally have neither doubts nor diverse opinions about the principles that intelligence tests should be administered so as to elicit optimum motivation in those being tested, and that scores should be interpreted with reference to the scores of others.[1] They do, however, argue about and seek to evaluate diverse views on the nature and determinants of various intellectual skills. In this chapter, my concern is with the development of conceptions of such intellectual abilities.

To keep this distinction clear, I use the term *conceptions of intelligence* to refer to views about the nature and determinants of various intellectual skills—the properties of these skills and the ways they can be developed. Do students, for example, distinguish aspects of intelligence involving reasoning and problem solving from those that reflect the amount of information a person can recall about specific topics? If this distinction is made, how might the possibility of change in these different aspects of intelligence be construed? The term *conceptions of ability*, on the other hand, refers to understandings relevant to the immediate or proximal causes of performance. The conception of ability as capacity, for example, concerns the dynamics of effort and competence in determining performance. Accordingly, the stimuli and questions we used to assess this conception were designed to focus students' attention on the immediate effects of effort on performance, not on the long-term development of abilities. The specific characteristics of the skill involved were not of concern in the interviews about conceptions of ability and effort. Conversely, the interview we (Nicholls, Patashnick, and Mettetal, 1986) developed to assess conceptions of intelligence focused on the specific properties of various intellectual skills and on how these might be improved.

Different cultures include different forms of competence under the term "intelligence" (Berry, 1984; Goodnow, 1980). Our society also admits variation in the types of competence that are referred to as intelligence. Adults are readier to take social competence as an indication of intelligence in young children than in adolescents (Siegler and Richards, 1982). Adolescents employ the term with more discrimination than do eight-year-olds (Murray and Bisanz, 1987). Across this age span students use the term "intelligence" to describe examples of competence at academic and mental activities, but older students are less likely to apply the term to examples of social and physical ability. Our work has been restricted to the development of the understanding of competencies that, in this society, would clearly be considered intellectual skills by children and by adults.

A starting point for our work was Sternberg, Conway, Ketron, and Bernstein's (1981) evidence that both expert and lay North American adults conceptualize intelligence as "fluid" and "crystallized." Fluid intelligence consists mainly of abstract, nonverbal reasoning and problem-solving skills, whereas crystallized intelligence pertains mainly to verbal skills such as vocabulary and comprehension. According to Horn (1968), "a relatively large proportion of the reliable variance in fluid intelligence reflects a pattern of physiological influences and a relatively small proportion of this variance reflects acculturation, whereas the opposite emphasis occurs for crystallized intelligence" (pp. 247–248).

Because most adults describe intelligence in terms analogous to the fluid and crystallized distinction, we evolved a method we hoped would reveal such concepts in students who had them, but which could also detect other ways of construing these two aspects of intelligence. A fundamental decision concerned the stimuli about which we questioned students.[2] We chose items from a verbal and from a nonverbal intelligence test that illustrates crystallized and fluid intelligence respectively. In each item of the verbal test, a group of words was shown in heavy type and a further word—nearest in meaning to those in heavy type—had to be selected from a second group of words in lighter type. The nonverbal test was essentially the same except that unfamiliar abstract figures were employed instead of words.

Students from first grade through college were interviewed about two other students, one of whom was represented as more able than his or her classmates on the verbal test and less able on the nonverbal test. The second student's standing on these tests was the opposite. The following extract from the transcript of an interview with a sixteen-year-old illustrates our finding that conceptions akin to fluid and crystallized intelligence were common at (and after) this age. (The full schedule of questions is given in Nicholls et al., 1986.)

"What if these two children wanted to be near the top of their class on both tests. Could they both get better at the one they are bad at?"

"Yes."

"Would it be easier for one of them to get better?"

"Be easier for the one who is low on words." (*Students referred to the verbal test as "words" and the nonverbal test as "shapes."*)

"How can you tell?"

"The words are just memorizing. Shapes need more judgment. It's not memory so it'd be harder. You could get better [at shapes] but it still would be tough to do."

"What if a new student comes to your class and the teacher could use only one test to see how intelligent or clever the student is. Would one test be better for this?"

"Shapes show judgment, common sense. Words show what they've been taught. Shapes would be better if you wanted to not be biased by the person's background. If they are high on this, they have ability if they want to use it."

"Do you think one of these children is smarter or more intelligent than the other one?"

"Yes and no. More judgment is shown on shapes . . . [but] they are both intelligent in different ways."

Most undergraduates gave similar responses. For example: "There really aren't specific things to learn [for the shapes test]. In that way, it's more reasoning [than words] and it's harder to teach reasoning than facts" and "the words test is more or less memorization. For the shapes you have to analyze. [The person who is good on shapes] is more analytical."

These excerpts illustrate the most differentiated of the three levels of conception of verbal and abstract (nonverbal) intelligence that we isolated (level 3b). The essence of this conception is that accumulated information or the content of memory is distinguished from reasoning, problem solving, or (as a few students put it) creative thinking.

Conceptions of Verbal and Nonverbal Intelligence

1. *Intellectual skills are evaluated in terms of their subjective difficulty.*

Verbal and abstract reasoning tasks are distinguished on the basis of how hard they seem to the subject. The intrinsic properties of the different skills are not referred to. Most children judge the verbal test as harder but not because words have meanings that must be learned and remembered. Some fluctuate in their choices. The identifying factor, however, is the self-referenced or tautological nature of the explanations for why one skill is harder.

2. *Intelligence involves effortful learning or acquisition of information.*

a. Verbal intelligence is seen to require learning and retaining many specific word meanings. It is acquired through teaching and depends on systematic or conscious attempts to learn. Abstract stimuli are not seen to have specific meanings that must be learned or remembered. Abstract reasoning can be done with little or no learning, memory, or effort and is regarded as easier to improve. The implication is that abstract reasoning is not a real or significant form of intelligence.

b. Verbal intelligence and abstract intelligence are not seen as inherently different. Both require systematic efforts to acquire information and can be improved by direct teaching. Each type of intelligence is seen as requiring the same amount of learning and the rate of improvement of each is dependent on amount of effort (and teaching) to the same extent.

c. Verbal and abstract intelligence are both seen as dependent on acquisition of information and are not viewed as inherently different from each other. Opportunities to acquire them, however, are seen as unequal. Dictionaries and many other opportunities exist to learn words. Fewer opportunities are available to learn abstract stimuli, making it harder to improve abstract reasoning.

3. *Acquisition of information is distinguished from problem solving.*

a. Verbal material can be memorized because words have specific meanings. Abstract stimuli, lacking meanings, are harder to compare, are more confusing, or require more concentration to permit mental comparisons. Thus abstract intelligence would be harder to improve.

b. Verbal reasoning reflects memory whereas abstract reasoning reflects problem-solving ability. Words have specific meanings. They can be learned by memorizing or by a planned effort to learn. Abstract reasoning is more a matter of thinking ability. Rather than memory, it reflects common sense, creativity, or general experience. Thus (as in 3a) it would be harder to improve abstract intelligence.

The distinguishing features of the second (middle) level are an absence of the distinction between reasoning ability and the contents of memory, and the construal of intellectual abilities in terms of the amount of memorization involved. Some students at this level see the verbal test as requiring more information than the nonverbal test (level 2a). Extracts from three interviews illustrate this position: "Shapes are easier [to improve on]. All you have to do is look at them . . . The words test tells more of what you know. The other is just shapes." You could improve "on shapes faster. You've got to put just shapes together. Not [like] words that you sometimes can't pronounce. You might not know the words . . . [It would be easier to teach someone how to do shapes because] the teacher could tell them to just look at the outside texture [of the shapes] and then go to the inside." Again, "Shapes are easier [to improve on]. For words you have to remember the long word and the definition . . . You just have to look at the shapes."

Students at level 2b see the two tests as requiring similar amounts of information. For example:

"It would be equally easy for them [to improve on either test] if they practice enough."
"How could this one [who is poor at words] get better?"
"By looking up words. Use a dictionary."
"How could this one [who is low on shapes] get better?"
"Practice looking at shapes."
"If the teacher tried to help them both, might she be able to improve one of them more than the other?"
"Equal if they both try."
Another example.
"Would it be easier for one of them to get better?"
"Be the same."
"Why?"
"If they both study hard they'd be better equally."
"How could this one [who is poor at shapes] get better?"
Look in books of shapes. Ask someone to help."
"How could this one [who is poor at words] get better?"
"Study. Look up in the dictionary."

The students at level 2c, fewer in number, differ from the 2b subgroup only in that they see fewer opportunities to "look up" or learn shapes. There are "no shapes in the dictionary." "It's harder to look up shapes." "Mostly you'd have to find it [shapes] in math books. It's easier to get reading books."

What sets levels 2a, 2b, and 2c apart from each other are distinctions in content or interpretation of specific tasks, not differences in interpretational framework. For students at each level, interpretations hinge on the amount of information that seems to be required and the assumption that this is acquired through conscious effort or direct teaching. This is a quiz-show or Trivial Pursuit game conception of intelligence. Our interview was designed to make it easy for students to distinguish reasoning skill from the contents of memory, but level 2 conceptions are marked by an absence of such a distinction.

Students at the lowest level made almost no reference to the inherent properties of the different skills in explaining why it might be harder or easier to improve on the task. At this level, subjective judgments of difficulty predominate and explanations are tautological. For example:

> "Would it be easier for one of them to get better?"
> "Easier on the shapes."
> "Why?"
> "'Cause shapes are easier."
> "What makes them easier?"
> "This one [verbal test] has words." (*Rephrasing of questions produced repetition of these answers.*)
> "Would one of these tests be better . . . to find out how smart [a new student is]?"
> "Words."
> "Why?"
> "It uses words. They'd probably need help on words."
> "Why not on shapes?"
> "They probably know them."
> *Another example.*
> "Shapes are easier."
> "How can you tell?"
> "'Cause shapes are easier."
> "Why are they easier?"
> "This [verbal test] has hard words."

At level 1 children make almost no reference to the inherent properties of different types of intellectual ability; the subjective sense of difficulty predominates. Level 2 represents a conceptual advance in that it involves a specification of what makes intelligence difficult to acquire—namely, the amount of information that must be acquired through effort. Level 3b, which more or less differentiates fluid and crystallized intelligence, represents an advance over level 2 in that memory is clearly distinguished from problem solving or reasoning ability. Level 3a appears as a less complete or transitional construction of this distinction. Although abstract reasoning is seen as a significant type of skill and as more difficult to improve, it is not explicitly described as a problem-solving ability.

The ages of students corresponding to each conception of intelligence are shown in Table 5.1. The association between conceptions of intelligence and levels of differentiation of effort and ability is shown in Table 5.2. Analyses of the data of these two tables support the view that the conception resembling fluid and crystallized intelligence (3b) is the most mature one, that 3a is close to it, and that the conception based on subjective difficulty (level 1) is the least mature (Nicholls et al., 1986).

Table 5.1 Conceptions of Intelligence as Function of Age

Age	As judged on basis of subjective difficulty (1)	As information acquisition			As fluid and crystallized[a]		N
		(2a)	(2b)	(2c)	(3a)	(3b)	
6–7	21	—	1	—	—	—	22
8–9	14	2	6	1	—	—	23
10–11	2	5	8	3	2	—	20
12–13	2	10	11	2	4	1	30
14–15	1	3	3	—	9	3	19
16–18	—	6	9	1	4	9	29
19–22	—	3	1	—	3	20	27
N	40	29	39	7	22	33	170

Note: Values are numbers of students: Those younger than nineteen were in public schools and those nineteen and older, in college.
  a. The conception is only partially developed at level 3a.

Intelligence and Ability

The conceptions of intelligence show some parallels with the conceptions of ability and effort. For example, the level 2 conception of intelligence as based on effortful acquisition of information parallels the level 2 conception of ability where effort is seen as the prime determinant of task outcomes.[3] At the other end, a belief in the limited value of effort for improving abstract intelligence is most evident in the most differentiated conception of intelligence (3b). This parallels the mature conception of ability as capacity, which recognizes the limited effect of effort on performance. However, these conceptual parallels are not expressed as empirical parallels. As we observe in Table 5.2, the most differentiated conception of ability emerges before the corresponding conception of intelligence.

This finding is not surprising, because the understanding of

Table 5.2 Conception of Intelligence as Function of Conception of Ability

Conception of ability	Conception of Intelligence						
	Subjective difficulty	Information acquisition			Fluid and crystal- lized		
	(1)	(2a)	(2b)	(2c)	(3a)	(3b)	N
Schoolchildren							
At level 1[a]	16	1	4	—	—	—	21
At level 2	22	9	16	2	4	—	53
At level 3	2	6	7	2	3	1	21
At level 4	—	10	11	3	12	12	48
College students							
At level 4	—	3	1	—	3	20	27
N	40	29	39	7	22	33	170

a. Conception of ability at level 1 is the least differentiated; level 4 (ability as capacity) is the most differentiated.

intelligence presumably depends on understanding both the dynamics of performance on tests (conceptions of ability) and how individuals acquire the skills they bring to testing situations. Furthermore, circumstances that "demand" the conception of ability as capacity appear both ubiquitous and logically compelling: one can often observe individuals expending more or less effort for the same accomplishment. No such decisive or frequent occurrences "demand" the conception of fluid and crystallized intelligence.

The conception of ability as capacity clearly embodies a more adequate explanation of the specific phenomena it addresses than do the less differentiated conceptions of ability. Furthermore, the logic implicit in the conception of ability as capacity closely resembles that of early formal operations, while the earlier conceptions correspond to the earlier stages of logical thought described by Inhelder and Piaget (1958) (Nicholls, 1978, pp. 801, 805). The various conceptions of intelligence, on the other hand, appear not to correspond well to levels of Piagetian operational logic. It is also less clear that the most mature conception of intelligence embodies the most adequate solution to the questions it addresses. Although concepts like fluid and crystallized intelligence are found among experts (Sternberg et al., 1981), there is no unanimity among them about how verbal and abstract intelligence should be construed. It is also easier to visualize possible cultural variations in conceptions of intelligence than in conceptions of ability. In these respects the conceptions of ability and effort seem to correspond to what Kohlberg, Levine, and Hewer (1983) term hard "stages," whereas the conceptions of intelligence appear to be softer "stages."[4]

Evaluations of Intellectual Abilities

We have observed how different conceptions of ability are accompanied by different evaluative judgments. A similar pattern was expected to emerge with conceptions of intelligence. At the end of the interview about intelligence, students were asked whether they would rather be good at the verbal or the abstract intelligence test. Overall, 67 percent of the students with conceptions akin to fluid and crystallized intelligence (level 3b), but only 16 percent of the ones on levels 1 and 2 preferred abstract intelligence (Nicholls, et al., 1986).

Convergent findings were obtained in a study of Taiwanese and Australian sixteen-year-olds and college students (Chen, Braithwaite, and Jong, 1982). Some differences appeared in valuing of skills—the Chinese valued factual information more highly than did Australians. But the similarities were more striking. Both groups saw abstract (spatial) reasoning as more important than verbal-educational ability and rote memory.

In Western culture disciplines that seem to involve abstract reasoning have long been accorded special status. Plato exalted rational contemplation over other forms of thought. He saw many socially indispensable skills as trivial and devised a course of education, culminating in mathematics and philosophy, that served to separate common people from aristocrats. Similarly, the seven liberal arts of the medieval curriculum were divided into an introductory or basic trivium and a more advanced quadrivium. (Trivium is perhaps the source of our word trivial; Safire, 1980. p. 277.) The four subjects of the more advanced and more esteemed quadrivium were the "mathematical arts"—arithmetic, geometry, astronomy, and music (Eby and Arrowood, 1940). A person who can distinguish fluid from crystallized intelligence is not bound to embrace this hierarchy or the Platonic framework. But Plato's position would more easily be adopted by individuals who could make such a distinction than by those who could not.[5]

The greater value placed on abstract reasoning that accompanies the differentiation of concepts of intelligence might also make academic subjects such as mathematics especially threatening to students who doubt their fluid intelligence. When ability is seen as capacity, the consequences of low perceived ability become more negative. The concept of fluid intelligence might, similarly, have especially negative emotional consequences for those who believe they are deficient in this aspect of intelligence. This could lead to a choice of academic subjects and occupations that seem to demand little fluid intelligence. Those who see themselves as high in abstract reasoning might seek to enhance their self-esteem by a choice of subjects and occupations that appear to demand this form of intelligence.

Conceptions of intelligence might also be expressed in student attitudes to diverse teaching methods. For example, provided they do not doubt their own competence, students with conceptions akin to fluid and crystallized intelligence appear more likely than others to favor teaching that fosters problem finding and solving rather than memorization. One high school student's comment illustrates this point: "The way teachers are, they'd be more impressed with someone who was good with words. They don't pay attention to the way you think, just what you absorb." Younger children gave no hint of such an attitude. Their conceptions of intelligence appear to dispose them to see virtue in memorization. Indeed, level 2 (quiz-show) conceptions of intelligence probably contribute to the resistance that teachers who attempt to encourage self-directed problem finding and solving may encounter from younger students. On the other hand, level 2 conceptions of intelligence might be strengthened by the emphasis on memorization and on the following of teachers' rules that prevails in the schools (Goodlad, 1983).

Conceptions of Knowledge

Just as questions about intelligence go beyond questions about ability (as I use this term), so do questions about the nature of knowledge go beyond those I have discussed under the heading of intelligence. The fact that a student can conceptualize two types of intelligence would not tell us much about her conception of knowledge. It would not tell us, for example, how she might interpret statements such as "the theory of evolution is just a theory"; "psychology is not a real science because its measurements are not exact"; or "moral philosophy, social science, and literature are all ways of figuring out how we should relate to others."

In their research on the development of knowledge, William Perry and his associates (1970, 1981) employed wide-ranging interviews of college students. The first position described by Perry (1970) is a dualist one: knowledge is either good or bad, right or wrong. Right answers to problems exist somewhere and are known to the proper authorities. Knowledge is acquired by hard work and mastery of the answers that good authorities provide. The dualist, black-white, right-wrong conception of knowledge begins to be transformed as students recognize the diversity of views that exist on any given topic. Initially, this diversity is not seen as legitimate. Instructors who present diverse perspectives without saying which one is "right" are seen as poor authorities. Academic disciplines are evaluated in the same way. For example: "I'll tell you the best thing about science courses: their lectures are all right. They sort of say the facts. But when you get to a humanities course, especially—oh, they're awful—the lecturer is just reading things into the book that were never meant to be there" (Perry, 1981, p. 82). But even science can fail. "They're supposed to teach you to arrive at more logical conclusions and look at things in a more scientific manner. Actually, what you get out of that course is that science is a terrifically confused thing in which nobody knows what's coming off anyway" (p. 82).

Gradually students come to accept the existence of diverse viewpoints as legitimate, but only in areas where they believe the right answers have not yet been discovered. As the frontiers of knowledge are extended, the grounds for legitimate diversity will, in this view, be reduced. But where right answers have not yet been established, one opinion can be as good as another. Although legitimate diversity is recognized, it is seen as more or less temporary or extrinsic. It is not construed as an inherent or fundamental characteristic of human understanding.

Eventually, and by no means for all college students, an understanding of relativity as an inherent feature of knowledge emerges: "So here were all these theorists and theories and stuff in [economics] and psychology and historiography—I didn't even take any straight philosophy—and hell, I said, 'These are *games*, just *games*, and everybody makes up their own rules! So it's gotta be bullshit!' But then I realized, 'What else have we got?'" (p. 89).

Without the one right, objective view on any major topic, students face the prospect of leaving the Eden of right knowledge and good authorities. When the fruit of the tree of knowledge is not marked "good" and "evil," "right" and "wrong," each individual faces the responsibility for choosing a perspective, an interpretational framework. This is threatening for many and not all can face it (Perry, 1981). But for those who do, it can mean new freedom and excitement. These are the students who are likely to see, as Lewis Thomas (1982) wishes more of them did, science as a high adventure in which the issues often have every-one baffled, where new work can turn a whole field upside down, and where something that looks like an important answer even-tually turns into a question. On the other hand, for students with the earlier, dualist views of knowledge, Thomas's views about science might raise doubts about his status as an authority on the subject.

In the dualist conception, acquisition of knowledge is a matter of accumulating a body of correct answers by hard work. This parallels the view of intelligence (level 2) as a reflection of the amount of information one has memorized through conscious effort. A further—though conceptually more remote—parallel can be drawn with the imperfectly differentiated conceptions of ability and effort (level 2) wherein effort is seen as the prime determinant of performance: effortful accomplishment is equated with ability. The dualist conception of knowledge is a later formulation than the information-acquisition conception of intelligence, which, in turn, comes after the concepts of effort and ability have become differentiated. Yet each of these conceptions—more than the sub-sequent conceptions in each domain—appears to dispose students to see virtue in what might be termed authoritarian approaches to education. These include an emphasis on dogged persistence and, in the case of the latter two, an orientation to authority and "established" facts rather than to conceptual coherence and con-sidered individual judgment and responsibility. Conversely, more differentiated and integrated conceptions of intelligence and (more markedly) knowledge bring with them new opportunities for the exercise of individual judgments about what makes sense and what is worth knowing. Together with these comes an aware-ness of new responsibilities for making such judgments about logic and meaning. With it, our picture of the ideal educator changes to that of an adviser or collaborator rather than a law-giver or a source of facts.

Conclusion

Perry's account of the development of conceptions of knowledge brings the story back to one of the key points of my introduction. The dualist conception of knowledge is analogous to the conception of science as a value-neutral activity in which unbiased scientists observe *the* facts and, from these, deduce the nature of reality in a rational, logical fashion that differs fundamentally from the way we think, for example, about literature. This view of science is in sharp contrast to the postmodern view of writers such as Rorty and Toulmin, for whom scientific activity always involves the adoption of some interpretive stance. They deny that there must be one objective view of reality, and argue that a sharp distinction between objective scientific knowledge and hermeneutic relativity does not hold up. This more recent view of science is analogous to the relativistic conception of knowledge, which is late to emerge in individual development (Kurfiss, 1977; Perry, 1981).

But I have not discussed conceptions of knowledge merely to bring the discussion back to the themes with which I started. My main focus in Part I has been on conceptions of ability. The development of concepts of intelligence and knowledge was brought in partly to remove confusion about what conceptions of ability involve. It is especially easy to confuse ability attributions with the meaning of ability, and both are commonly confused with concepts of intelligence. The description of conceptions of intelligence and knowledge ought to make it clearer what conceptions of ability do not encompass. Later, when we consider the role of motivation in education in Part III, students' and teachers' views of knowledge and intelligence will be of much importance. An exclusive focus on conceptions of ability would provide a rather thin basis for discussion.

Nevertheless, as a matter of choice, it is conceptions of ability or competence that are the central concern in this book. This choice partly reflects the fact that matters relating to ability have more general applicability than issues of intelligence and knowledge. People can feel able or incompetent in a vast number of areas. Activities as diverse as athletics, gardening, cooking, carpentry, writing, drawing, speaking, singing, music appreciation, motorcycle riding, and sexual intercourse can become domains in which we wrestle with feelings of competence or incompetence. And the developmental evidence I have reviewed indicates that the various ways of construing ability have related consequences for individuals and for societies.

II

Achievement Motivation

6

The Task and the Self

I have gone to some trouble to describe a process of development from less to more adequate ways of construing competence. This picture of individual development might appear to parallel the view of science as a linear progression toward more objective representations of reality. But this parallel is misleading. The series I have described is better thought of as a sequence of increasingly adequate answers to only some of the many questions one could ask about competence and accomplishment. In fact students did sometimes answer questions other than the ones we had posed. Our attempts to ensure that they answered our questions instead of theirs sought to keep our data comprehensible, not to assert that our questions were the only legitimate ones. Indeed, one of my themes in Part II is that excessive preoccupation with issues of personal capacity has unfortunate consequences for individuals and societies.

Just as a given scientific approach may be useful for some purposes and not for others, so the conception of ability as capacity is useful for thinking about certain types of problems but not others. One should not leap from the premise that more differentiated conceptions of ability embody more conceptually adequate solutions to one type of question to the conclusion that individuals either should or always will employ the most differentiated conception available to them. What we do and the concepts we employ depend on our purposes—on what we want to accomplish or on what question we want to ask.

Empathy for the "Subject"

The attempt to understand thought and action in terms of individuals' purposes can be termed an intentional approach (Dennett, 1978). It assumes that thoughts and actions are rational and economical attempts to attain certain goals. These means might not suffice to accomplish the desired goals, but they cannot be useless in the sense that they would be if they were not "designed" to serve some purpose. In other words, I am using the term "rational" to refer to the way a goal is pursued rather than to the advisability of having or pursuing a particular goal. For example:

> Some young mathematicians had inveigled the great mathematician Johnny von Neumann, who invented game theory with his elegant "minimax" theorem, into playing poker with them . . . That night, von Neumann raised every bet an opponent made. He seemed to bet without looking at his cards. Within thirty minutes, he had lost all his chips, paid the winners, and excused himself, muttering about some problems on his mind. At first, the remaining players were stunned, then they occupied themselves with an analytic recapitulation of his strategy. Finally, one player worked out the solution: "Hell, he wasn't trying to maximize his money, he was minimizing his time."   (Ankeny, 1982)

To a committed poker-player taking it for granted that von Neumann's purpose was to win, the mathematician's actions might seem irrational. But his actions can be seen as rational or efficient attempts to achieve a different goal—to leave the game without seriously offending the other players.

It is interesting to note that when a person tries to empathize with another, she tends to adopt the intentional perspective: she seeks to interpret the other's actions in terms of the other's purposes. When, on the other hand, that person tries to predict behavior, she is less likely to think about the other's goals or the meanings that actions have for the other (Hoffman, Mischel, and Mazze, 1981). Among academic psychologists, empathy has not been widely approved as a perspective for understanding people, let alone rats. Yet John Garcia (1981) owns that "I always use anthropomorphism and teleology to predict animal behavior because this works better than most learning theories. I could rationalize this heresy by pointing to our common neurosensory systems or to convergent evolutionary forces. But, in truth, I merely put myself in the animals' place" (p. 151).

The intentional approach does not depend on the assumption that people or animals are conscious of their goals. When playing chess with a computer, for example (Dennett, 1978), we are more likely to anticipate its moves and beat it if we act as if the computer is trying to play by the rules with the purpose of winning; it will not help to study its wiring or program. Yet this does not mean we must believe that the computer is consciously attempting to beat us. Like Freud, most of us will at times attribute to others purposes of which they appear to be unaware.

Of course if we are attempting to repair our computer, the intentional perspective will be of little value. In this case we will do well to study the hardware. This illustrates once again the point that a given way of construing anything is not categorically better or worse than all others. The value of any interpretive stance depends on the purpose for which it is employed.[1] The attempt to understand and predict cognition and action by way of empathy—by trying to put oneself in the shoes of our "subjects"—may not satisfy those who think that psychology is only good science when it is comfortless and impersonal. Yet I hope to show that this intentional or empathetic perspective may advance us toward other useful goals, including predictions of action and accomplishment—an enterprise that is dear to the hearts of most researchers, even those who eschew the strategy of empathy.

One of my goals in constructing the theory presented in this section derived from the observation that the different approaches to achievement motivation (noted subsequently) each dealt with important aspects of the topic that were overlooked by others. "A comprehensive framework for the analysis of achievement motivation should combine the strong features of the different approaches" (Nicholls, 1980c, p. 2). But the judgment of what is an important aspect of a theory depends partly on what one wants to accomplish. Previous approaches were of limited value for helping us to understand inequality of motivation for intellectual development and for deciding what might best be done to foster optimum motivation in students of all levels of ability (Nicholls,

1979b). I sought a theory that would do these things. The keys to the resulting theory are the intentional perspective and the distinction between more and less differentiated conceptions of ability.

Task Involvement and Ego Involvement

Self-Evaluation. Suppose you asked a friend who had recently joined a chess class how she was finding it. One of many possible answers that would make sense is "I'm really pleased because I've just mastered some new and interesting opening gambits." However, if your friend gave this as an answer to the question "How good are you at chess?" you would have cause to ask the question again. The information that someone is pleased that she learned something tells us little or nothing about how able she is (Jagacinski and Nicholls, 1984a). If she answered, "Well, I've always beaten everyone except one person in the class and I know he's been spending a lot more time on it than I have," our question about her competence would have been answered more adequately. When we are explicitly seeking to evaluate our own or another's ability, we must depend on the most differentiated conception: ability as capacity. That is to say, we need to make sure we are evaluating ability and not effort or task difficulty (or ease).

A common situation that would induce concerns about the adequacy of our ability is what we call *a test.* The more highly an individual values the skill being tested, the stronger these concerns about competence are likely to be. In our culture, for example, such concerns are not likely to be aroused in adolescent males by a test of sewing ability. On the other hand, the announcement that a task is a measure of intelligence or a test "to see how good you are at schoolwork" would usually induce such concerns. Interpersonal competition on skill tasks also directly raises the issue of who is best and is virtually the same as a test. For example, "We are going to have a race to see who is fastest. Everyone line up here," amounts to the statement that "We are going to test everyone's running ability." Interpersonal competition, especially when valued skills are involved, is apt to increase explicit concerns about how able one is and, thereby, induce self-evaluation in terms of the conception of ability as capacity. Public occasions can also arouse explicit concerns about one's ability: facing an audience, for instance, or making a video recording (Carver and Scheier, 1981). In these situations concerns about how one might appear from the perspective of others are high. Therefore, in a performance involving valued skills, anything that increases public self-awareness will increase the focus on the adequacy of ability and, consequently, increase the tendency to evaluate oneself in terms of the conception of ability as capacity.

On the other hand, if we are concerned only about learning, understanding something more fully, solving a problem, or performing a specific action, the conception of ability as capacity is irrelevant. This is because in such cases we can evaluate our performance perfectly well simply by noting whether our level of performance is improving, whether we are gaining in understanding, or whether we can perform the task with less effort. We need not ask whether we have performed better or with less effort than our peers. Indeed, such information is irrelevant. In other words, when our aim is to solve a problem, to learn, or to increase our understanding, we become like little children for whom competence is signalled by gains in level of performance or by increases in the sense of certainty that they can understand or do something.

In very young children, ability and difficulty are self-referenced: tasks are seen as more difficult if failure appears more likely and the more difficult tasks appear the more does success indicate high ability. Accomplishing tasks that one feels uncertain of being able to complete (which, if performances are repeated, is the same as a greater gain in mastery or a greater reduction in the time or effort needed to master a task) indicates greater competence. Furthermore, because more effort is seen to lead to more learning (or because a need for greater effort indicates a harder task), the more effort expended in completing a task, the higher the perceived ability. That is, the feeling of effortful accomplishment is the feeling of competence.[2]

Many observers have noted that humans (and monkeys) will spontaneously attempt to improve their levels of performance or understanding when they get tasks that present them with a moderate challenge (Asch, 1952; Deci, 1975; Elkind, 1971; Harlow,

1950; Hunt, 1963; Stott, 1961; White, 1959). The tendency to seek competence in this undifferentiated sense is, it seems, one of our basic inclinations. Yet it does not seem possible to induce it in the direct way that explicit concerns about one's capacity can be induced—by, for example, announcing an IQ test. Instead, all we can do is to present suitable tasks that offer some challenge or a chance for growth in competence and reduce factors (such as physiological stress and task-extrinsic incentives) that would undermine or transform the desire to improve one's skills or understanding of the world (deCharms, 1984, p. 276).

All this adds up to the prediction that we will tend to employ the undifferentiated conception of ability when we are engaged in suitable tasks without evaluative cues (or task-extrinsic incentives or physiological stress). Use of our most differentiated conception is, especially when valued skills are involved, predicted to be increased by evaluative, test-like cues, an emphasis on interpersonal competition or social comparison, and by events (audiences or recordings) that heighten public self-awareness.[3]

Interest. Working under these different conceptions of ability will have related consequences for the experience of interest or enjoyment in a task performance. When we have the goal of establishing high capacity, effortful accomplishment is not enough. This is because, even if we accomplish something that is very difficult for us, this might not indicate that we have high capacity. If others find the task easier than we did, our great effort to complete the task would indicate low ability on our part. When our concern is to establish that our capacity is high, we must calculate whether our effortful accomplishment will be adequate to this purpose; our striving will tend to be experienced as the means and not as an end in itself. This state is nicely illustrated by a character in the film *Chariots of Fire* who, after losing a race, announced, "I won't run if I can't win." (Deci and Ryan, 1980, use different reasoning to develop a similar prediction about competition and intrinsic motivation.)

On the other hand, if our goal is defined in terms of the less differentiated conception of ability, to accomplish, learn, or understand something we were not sure we could do is to be competent. In the very act of accomplishing, understanding, or learning we achieve a sense of competence. That is, the activity will be experienced more as an end in itself—it will be more intrinsically satisfying.

The Terms. I label the state where the less differentiated conception defines the goal as *task involvement* and the state where the differentiated conception describes it as *ego involvement*. Ego involvement connotes the desire to enhance the self by establishing one's superiority relative to others, even when one might not be directly competing with or even imagining any specific others—while taking an individual intelligence test, for example. This reflects popular usage of the term "ego." For example, Royal Robbins says of the people he meets when kayaking: "there are some ego-maniacs who are only interested in how great they can look. But . . . kayaking has put me in contact with many people . . . who aren't interested in making money or dominating others" (Clark, 1982, p. 8). Similarly, Einstein argued that "the desire to be acknowledged as better, stronger, or more intelligent than a fellow . . . easily leads to an excessively egoistic psychological adjustment" (1956, p. 34).

This usage of ego involvement also has a history that is, for the field of psychology where it sometimes seems that all researchers seek new names for the phenomena they study, unusually long. (Alper, 1946; Asch, 1952; Ausubel, Novak, and Hanesian, 1978; Crutchfield, 1962; DeCharms, 1968; Klein and Schoenfeld, 1941; Maehr and Braskamp, 1986; Nicholls, 1979b; Ryan, 1982; Weiner, 1970). Klein and Schoenfeld (1941), for example, spoke of ego involvement as a state where "social prestige, self-esteem, fear of academic standing are closely bound up in . . . tasks" (p. 249) and induced ego involvement by presenting a task as "an intelligence test, the results of which were to be recorded . . . in the Personnel Bureau of the college" (p. 253). There is, it seems to me, some advantage in maintaining our links to our predecessors by retaining their terms, especially when they resonate with common usage. It should be noted, however, that "ego" can have other connotations (Greenwald, 1982).

In some early usages (Alper, 1946) task involvement implies that a task or the skills it demands are of little importance to the person. In this usage, task involvement is a polar opposite of ego involvement. But, as Asch points out, the conception of involvement as a single continuum running from high to low eliminates the distinction between types of involvement or importance. It also makes the unjustified assumption that the only sense in which the achievement of a task can be important to us is as a vehicle for demonstrating our superiority over others. Furthermore, if a task is unimportant to a person, it is strange to describe such a person as task-involved. These problems are absent from the use of the term by Asch (1952), Crutchfield (1962), Covington and Beery (1976), Nakamura and Finck (1973), Ausubel et al. (1978), Maehr and Braskamp (1986), for whom task involvement implies a state where performing, understanding, or completing tasks is important in its own right, not as a means to establishing one's superiority over others. The logic of this usage is captured by Koch (1956) describing a state wherein the person is dominated by the problem context "or, better by a certain direction defined by the problem context . . . All systems of personality seem 'polarized' into the behavior . . . [In this state] you do not merely 'work at' or 'on' the task; you have committed yourself to the task, and in some sense you are the task" (p. 67). Similarly, Asch (1952) speaks of task orientation as a state where the task "becomes the center of concern. We may speak here of intrinsic interest, in contrast to that which grows solely out of the rewards reached at the end of the task" (p. 303). In this sense, task involvement does not imply that accomplishment is not important to the individual. It does imply that individuals do not consciously focus on questions about their competence as they do when their egos are involved.[4]

An innovation here with respect to task and ego involvement is that I have explicitly related these states to more and less differentiated conceptions of ability. This and the systematic use of the intentional perspective to develop predictions distinguishes the present (Nicholls, 1980d; 1983; 1984a; 1984b) from previous discussions of these motivational states.

Finally, as others (for example, Ausubel, et al., 1978) imply, it is useful to distinguish ego involvement from other extrinsic work-inducing factors such as coercive teaching or offers of rewards (Deci and Ryan, 1985; Kruglanski, 1975; Lepper and Greene, 1978). It might also be noted that drawing distinctions between task involvement, ego involvement, and other forms of extrinsic involvement does not mean that such states exist in isolation. We can fluctuate between states and experience combinations of different levels of them.

Determinants of Self-Evaluations and Interest

I have argued that people use either more differentiated or less differentiated conceptions of ability to evaluate their performance.[5] I have also argued that the conception of ability as capacity (or the person's most differentiated conception) will be activated when, instead of being presented in a "neutral" fashion, tasks that involve valued skills are presented (a) as tests of those skills; (b) in a context of interpersonal competition or comparison; or (c) in situations that increase public self-awareness. Ego-involving conditions were also predicted to diminish intrinsic interest in task performance. How do these predictions stand up in the face of data?

Self-Evaluation. Butler (1987) obtained findings concerning students' goals in conditions that would favor task versus ego involvement. Using factor analysis, she found that students' attributions of their effort to interest in the task were associated with attributions of effort to a desire for improved performance. Attributions of effort to desires to perform better than others and to avoid doing worse than them formed a separate cluster. In other words, the distinction between task involvement and ego involvement was manifest in students' reasons for their own efforts. Butler also found that students' attributions of their successes to interest, effort, and learning were highly associated. These results are consistent with the proposition that task involvement is marked by intrinsic interest and a desire to improve through effort. Also consistent with the distinction between task and ego involvement is the finding that attributions of success to high ability and to the relative performance of other students (indicating ego involvement) were associated with each other but independent of attributions of success to interest, effort, and practice (which would indicate task involvement). Butler was then able to use these associated attributions to form separate scales for task and ego involvement. Using these indices, she found higher levels of ego involvement in students who received grades indicating their standing relative to others, and higher levels of task involvement in students who received only task-focused comments on what they had done well and how they might improve. This study supported the meaningfulness of the concepts of task and ego involvement and the prediction that an emphasis on social comparison would increase ego involvement.

Jagacinski and Nicholls (1984a) asked undergraduates about their feelings of competence after a variety of imagined or recalled activities involving either high or low effort. The students expected higher effort to lead to greater gains in competence. In competitive (ego-involving) situations, however, students anticipated feeling less able when their effort was high and that of others was low. This indicates self-evaluation on the basis of the conception of ability as capacity, according to which higher effort implies lower capacity. In learning for learning's sake situations, high effort (in self-referenced terms) occasioned perceptions of high competence.[6] Furthermore, pride and a sense of accomplishment were stronger when effort was higher on task-involving activities and lower when effort was higher on ego-involving activities. These findings indicate that the meaning of effort changes with the situation in the predicted fashion and support the thesis that competitive more than learning-oriented conditions engage the conception of ability as capacity.

In a comparison of task-involving and ego-involving situations, Koestner, Zuckerman, and Koestner (1987) obtained similar trends to those of Jagacinski and Nicholls. These trends, however, were not significant, perhaps because the task-involving context had some emphasis on social comparison. But a related finding was, though not specifically predicted, supportive of our framework. Students who were told they were working hard subsequently spent relatively more time in the task-involving than the ego-involving condition, whereas those told they were highly able spent more time in the ego-involving condition. If people are encouraged by being told they are what they hope to be, these results suggest that task-involving conditions increase the desire for effortful accomplishment, whereas ego-involving conditions increase the desire for superior ability.

When Diener and Srull (1979) made television and voice recordings of students—a method that appears to induce public self-awareness (Carver and Scheier, 1981, chap. 16)—the students rewarded themselves if their performance surpassed peer norms. If no recording were made, however, students were more inclined to reward themselves when they improved their performance (indicating self-evaluation in terms of the less differentiated conception). When self-awareness was manipulated and individual variations in public self-awareness were assessed, Scheier and Carver (1983) also found self-awareness to be associated with more attention to social comparison norms. These results support the hypothesis that public self-awareness increases use of more differentiated conceptions of ability to evaluate one's performance.

Patten and White (1977) found that presenting a task as an intelligence test (which should create ego involvement) and asking students to make causal attributions for their performance yielded the same effects on performance. (Performance differed in a neutral condition.) When attributing one's outcomes to ability, effort, or difficulty, the differentiated conception of ability must be activated if is to respond meaningfully. Thus Patten and White's finding is consistent with the view that presentation of tasks as tests of a valued ability, more than a neutral presentation, is likely to activate the conception of ability as capacity.

Comparisons of competitive and noncompetitive conditions indicate, likewise, that in noncompetitive situations self-evaluation is more often based on the less differentiated conception of ability, wherein effortful accomplishment occasions feelings of accomplishment. More effort attribution (Ames and Ames, 1981) and a stronger positive association between perceived effort and satisfaction (Ames, Ames, and Felker, 1977) emerged in noncompetitive conditions. In competitive conditions, however, satisfaction was associated with perceived ability, not effort (Ames et al., 1977). In the above studies, experimenters elicited attributions. When students could report either attributions or thoughts about how to do the task, a complementary pattern emerged (Ames, 1984a). Competition produced more explanations in terms of ability and difficulty of tasks than did an individual goal condition, which produced more effort attributions and more thoughts about methods of performing the task. In summary, the focus tends to be on effort in noncompetitive conditions and on capacity in competitive conditions (Ames, 1984b).

Interest. Evaluative, competitive conditions have been found to diminish intrinsic interest. Maehr and Stallings (1972) and Salili and colleagues (1976) compared the effects of students' evaluations of their own learning with effects of public evaluations by a teacher. The latter condition, predicted to induce more ego involvement, produced less interest in further learning. Similarly, Ryan (1982) found more interest in puzzles after performance in a neutral condition than after a condition where the puzzles were said to be an intelligence test. This finding was replicated by Koestner, Zuckerman, and Koestner (1987). Deci et al. (1981) found more interest in puzzles after individual performance than after competitive success. Harackiewicz, Manderlink, and Sansone (1984) found that the expectation of being told how one's performance at pinball compared with that of others reduced subsequent interest in the game. Harackiewicz, Abrahams, and Wageman (1988) found that enjoyment of word puzzles diminished when students were told their performance was to be evaluated relative to that of other high school students, but not when a fixed standard of evaluation was mentioned. Csikszentmihalyi (1977) also found lower intrinsic involvement (flow) in activities when interpersonal competition was emphasized.

Evaluation on the basis of social norms has been linked to low intrinsic involvement. Teachers' reports of their use of social comparison to control children were more highly correlated with reports of use of coercive methods than with use of noncoercive methods (Deci et al., 1981). Furthermore, children whose teachers used higher levels of social comparison and coercion (not separated in analyses) reported less intrinsic interest in school.

Finally, three experimental studies evaluated feedback in the form of socially comparative grades compared with comments that focused on the positive features of students' performances and on aspects that might be improved (Butler, 1987; 1988; Butler and Nisan, 1986). In each case, students who received grades showed less interest in continued work on the tasks.

There is, then, support for the claim that both undifferentiated and differentiated conceptions of ability can define individuals' goals. Evaluative, interpersonally competitive conditions and those that induce public self-awareness increase the extent to which competence is evaluated in terms of the conception of ability as capacity. At the same time, these conditions decrease intrinsic involvement in the process of performing tasks or understanding things.

The Wisdom of Using Less Mature Conceptions of Ability

The conception of ability as capacity might appear to be a product of Western cultures. I know of no evidence that indicates clearly that this concept is absent in non-Western societies. Such an absence would certainly not be established by evidence that some societies are not interpersonally competitive or avoid social comparison of abilities. Nor, as some imply (for example, J. G. Miller, 1984), can cultural differences in conceptions be established by evidence of cultural differences in the ways complex or ambiguous social events are accounted for. As we have seen, causal attributions fluctuate with situations. It does not follow that individuals' knowledge or conceptual competencies undergo the same fluctuations. Rather, our use of our concepts changes as our purposes change. Similarly, individual differences in achievement goals are associated with individual differences in interpretations of the roles of effort, luck, and other factors in academic success. For example, high school students who desire to get out of schoolwork are less inclined than others to believe that hard work at one's lessons leads to success in school. For them, a successful school day is one where they manage to avoid doing schoolwork. This is not to say that students who like to avoid schoolwork have different understandings of the nature of effort from those who are habitually task-involved. It is easier to assume that beliefs about the usefulness of effort in school depend on what one wants to do in school. Yet we seem ready to leap from cultural diversity of interpretations of ambiguous social events to judgments of diversity of basic concepts. Cultural differences are more likely to manifest themselves in the ways basic concepts or processes are deployed than in these concepts or processes as such (Cole and Scribner, 1974).

Societies vary in the extent to which their members are preoccupied with hierarchies of competence (Duda, 1986; Maehr and Nicholls, 1980). My hunch is that in all societies most adults will understand ability as capacity, but in a number of cultures our preoccupation with who has more capacity will seem foolish if not barbarous. Rather than being incapable of construing ability as capacity, others might less frequently use this conception to evaluate one another.

In our society, the differentiation of the concept of ability is likely to mean that more students will judge themselves as lacking in ability. The consequences of low perceived ability for self-esteem and performance tend to become more negative as the concept of ability becomes more differentiated. Yet it would not be useful to attempt to retard the development of more differentiated conceptions or to teach the view that one's abilities have no limits. For one thing, the negative effects of ego involvement are already evident in young children (see chapter 1). Retardation of the differentiation of conceptions of ability might reduce, but would not eliminate them. Furthermore, the conception of ability as capacity provides a more adequate explanation of individual differences in competence than do less differentiated conceptions of ability. To advocate retardation of the development of the concept of ability would be to advocate ignorance. Likewise, it does not appear constructive to suggest that schools ought to prevent students from thinking they are below average (Rosenholtz and Simpson, 1984). Instead, students as well as educators and parents might do well to accept and find fair ways of living with the fact that everyone can't be above average. To this end we might construct interpretive frameworks that give our differences in competence a more communal function. Competence need not dominate; it can also serve. It is not likely that the injustice of competitive, ego-involving schools and societies will be alleviated by the expectation that everyone can make it to the White House or to the top of the class.[7]

No easy way is at hand to promote optimum motivation in all students. Yet there is hope in the evidence that the possession of the conception of ability as capacity does not mean that this conception must always provide the basis for self-evaluations. When we are explicitly concerned about our competence we tend to employ the conception of ability as capacity. But we can also find learning and the exercise of our skills inherently satisfying and gain a sense of competence and accomplishment in the absence of explicit concerns about our ability—without reflecting on how we stand relative to our peers. Task involvement and feelings of competence and accomplishment may be available even to those who, upon reflection, recognize that they are clearly below average in ability. We do not have to create the illusion that everyone is or (if they work hard enough) can be above average to sustain equality of optimum motivation and sense of accomplishment.

Task Orientation and Ego Orientation

So far I have written as if task involvement and ego involvement are purely a reflection of properties of the situations in which people find themselves. Things can hardly be this simple. Individual differences in proneness to the different types of involvement also exist. To mark this distinction, "task orientation" and "ego orientation" are applied to individual differences in proneness to the two types of involvement, and "task involvement" and "ego involvement" refer to the states that people experience in a given situation.

Individual differences in task orientation and ego orientation are measured with questionnaires that ask individuals about their usual achievement-related concerns or criteria of success. Helmreich and Spence (1977; 1978; Spence and Helmreich, 1983) designed such a questionnaire. One of its scales assesses competitiveness—the desire to compete with and perform better than others. Two other scales that are normally combined encompass the concept of task orientation: Work—the desire to work hard, do one's best, and improve—and Mastery—the desire for challenge, keeping busy, and completing work. As we will see, Spence and Helmreich's scales have interesting correlates that confirm the importance of distinguishing the two motivational orientations. Maehr and Braskamp (1986) have developed similar (and additional) scales for the study of motivation in the workplace. Parallel distinctions hold up in the domain of sport (Duda, 1985; 1988; Ewing, 1981).

We constructed scales to distinguish the two orientations among high school students (Nicholls, Patashnick, and Nolen, 1985). Task orientation was assessed with items such as "I feel most successful [in school] if I get a new idea about how things work; I feel most successful if something I learned really makes sense to me; I feel most successful if something I learned makes me want to find out more." Sample ego orientation items were: "I feel most successful if I score higher than the other students; I feel most successful if I do the work better than other students." A further scale was Work Avoidance or academic alienation. Items from this scale included: "I feel most successful if I get out of some work; I feel most successful if I fool around and get away with it; I feel most successful if all the work was easy."[8]

Associations of Task Orientation with Ego Orientation (Nicholls et al., 1985) were low to moderate (see Table 6.1). And, as one would expect if a task orientation more than an ego orientation reveals intrinsic satisfaction with work, Work Avoidance was negatively associated with Task Orientation (but not with Ego Orientation). The finding that Task Orientation (but not Ego Orientation) was associated with satisfaction with school learning and, less consistently, with plans to attend college also indicates a stronger link of task orientation with interest in learning (see Table 6.2. Similarly, Maehr and Braskamp (1986) found occupational satisfaction more highly associated with task than with ego orientation.)

Modified versions of these scales produced similar results with a sample of fifth graders (Nicholls and Thorkildsen, 1987). Another version, revised specifically to apply to early elementary school mathematics, also produced similar findings with second-grade students (Nicholls et al., 1988b). (The various scales mentioned above are shown in Appendix A.) In each case Task and Ego Orientation were only slightly correlated, and Work Avoidance was associated negatively with Task Orientation. There are considerable changes in the meaning of ability over the school years. Yet at all levels (at least after grade 1) individual differences in concern about having superior ability are evident and almost independent of task orientation.

Task orientation was only slightly associated with self-perceived competence of high school students (Table 6.2), and fifth and

Table 6.1 Correlations among Motivational Orientations

	Ego orientation				Task orientation			
	School A grade		School B grade		School A grade		School B grade	
	9th	12th	9th	12th	9th	12th	9th	12th
Work avoidance	00	21	08	07	-47^c	-39^c	-43^c	-26^b
Ego orientation	—	—	—	—	29^c	17^a	23^c	29^b

Note: Decimal points have been omitted. For School A, N = 130 and 121 for 9th grade and 12th grade respectively; for School B, N = 185 and 151. School A was in an upper-middle-class area; School B, in a mixed area.
a. $p < .05$.   b. $p < .01$.   c. $p < .001$.

second graders. Gottfried (1985) and Harter and Connell (1984) report higher associations of indices of intrinsic motivation with perceived competence.[9] The associations of Task Orientation with satisfaction with school learning and plans to attend college remained when perceived ability was partialed out. In other words, a task orientation might, to some degree, insulate students from the negative consequences of low perceived ability.

One should not leap from the above evidence to the conclusion that perceived ability plays no significant role in task involvement or enjoyment of learning. Ego-involving situations probably make it especially difficult for students who doubt their ability to maintain an active, unselfconscious involvement in performance. This thesis is supported by Sansone's (1986) evidence that undergraduates with low perceived ability enjoyed a task less than those with high perceived ability when the task was presented as a measure of their standing on creativity and intellectual flexibility, but not when this ego-involving emphasis was absent. In another study of undergraduates (Nicholls et al., 1988a), Perceived Ability and Task Orientation scales were uncorrelated, as they were in the studies cited above. When students performed a test, however, those with lower perceived ability reported less task involvement. Students who were high on the Task Orientation scale were inclined to be more task involved on the test, but perceived ability was equally important as a predictor of task involvement.

The Science and Values of the Lay Social Psychologist

Attribution theorists (such as Kelley, 1973) have popularized the hypothesis that ordinary individuals' way of analyzing the causes of events resembles the way scientists approach their research questions. How we respond to this hypothesis depends on how we construe scientific inquiry. Attribution theorists have generally distinguished scientific interpretations from those that are biased by personal motives. In this vein, they have attempted to establish when and to what extent individuals' interpretations are biased by self-interest.

But the utility of a categorical distinction between scientific and personal influences in reasoning is questioned by others. Toulmin (1983) implies that the choice or construction of a research question is a critical part of the research process, and that this choice reflects the scientist's value judgments about what is important. The scientist's values thus shape her or his analysis. If an analogous process works with nonscientists, we should find that their analyses of what leads to social or academic outcomes are meaningfully related to what is important to them. People would gather data that is relevant to their purposes and analyze it in ways that help them accomplish these purposes.

Accordingly, we (Nicholls et al., 1985) examined the relations between motivational orientations and beliefs about what leads to success in high school (see Table 6.3). Students who scored high on Task Orientation were also likely to agree that the students who do well in school are the ones who work cooperatively, work hard, are interested in their work, and try to understand their work rather than just memorize it. In short, the more students wanted to learn and understand, the more they thought that success in school followed from attempts to do these things. The consistency between personal goals and beliefs about the nature of success in the classroom is obvious.

Ego Orientation, on the other hand, was positively associated with the beliefs that success comes to those who are intelligent, try to do better than others, have teachers who expect them to do well, know how to impress the right people, and act as if they like the teacher. Again, what students want is meaningfully related to what they believe one must do to succeed. The Avoidance

Table 6.2 Correlations of Motivational Orientations with Satisfaction with School, Plans to Attend College, and Perceived Ability

| | Work avoidance | | | | Ego orientation | | | | Task orientation | | | |
| | School A grade | | School B grade | | School A grade | | School B grade | | School A grade | | School B grade | |
	9th	12th	9th	12th	9th	12th	9th	12th	9th	12th	9th	12th
School satisfaction	-44[c]	-48[c]	-55[c]	-51[c]	11	02	-07	05	53[c]	50[c]	49[c]	45[c]
College plans	-38[c]	-25[c]	-38[c]	-28[c]	-10	-05	-13[a]	14[a]	31[c]	28[c]	25[c]	27[c]
Perceived ability	-17[a]	-18[a]	-22[c]	-22[c]	16[a]	03	04	29[c]	24[b]	12	21[b]	17[a]

Note: Decimal points have been omitted. For School A, N = 130 and 121 for 9th grade and 12th grade respectively; for School B, N = 185 and 151. School A was in an upper-middle-class area; School B, in a mixed area.

a. $p < .05$.   b. $p < .01$.   c. $p < .001$.

of Work (academic alienation) scale was positively associated with beliefs that success is more likely if students act as if they like the teacher, know how to impress the right people, and are lucky. This scale was negatively associated with the beliefs that success is attainable by hard work and interest. These views are hardly likely to promote understanding and learning of academic tasks, but then, that is not what the work-avoiding students want to do. Thorkildsen (1988) found parallel associations between motivational orientations and beliefs about the causes of success with academically gifted students.

Similar findings were obtained with slightly revised scales and a large sample of fifth-grade students (Nicholls and Thorkildsen, 1987). Task Orientation was associated with the belief that success in school depends on helping each other, interest, effort, and attempts to understand. Conversely, it was associated with rejection of the beliefs that success is fostered by knowing how to impress and pretending you like the teacher. Ego Orientation and Work Avoidance were both associated with the beliefs that success results from being smarter than one's peers and beating them. Work Avoidance was also associated with the belief that success followed from knowing how to impress and pretending to like the teacher. A second-grade sample produced almost identical results for orientations to mathematics and beliefs about the causes of success in mathematics (Nicholls et al., 1988b). (The scales measuring perceptions of the causes of success in school are shown in Appendix B.)

The worlds students see are, to a significant degree, the worlds they want; their views about the way things are relate meaningfully to their personal goals. And who is to say that these diverse views about what leads to success in school are incorrect? There is not one form of success or one truth about success in the classroom any more than there is one objective, scientific view of the world. Yet researchers (Nicholls [1975] included) working in the tradition of attribution theory (Kelley, 1973) have assumed that there is one form of success and that the research problem is to ascertain how individuals explain success or failure. Apart from an occasional mention (Frieze, Francis, Hanusa, 1983; Maehr and Nicholls, 1980), the prior problem of deciding what success is and how it is construed has been ignored.

Table 6.3 Correlations of Motivational Orientations and Perceived Causes of Academic Success

	Avoidance of work				Ego orientation				Task orientation			
	School A grade		School B grade		School A grade		School B grade		School A grade		School B grade	
Students succeed if they:	9th	12th	9th	12th	9th	12th	9th	12th	9th	12th	9th	12th
Show liking of teacher	31[c]	28[c]	14[a]	15[a]	25[b]	30[c]	11	20[b]	-06	-07	00	29[c]
Can impress right people	32[c]	21[a]	40[c]	32[c]	19[a]	30[c]	23[b]	20[b]	-06	-05	-13[a]	09
Dress and behave nicely	23[b]	03	21[b]	14[a]	-06	18[a]	21[b]	11	-02	-03	06	15[a]
Are lucky	24[b]	31[c]	44[c]	28[c]	01	01	-03	21[b]	-05	-22[b]	-30[c]	-02
Are intelligent	-02	14	12	05	36[c]	08	28[c]	32[c]	29[c]	-01	08	23[b]
Are expected to, by teachers	17[a]	11	24[c]	06	21[b]	19[a]	26[c]	20[b]	-06	16[a]	09	18[a]
Try to beat others	22[b]	13	01	18[a]	35[c]	14	21[b]	27[c]	06	02	00	00
Are good at tests	-04	16[a]	17[b]	07	12	15[a]	20[b]	01	18[a]	08	10	01
Work cooperatively	-18[a]	-04	-13[a]	-09	-03	08	19[a]	09	45[c]	10	36[c]	36[c]
Work hard	-21[b]	-04	-24[c]	-23[b]	27[c]	10	25[c]	-02	44[c]	18[a]	43[c]	32[c]
Are interested	-21[b]	-19[a]	-31[c]	-17[b]	14	02	19[a]	11	44[c]	28[c]	37[c]	38[c]
Try to understand	-18[a]	-24[b]	-24[c]	-08	-11	06	18[a]	04	30[c]	33[c]	36[c]	33[c]

Note: Decimal points omitted. Values are italicized when $p < .05$ for all four samples and $p < .01$ for at least three of the four samples. The "Causes of Success" items are slightly abbreviated. School A was in an upper-middle-class area; School B, in a mixed area.   a. $p < .05$.   b. $p < .01$.   c. $p < .001$.

The assumption of one objective criterion of success is most obvious in the considerable body of research that seeks to establish the extent to which people's causal attributions are logical or unbiased—as opposed to being influenced by self-interest. In taking for granted that only one scientific or logical analysis applies to any social phenomenon, this tradition embodies an impoverished view of science as well as social life (Semin, 1980). When scientists and nonscientists fudge or fake their data, we can speak of bias. But even the relatively constrained world of high school is susceptible to more than just one meaningful interpretation. As advocates of the ecological perspective on social perception argue, an individual is necessarily sensitive to adaptively relevant information rather than to all possible information. And relevance depends upon the perceiver's goals (McArthur and Baron, 1983). Our findings indicate that different motivational orientations are not just different types of wants or goals. They involve different world-views. Like scientists with different research questions, students with different motivational orientations collect different data and interpret them differently.[10]

Graduate students, for example, sometimes act as if they believe that the way to get a Ph.D. and a desirable academic job is to set about doing exactly what their professors appear to want rather than to develop their own understanding of their subject. They will even advise other students that this is the way to succeed. Although most students and academics will have observed occasions when this view of reality was sustained, professors can sometimes be favorably surprised and impressed by students who come up with good reasons for positions that initially seemed inadvisable. Yet it is not convincing to tell students that trying to please professors does not lead to "success." It does make sense, however, to ask the ethical question of whether it wouldn't be appropriate for students to have a purpose other than pure professor-pleasing; to construe success in another way; to seek to think critically about their subject and to make a constructive contribution to it.

I count myself among those who advocate task orientation rather than ego orientation. I consider that, ethically, it is more desirable. I can argue that ego orientation and academic alienation are unfortunate and cynical approaches to academic life. But I can hardly argue that these orientations are false, biased, or not objective. Instead, I argue that these unfortunate realities are more pervasive because people who are highly competitive or alienated claim that impressing the "right" people and beating others is the way to success. The claim "that's the way things are" often conceals a moral preference for "that way." And "that way" reduces the chances of intrinsic motivation to learn. As I will later argue, it also diminishes the quality of our accomplishments.

Amundsen and Scott: A Moral Tale

In Roland Huntford's (1983) account, Roald Amundsen and Robert Falcon Scott, leaders of the first and second parties to reach the South Pole, exemplify the contrast between task and ego orientation.

Amundsen's ambition for polar travel formed early in life, and he took every opportunity to penetrate its secrets (Huntford, 1983). His early cross-country ski trips were each "an exercise in applying lessons learned" (p. 57). At the age of twenty-one, writing to satisfy his brother's interest about his first trip to the Arctic (on a seal-hunting ship), his preoccupation was with what he learned. In his letter, "Everything is to the point. He shows a capacity, even a determination, to learn from what he sees and hears . . . [it] reads like a student's notebook" (p. 51). On his first trip to the Antarctic he was one of those who made the first sled trip in the history of Antarctic exploration. "After eight hours' incessant battling with the ice, constantly in danger, they finally returned to camp. 'These excursions are wonderful,' was Amundsen's comment, 'and I hope to have frequent opportunities for more.' [In recording his experiences] he ignores the historic significance of what he has helped to do. He does not expatiate on the glories of discovery, there are no rhapsodies on the sensation of treading where human feet have never trod before. He is wholly and soberly occupied with the lessons he has learned" (p. 68). Back in the Arctic, making the first completion of the North-West Passage, he lived with and observed Eskimos. "These would be his masters in the art of living in deep cold. After a decade of preparation, he was still acutely aware of the defects in his technique" (p. 101). On the great trip to the South Pole, lessons were still being learned. For example, he had gone to great pains to design special boots. But even after he reached Antarctica, these were modified four times (p. 384). Amundsen and Scott were both bent on reaching the Pole first. Neither was devoid of elements of ego involvement. But the details of polar travel were intrinsically meaningful to Amundsen. He mastered these details and accomplished his mission with a margin of safety—losing no lives. And, despite hardships, he and his men had their share of sheer pleasure getting there and back.

For Scott, polar travel was a means to an end: the details of exploration were of no consequence, getting there was no fun at all, and he never did get back. At the age of thirty, Scott was a British naval lieutenant with an "inchoate passion to get on without any definite aim" (p. 125). On receiving a promotion, "He was not satisfied with having caught up with his contemporaries, he wanted to leave them behind" (p. 134). When a British Antarctic expedition was announced, he "saw in it the much sought passport to promotion" (p. 132). But in contrast to Amundsen, Scott's ambition lacked the leavening of an interest in travel on snow and ice. Before his second (and last) trip to the Antarctic, he had known for four years that he would return. "He could have visited Norway or the Alps; learnt to ski and drive dogs himself; acquired a grounding in the internal combustion engine . . . or even tried some mountaineering. He had done none of these things. Incompetent design penetrated into most details of equipment. Scott had learned nothing and forgotten nothing" (p. 393). While Amundsen constantly sought improvement, Scott "had long ago decided that his equipment was incapable of being improved" (p. 391). Where Amundsen strove to create a little democracy, a cooperative enterprise, Scott "was a man who always raced; against a rival, a friend" and the members of his own expedition (p. 436). Amundsen rarely wrote a letter. He "squandered his talent on his deeds" (p. 526). When Scott could have been preparing for his expedition, he wrote letters, "looking over his shoulder at an unseen audience, concerned more with his reputation than his actions." His lack of preparation caught up with him and the men who had trusted him. But even as he lay dying in his tent, having failed to accomplish his return, Scott wrote—selecting the evidence—to enhance his reputation. In this he lacked no determination. "Scott turned polar exploration into an affair of heroism for heroism's sake" (p. 523).

In a real sense, each man got what he wanted. In Amundsen's case this is clear. Scott, obviously, would rather have been a live hero than a dead one; he would rather have reached the Pole first. But his failure on these points reflected his purposes as truly as did his success in securing the leadership of two British Antarctic expeditions and his posthumous lionization by the British press and public. His guiding motives, ones that propelled him to his position as expedition leader, were of no value when it came to polar travel. The notion that different ambitions produce different actions and that these produce different accomplishments is not novel. This unsurprising notion, that even apparently irrational actions make sense when we understand the actor's purposes, is the kernel of the intentional approach to predicting action and accomplishment. It is not that things come out the way we want. We can misunderstand and miscalculate. Circumstances can, even when they don't conspire against us, prove too much for us. But even the choice of circumstances that are clearly too much for us can be rational.

7

Choosing a Level of Challenge

According to the intentional perspective, an adequate description of what individuals want will, in conjunction with a description of their understanding of what they might do to get what they want, enable us to derive predictions of their actions. Here, this perspective is applied to choice of difficulty level or preferred level of challenge. (Predictions of performance and accomplishment are taken up in the following chapter.)

In school and at work we are often assigned tasks, but we also face minor and major choices of related activities. Students' choices of library books can affect their enjoyment and learning. Choices of college majors and of careers can mark turning points in lives. Most theories of task choice or level of aspiration focus on one dimension of such choice situations—the difficulty of the task.

From my perspective, a reading of theory and experimental research on this topic is complicated by the variety of conceptions of difficulty and ability. Atkinson (1957, p. 362), for example, explicitly bases his definition of difficulty on the five-year-olds' undifferentiated conception: "hard" is not distinguished from "hard for me." He states that task difficulty is inversely related to the individual's subjective probability of success—difficulty equals one minus subjective probability of success. Some researchers testing Atkinson's predictions about the levels of difficulty that adults will prefer have taken moderate difficulty to mean moderate subjective probability of success (Hamilton, 1974; Moulton,

1965). Others have taken it to mean moderate normative difficulty (Trope and Brickman, 1975). Atkinson himself is not consistent on this point when he acknowledges that what is "hard" for one person might be "easy" for another—an implicit recognition that task difficulty should not be confused with subjective probability of success.

Variation in the use of conceptions of difficulty is also evident in the work of Meyer, Folkes, and Weiner (1976). In predicting that individuals will prefer tasks of intermediate difficulty, these writers explicitly refer to the performance of others as the basis for judging task difficulty (p. 414). But in their four experiments they translate their prediction into the hypothesis that individuals will prefer tasks on which they have intermediate expectations of success. That is, they employ the undifferentiated conception of difficulty when testing predictions which they generated in the framework of the differentiated, normative conception.

My argument is that these different conceptions of difficulty both have a place in our thinking about task choice and related topics. But the place of the less differentiated, self-referenced conception is in task involvement, whereas the normative conception is relevant to ego involvement.

Anticipating the exposition that follows, the essence of my argument is that a person who is task-involved will choose any task that she believes offers an opportunity to exercise or extend her competence. But a person who is ego-involved may have to face the prospect that a gain in competence or a best performance will still leave her feeling incompetent. In ego involvement (but not in task involvement) we sometimes make choices which avoid the unhappy prospect that we might perform less competently than others, but which simultaneously prevent us from exercising or developing our competence.

Predictions

To simplify the following discussion, I assume that tasks vary in difficulty (in any sense) and provide only dichotomous, success-or-failure information. In reality many tasks provide feedback about how clear our successes are and how close our failures are to being successes. For example, I can observe how close I come to hitting a target with an arrow and whether I am getting closer on successive attempts. This is equivalent—when tasks varying in difficulty provide only dichotomous success-or-failure information—to observing how much effort the tasks we can master demand for us, and whether the effort we need for mastery decreases on successive attempts.

Task Involvement. Let us assume that individuals are able to make repeated attempts at tasks. In this case, task-involved individuals should seek tasks where they expect to be able progressively to reduce the amount of effort needed for success—such a reduction being an indication of competence in the undifferentiated sense. A task that we believe will demand a negligible level of effort will appear to offer a negligible chance of a more effortless performance. Similarly, tasks where success appears bound to be beyond our best efforts will also appear to offer no chance of reducing the effort needed for success. Tasks that appear likely to yield, but only to high effort, offer the greatest scope for progressively reducing the effort we need for success. We should, therefore, prefer such tasks when we are task-involved.

The same logic applies to situations where repeated attempts at a given difficulty level are not possible. Because our judgments of task difficulty are self-referenced, if we are sure we can succeed on a task we will also expect that success will not occasion a significant feeling of competence. That is, if we think we can master a task with little effort, we will anticipate but slight feelings of competence upon mastery. Or, if a task seems easy in the undifferentiated sense, its mastery will not appear to demand much ability. At the opposite extreme, if the prospect is of certain failure (if our best efforts appear bound to produce nothing), the task will offer no prospect of a sense of competence or accomplishment. We cannot establish evidence of our competence at tasks on which we can have no impact.

Tasks that appear likely to yield to high effort will, on the other hand, present the likelihood that high effort will lead to a sense of competence. That is, success on tasks that appear difficult in the undifferentiated sense will indicate competence. Tasks will be most attractive when we believe that high effort is needed to produce success—when neither success nor failure seem certain.

Different individuals will select tasks of different levels of objective or normative difficulty, but they will prefer tasks they believe will demand high effort—personally challenging tasks.

Ego Involvement. In this state our judgments of our own competence depend on the competence of others. Thus a task that most of our peers can master easily will not offer significant feelings of competence because success can be attributed to the ease of the task. Anyone who expects to fail at it, however, will face the prospect of feelings of incompetence. Tasks that are extremely normatively difficult, on the other hand, present no threat of feelings of incompetence because most people will fail at them. Success on such tasks will, however, indicate very high ability. The perception of our ability and the anticipated feelings of competence or incompetence will thus depend on how well we expect to perform relative to others.

People who are ego-involved and have high perceived ability will have moderate expectancies of success on normatively moderate to difficult tasks where success indicates high ability. They are likely to prefer tasks at or above (depending on how able they believe they are) moderate difficulty levels. After successes at any level, they can gain in perceived ability by attempting more difficult, effortful, and personally challenging tasks. In this respect, individuals with high perceived ability will behave similarly whether ego- or task-involved. Personally challenging tasks will be chosen in each case.

The picture is more complex if we believe our ability is low. In this case, when we face tasks of moderate normative difficulty we will expect to fail and to feel incompetent. We have therefore good reason to avoid levels of moderate difficulty. Choice of either very easy or very difficult tasks would avoid decisive evidence of our incompetence. Which tasks we choose will depend on how certain we are that we lack ability, and on how much we are committed to establishing our competence or to avoiding implications of incompetence.

It is possible to be committed to goals one does not expect to attain (Klinger, 1975; McFarlin and Blascovich, 1981). But ultimately, the rational response to a goal that is unattainable is rejection of that goal and selection of the next most attractive goal

(Klinger, 1975). (There is, in the intentional view, no chance of our acting without a purpose.) If it becomes increasingly clear that we do not have high ability, we would tend to adopt the lesser goal of avoiding indications of our incompetence. This less attractive goal must, in turn, be relinquished as hope of attaining it dies.

For people with low perceived ability who still want to establish themselves as competent, the choice of easy tasks would be irrational in that it could not lead to evidence of high ability. Only normatively difficult tasks can supply this evidence, so people who suspect that their ability is low but are committed to proving themselves should prefer such tasks. In making the attempt failure cannot indicate incompetence, while success cannot be clearly ruled out.

Repeated failures or other experiences can, however, produce the virtual certainty of having low ability. The intentional framework leads to the prediction that people in this category will have little commitment to establishing their competence and will wish to avoid the implication of low ability by withdrawing from the situation. If a choice is mandated, as it often is in school and in psychological experiments, the rational choice is a normatively easy task that demands little effort. The same choice is rational for people in a more extreme category—those who are certain their ability is low but are not committed to avoiding the implication of incompetence. They should see very easy tasks as offering the most economical way of leaving the situation.

In summary, individuals with high perceived ability should prefer personally challenging tasks. Among those with low perceived ability, those who retain some hope of establishing their competence and are committed to this goal should be more inclined to select normatively difficult tasks where success will seem unlikely. Others, more certain that their ability is low and less committed to the whole enterprise, should tend to prefer normatively easy tasks where they will expect success.

Competence by Any Other Name: A Digression on the Measurement of Perceived Ability

For testing of the predictions for task involvement, estimates of individuals' perceived ability (in the undifferentiated sense) can be based on their expectations of success. An index of perceived ability relevant to ego involvement should indicate individuals' evaluations of their ability relative to that of others and predict expectations of success (or perceived ability) on experimental tasks. Before I can examine evidence bearing on the predictions of task choice, I must spend a little time on matters of measurement, including measures of self-esteem or self-concept, test anxiety, and resultant achievement motivation.

Self-esteem or self-concept scales serve effectively as measures of perceived ability relative to the ability of others. Such scales refer primarily to the adequacy of one's competence (Crandall, 1973), and researchers (for instance Brockner, 1979; McFarlin and Blascovich, 1981; Shrauger, 1975) commonly employ and describe them as perceived competence measures. The fact that they predict perceived ability on experimental tasks (McFarlin and Blascovich, 1981) supports their validity for the present purpose.

Jagacinski and Nicholls (1984a) also found that college students interpreted a statement that someone is able as meaning that this person has high ability relative to others. Conversely, a statement that someone succeeds through high effort was not interpreted as implying that they have high ability. It is a valid assumption that typical self-esteem items would elicit evaluations of ability in the differentiated sense. High correlations between students' ratings of their academic ability relative to that of others and their self-ratings on a scale (running from excellent to very poor) involving no reference to others (Nicholls et al., 1985, p. 685) are consistent with this assumption. Furthermore, conventional self-concept scales contain numerous items concerning competence. Many questions about one's competence would heighten a self-evaluative stance and amplify the tendency to employ the conception of ability as capacity. Significant associations between conventional self-concept scales and ratings of own skill relative to that of others (Clinkenbeard, 1982; Roberts, Kleiber, and Duda, 1981) support this conclusion more directly. So too does evidence that students' ratings of their ability as simply high versus low load on the same factor as ratings of their ability relative to others (Nicholls et al., 1988a).

Test-anxiety scales correlate fairly highly with self-concept or self-esteem scales (Crandall, 1973) and thus have questionable discriminant validity. But such correlations are virtually inevitable.

Although one would not guess it from the titles of test-anxiety scales, the content of these scales usually refers directly to perceived ability and expected adequacy of performance. These facts alone provide a case for considering them measures of (low) perceived ability. Moreover, in the case of one test-anxiety scale, it has been shown that perceived-competence content can account for the associations of the scale with performance and other variables that have been presumed to be a consequence of anxiety (Nicholls, 1976b). Similarly, Liebert and Morris (1967) separated test-anxiety scale content into worry and emotionality components. A number of studies show that worry rather than emotionality is related to performance and that worry but not emotionality scores are influenced by performance feedback in exactly the ways one would expect perceived ability to be affected (Morris, Davis, and Hutchings, 1981; Wine, 1971). But the term "worry" is misleading. Morris and coauthors characterized the tendency to worry as a tendency toward negative self-evaluation and negative expectation. Indeed, worry items are more accurately described as low perceived competence (for example, "I do not feel confident about my performance on this test"; "I do not feel self-confident"; Morris et al., 1981). Thus the active ingredient of test-anxiety scales is perceived competence. The validity of this conclusion is further confirmed by evidence that test-anxious students perceive themselves as less able on experimental tasks (Arkin, Detchon, and Maruyama, 1982) and as encountering more problems demonstrating ability on exams (Arkin, Kolditz, and Kolditz, 1983).

Resultant achievement-motivation scores (Atkinson and Feather, 1966) incorporate test-anxiety scores. For this reason and in accord with the evidence and arguments of Meyer (1987) and Kukla (1972, 1978), individuals scoring high in need for achievement and low in test anxiety (high resultant achievement motivation) can be considered high in perceived ability, while those low in need for achievement and high in test anxiety (low resultant motivation) can be considered low in perceived ability. Evidence that higher motivation is associated with higher expectations of success on experimental tasks (Atkinson, 1957, 1969; Feather, 1965) supports this view.[1] Klinger and McNelly's (1969) assertion that the measure of achievement motivation indicates an individual's perceived status is also consistent with this position.[2]

In summary, measures of self-concept, self-esteem, test anxiety, and resultant achievement motivation can be seen as instances of the same construct parading under different names. These measures are obviously not identical, but the case for hermetically sealed domains of research is not compelling.

Patterns of Task Choice

We will recall that the choice of the level of difficulty is thought to depend on the chooser's type of involvement. In task involvement, preference for a level promising intermediate chances of success is predicted for all individuals. In ego involvement, people whose perceived ability is high are predicted to prefer moderate expectations of success, while those with low perceived ability are predicted to choose the extreme levels. First, let us consider the evidence on the above general contrast between task and ego involvement. The extra predictions for ego-involved individuals with low perceived ability will then be examined.[3]

In one experiment Raynor and Smith (1966) presented puzzles as an intelligence test and emphasized the importance of the test. In another session, the experimenters acted in a nonevaluative manner and minimized the importance of the task. It appeared that students did not experience the contrast between the two presentations as strongly as Raynor and Smith intended (p. 187). Nevertheless, there was a strong tendency for low- more than high-resultant-achievement-motive students to select extreme probabilities in the more ego-involving condition. Preference for moderate probabilities was more evident in the neutral condition.

Schneider (1973, chap. 4), in a series of studies under neutral conditions, found no difference between individuals scoring high and low in resultant motivation. In one study (chap. 5), however, low-motive subjects preferred more extreme probabilities. This study differed from the others in that the experimenter was a teacher in the subjects' school rather than an unfamiliar, nonevaluative adult. This finding led to a further study comparing a nonevaluative presentation of a task with a presentation of the task as a valid test of ability. As predicted, more extreme probability preferences on the part of low- rather than high-resultant-motive students occurred only under the more ego-involving condition (Jopt, 1974, p. 196).

Studies with no direct comparisons of two conditions provide less adequate tests of the predictions. Nevertheless, they add confirming evidence to the theory. DeCharms and Dave (1965), Roberts (1974), and Hamilton (1974) studied men's choices of physical skill tasks. The very high value males place on physical skills (Roberts, 1984) and the fact that the performance outcomes were made public should have induced ego involvement. The same would be expected from academic material (deCharms and Carpenter 1968) and anagrams (Moulton, 1965) presented as important tests of ability. Brody (1963) gave undergraduates what was said to be a test of their ability, on which they recorded their names—both likely to induce ego involvement. Finally, Mahone (1960) studied occupational choices, which probably also stimulate that involvement. As predicted, in each of the above seven studies individuals with low resultant motivation preferred more extreme probability levels than did those with high resultant motivation.

Two studies appeared more likely to have allowed task involvement to predominate. Trope (1979) created a nonevaluative situation in which the task was said to be unrelated to intelligence and anonymity was assured. Thus it is probable that task involvement was maintained. Regardless of perceived ability, all of the subjects in this study preferred tasks demanding levels of ability closest to their own perceived level. With similar conditions, Buckert, Meyer, and Schmalt (1979) obtained the same results. These findings are consistent with choice predictions for task involvement.

The remaining question is whether there is evidence in support of predictions for ego-involved individuals who perceive themselves as low in ability. Among them, the individuals who retain a commitment to demonstrating high ability should choose tasks on which they have low probabilities of success. Those who are more certain their ability is low and whose commitment to prove the contrary is less should tend to choose tasks where their probabilities of success are high. Two studies with relevant data were found.

Sears (1940, 1941) gave nine- to twelve-year-olds academic tasks in a testlike, ego-involving manner. Children who chose higher and lower probabilities had failed consistently in school and would have lower perceived ability (Bloom, 1976; Nicholls, 1979a). Within this group, those selecting very low probabilities of success showed a stronger wish for high achievement in diverse activities and made more negative evaluations of their competence in these activities than did others. They acted "as if they never felt they were doing well enough" (Sears, 1940, p. 523). This indicates the predicted commitment to establishing high ability despite perception of low ability. Those selecting high probabilities showed greater responsiveness to nonachievement incentives and greater readiness to lower their goals after manipulated success (Sears, 1940, 1941). Both phenomena appear to indicate the predicted rejection of the goal of establishing one's competence at the task.

In Moulton's (1965) study of high school students' choices on tasks presented as valid tests of their intellectual ability, students low and intermediate in resultant achievement motivation chose more extreme probability levels than did high-motive students. Furthermore, the lowest group chose high probabilities more than the intermediate group, who favored low probabilities. Given that the lowest group was most certain that they lacked ability, these results also support the predictions.

In summary, the present theory successfully predicts choices in task versus ego involvement and, more specifically, high- versus low-probability choices in ego involvement. In so doing, this position solves one of the problems that occasioned its construction (Nicholls, 1980c, p. 9). It "resolves a major contradiction between Atkinson's (1957) and Kukla's (1978) predictions of level of aspiration. Atkinson predicts that individuals with low resultant achievement motivation . . . will choose extremely easy or difficult tasks. Kukla (1978), on the other hand, predicts that all individuals will prefer tasks with intermediate subjective probabilities of success and, therefore, that those with high self-concepts of ability will choose more [normatively] difficult tasks.[4] As noted, there is evidence in support of Atkinson's predictions . . . However, there are other studies where individuals with low resultant achievement motivation do not make atypical or excessively high or low level of aspiration choices (Kukla, 1978). Kukla may be right under conditions of task involvement, whereas Atkinson appears right under ego involvement. The present analysis also provides a basis for predicting when unrealistically difficult versus easy tasks will be preferred."

Doing What Makes Sense

Outside the "laboratory" goal selection is more complex, but the above themes can still be discerned. Virginia Valian (1977), for example, describes the competitiveness, the experience of learning as a means rather than an end, and the apparently self-handicapping goal-setting that is often characteristic of ego involvement.

> I approached [academic] work usually with two sorts of feelings. One was anger and resentment that I had to work; the other was a sense of competition as a life or death struggle—either I would kill others or they would kill me . . . For most of my life my way of coping . . . was . . . to be smart and clever but to accomplish nothing (p. 169) . . . Much of the time . . . I was preoccupied with questions about my ability . . . How smart was I compared to so-and-so? . . . I worried about whether I was smart enough to solve such-and-such a problem instead of getting on with trying to solve it (p. 172) . . . I resisted working my ideas out to the end . . . Many times I caught myself putting something away once the end was in sight (p. 173) . . . I almost never experienced impatience and eagerness to finish, unless there was a deadline . . . This was invariably at odds with what I said. Although I said that I wished I were finished with project X, I didn't feel the corresponding emotions . . . I made projects infinitely long.   (p. 174)

As she came to adopt the position that "The important thing is how much you can come to understand, which of your abilities you can develop, how far you can grow" (p. 172), the discovery of ideas and the understanding of problems became inherently satisfying and she was able to start projects more freely and complete them without feeling threatened by the implications of completion.

It would be easy to characterize as irrational the actions of ego-involved individuals who doubt their competence. Selection of tasks on which we can make no progress—either because we have already thoroughly mastered them or because they are so far beyond us we are almost certain to make no impression on them—is certainly not rational from the point of view of someone who thinks it makes sense to accomplish as much as possible. But if progress in one's work is not inherently satisfying and one's goal is to avoid accepting the prospect that one might be less able than others while maintaining some hope that one might be brilliant, it is rational to choose tasks that very few others can master. Similarly, a very easy task is a rational choice for someone who has no concern to establish competence in the skill involved but who is obliged to make a choice to escape from the experiment or the classroom.

Such choices are, indeed, irrational from the perspective of an observer who assumes that all people want to develop or exercise their powers as fully as possible or to accomplish as much as they can. If this is our goal for students, it would be irrational for us to promote competitive or publicly evaluative educational environments that induce ego involvement.

8

Accomplishment

It is common to assume that variations in level or type of motivation are only of interest if they produce results. Anything other than a concrete outcome—such as income, academic grade, test score, or attainment rank—is not seen as a real result. It is also easy to defend the opposing view: that income levels, grades, or test scores are only of interest if they enhance one's sense of accomplishment or make life more meaningful. What profit is it to men and women if they gain the whole world but no sense of accomplishment or meaning? This dualism, however, cries out for synthesis. What we presumably want, or should want, are "concrete" or visible signs that also enhance our personal sense of accomplishment and the meaningfulness of our actions. I have already given some attention to the factors that foster intrinsic interest or make achievement activities satisfying (Chapter 6) and will return to this topic later; the focus here is on the "bottom line" of visible accomplishment.

The logic of the analysis of task choice (Chapter 7) can be applied, with a few modifications, to the prediction of level of performance when people are assigned tasks of different levels of difficulty. Relevant experimental studies of performance in task- and ego-involving contexts will be considered in the first half of this chapter. The situations created in these studies differ from the real contexts of many significant accomplishments in that they allowed individuals no scope for initiative in finding or defining tasks or problems and no time for thinking about problems for days on end or seeking novel sources of insight and assistance. In short, these studies are better designed for establishing what impairs the short-term display of one's present skills than for ascertaining the conditions that promote significant accomplishment. (The question of significant accomplishment is taken up in the second half of the chapter.)

As was the case for task choice, the greater complexity of the conception of ability that is activated in ego involvement means that the predictions of performance on assigned tasks in the state of ego involvement are more complex than those for task involvement. And, paralleling the predictions of task choice, task involvement is held to be more likely than ego involvement to foster adequate performance—especially among those who perceive themselves as less competent than their peers.

Ego Involvement

The intentional approach implies that when we are ego-involved, we will apply high effort (and thereby perform effectively) if we believe high effort is necessary to establish that our capacity is high. On the other hand, performance will be impaired when we believe that our efforts will lead to outcomes that indicate incompetence on our part. The anticipation of feeling incompetent could impair performance by making effort appear fruitless for establishing our competence or by making the situation aversive or anxiety-provoking and, thereby, reducing commitment and attention to the task. These assumptions provide the basis for predictions of performance as a function of perceived ability and task difficulty.

It is claimed that in a situation of ego involvement, performance is impaired more by the expectation that failure will indicate one's lack of competence than by the mere expectation of failure to complete a task. This assertion is supported by the findings of Frankel and Snyder (1978). After a series of failures calculated to make the students doubt their ability, they were assigned tasks described as either normatively difficult or moderately difficult. Performance was not impaired in the difficult condition, where expectations of failure would be higher; as predicted, it was impaired in the perceived moderate difficulty condition—the only condition where failure would indicate low ability. These findings were replicated by Kernis, Zuckerman, Cohen, and Spadafora (1982) in a context where self-awareness was induced. In neutral conditions (minus the self-awareness) the two levels of perceived difficulty produced similar outcomes. (The dependent variable in this study was persistence instead of performance.) Kernis and coauthors confirm that the impairing effect of the expectation of incompetent performance demonstrated by Frankel and Snyder is more evident in ego-involving conditions.

Further support comes from a study by Miller and Klein (1986) assessing variation in ego orientation. Again, an initial failure at a test in an evaluative context was designed to shake students' confidence. A second test was then presented. Students who were high in ego orientation worked less when they were told the second test was moderately easy than when it was said to be hard for most people. They gave up more quickly in the condition where failure would indicate incompetence than in the condition where failure was more likely. This pattern was reversed for those who were low on ego orientation. They gave up more quickly when told the task was very hard for most people—a rational move for people who are not preoccupied with avoiding looking stupid but are inclined to desist when persistence appears unlikely to produce any result.

The additional thesis that the conception of ability as capacity (which, in adults, is engaged by ego involving conditions) plays a mediating role in the impairment of performance was supported by Arden Miller (1985). He replicated the findings of Frankel and Snyder (in clearly evaluative conditions) with sixth graders who had mastered the conception of ability as capacity. For these students, performance was impaired when (after an initial failure) they faced tasks at which about half their peers were said to succeed. No impairment was found when students were told hardly anyone their age could do well at the tasks they faced. Results differed for sixth graders who had not yet mastered the conception of ability as capacity. These students performed similarly in conditions of moderate and of high normative difficulty. The sixth-grade students with and without the conception of ability as capacity had similar levels of perceived ability, but expectations of incompetent performance (on tasks presented as of moderate normative difficulty) only impaired the performance of those who had attained this conception.

To summarize, performance in the context of ego involvement is most impaired: (1) by the expectation that an outcome will indicate incompetence—rather than a mere expectation of failure (Carver and Scheier, 1981) or a belief that one's actions will not alter a task outcome (Abramson, Seligman, and Teasdale, 1978); and (2) when ability is construed as capacity which, for adults, applies to ego-involved individuals.[1] This clears the way for consideration of the role of individual differences in perceived ability as well as variation in task difficulty.

In a situation of ego involvement, when individuals who perceive their ability as high face normatively moderate or difficult tasks, they will see high effort as necessary to confirm their competence. They should try hard and perform well. These individuals will spend little time and effort on easy tasks and on normatively difficult tasks where failure appears certain despite maximum effort. The picture is more complex for people who perceive their ability as low. When they face normatively easy or difficult tasks they will expect to be able to avoid the implication of low ability. To this end they will work hard (harder than the highly able) on easy tasks where failure—which would indicate incompetence—appears avoidable by high effort. If the task is seen as difficult, high effort will be forthcoming anyway (except at the very lowest level of perceived ability) because its absence would be inconsistent with the goal of performing competently. Accordingly, the performance of low-perceived-ability individuals should not be impaired whether they perceive tasks as normatively easy or highly difficult.

Impaired performance is likely when individuals with low perceived ability face tasks of intermediate normative difficulty. They will expect to fail, and thus to feel incompetent, on such tasks. But their performance will depend on how certain they are that they lack ability. Three levels of low self-perception might be distinguished. On the first level are those whose perceived ability is low, but not low enough to have extinguished their commitment to establishing competence on the task at hand. This commitment will keep up their effort. However, the prospect of feeling incompetent could produce the divided attention, negative affect, and impaired performance associated with test anxiety (Arkin et al., 1982; I. G. Sarason, 1975; Wine, 1971), despite a subjective experience of high motivation. Alternatively, the aversive prospect of feeling incompetent might lead to partial withdrawal of attention from the task (Carver and Scheier, 1981; Miller, 1986). Any of these processes—resulting from the prospect of feeling incompetent—would lead to impaired performance. (I make no attempt to separate these processes here.)

In a second category are the individuals whose perceived ability is extremely low. They would be less committed to establishing their competence. As certainty of incompetence at a task increases, the valuing of competence at that task should decline. But before certainty of incompetence is reached and all commitment is lost, individuals could retain some commitment to avoiding the implication of incompetence. The fact that, in ego involvement, failure implies low ability less decisively when effort is low might then give them an added reason for not trying.[2] Thus at moderate levels of normative difficulty, the probability of low effort and low performance should increase as perceived competence decreases.

Third are the individuals who are so certain that their ability is low that they have even given up avoiding the implication that they are incompetent. Despite conditions that would promote ego involvement, such individuals will seek to avoid involvement with the tasks in question. Their effort would be employed only to the degree that other incentives, such as the chance to leave the experiment or classroom, appear contingent on it. Even perception of the possibility of competent performance would not produce high effort in such extreme cases. The term "learned helplessness" might be used here, although in practice it has often been applied to any performance impaired by a perception that outcomes cannot be influenced by one's actions (Abramson, Seligman, and Teasdale, 1978). This could include perceptions that tasks are difficult or involve luck, not skill.

Most empirical studies of performance do not distinguish the different levels of low perceived ability or the effects predicted to be associated with them. Nevertheless, because impaired performance is predicted for all levels of low perceived ability (on moderately difficult tasks), such studies can be used to test the more general predictions concerning the effects of high versus low perceived ability.[3]

The Supporting Evidence. To recapitulate: in ego involvement, those who perceive themselves as able should perform their worst on tasks they perceive as normatively very easy, whereas those who perceive themselves as incompetent will perform their worst at moderate difficulty levels. If we perceive our ability as low we should perform better on tasks we see as normatively easy than if we have high perceived ability. These positions should be reversed at intermediate difficulty levels, where higher perceived ability should produce higher performance.[4]

In the following studies the experimenters manipulated normative difficulty cues and set up ego-involving situations, such as presentation of tasks as tests of intelligence. Karabenick and Youssef (1968) found that low-resultant-achievement-motive students performed most poorly and below high-motive students at an intermediate normative difficulty level. High-motive students performed worst at an easy level, but this performance was not, as predicted, below that of low-motive students. Comparing conditions of easy and intermediate normative difficulty, Kukla (1974) found all relevant predicted effects.[5]

I. G. Sarason (1961) found the anagram performances by test-anxious students (of low perceived ability) lower at moderate to moderately low-difficulty levels than at high-difficulty levels. Students who reported little anxiety performed better with moderate- than with high-difficulty instructions. These results accord with predictions made for the highly anxious, but not for the low-anxious students, for whom similar performance is expected in each case. However, the task was presented as an intelligence measure only in the condition of moderate difficulty. This could account for unanxious students' higher performance under conditions of moderate difficulty than under high difficulty. S. B. Sarason, Mandler, and Craighill (1952) found no difference between high- and low-anxious students in a normatively difficult condition, whereas low-anxious students outperformed those high in anxiety in an easy condition. If the easy task was seen as moderately easy, these results accord with predictions. Description of a task as highly difficult produced higher performance in test-anxious students than did a condition where difficulty was not specified but presumably seen as moderate (I. G. Sarason, 1958). As predicted, the less anxious students' performances were best in the latter condition. Though not perfectly consistent, most findings support my predictions that high perceived ability would be associated with higher performance at levels of moderate rather than low difficulty, and that this relationship would be reversed for those with low perceived ability.

Feedback and Performance. Information about how others perform can affect our own feelings of competence (in the differentiated sense). Normative feedback during performance indicates one's probable level of ability with little ambiguity and is also likely to increase or maintain ego involvement (Chapter 6). Therefore studies using normative feedback provide better controlled tests of the predictions of performance in ego involvement than do the studies reviewed in the preceding section.

We would expect individuals with low perceived ability who are told that their performance is below that of others to anticipate feeling incompetent, experience anxiety or reduced commitment, and perform relatively poorly. When their feedback indicates above-average performance, these individuals should believe that they are performing competently and apply high effort to maintain this state. Their performance should not be impaired. (If, however, people are certain they are incompetent, success feedback should not produce high effort.)

For individuals who believe they are competent, feedback indicating below-average performance would violate their expectations and produce high effort and effective performance. Positive normative feedback, on the other hand, would confirm their perceptions of competence, imply that high effort is not necessary, and thereby produce a relatively poor performance.

Results consistent with all the above predictions (except that in parentheses, which was not tested) were obtained by Weiner (1966). He told college students with high- and low-resultant-motivation that they were doing much better or worse than most others during their work on a task described as a test of general ability. The findings were replicated by Weiner and Schneider (1971). Perez (1973) and Schalon (1968) examined the performances of students of high and low self-esteem after telling them that their initial intelligence test performance was below average. The performance of students high in self-esteem improved. Performance of those with low self-esteem declined slightly.

Marecek and Mettee's (1972) study supports the further prediction that individuals who are certain their ability is low would not seek to establish their competence when the opportunity to do so arose. When told they had displayed above-average ability, most college students showed improvement on a retest. This was the case for students with high self-concepts and for those with low self-concepts who were uncertain about their negative self-evaluations. It was not the case, however, for students with low self-concepts who were certain about their negative self-evaluations. Finding that they did improve when their performance was represented as dependent on luck rather than on ability further supports the view that, in the skill condition, they would avoid trying to establish their competence. (There was, in this study, no evidence of the diminished performance predicted under ego involvement for students of high perceived ability after they received success feedback. However, ego involvement was probably not aroused on the pretest because the initially stated purpose of the session was to determine group baseline performance levels.)

Thus far, predictions for individuals with low perceived ability were confirmed with considerable consistency. The expected diminished performance of individuals with high perceived ability after feedback indicating that their performance was superior was not found in one of three cases. Variation in degree of ego involvement might have been responsible for this exception; the better controlled tests of the predictions of performance in ego involvement support the theory.

Performance Under Task and Ego Involvement

In the condition of task involvement the amount of effort should reflect the extent to which work appears likely to improve performance, increase efficiency, or help to accomplish tasks that we are not certain we can master. If we believe that much effort is necessary for mastery or improvement we will apply it. Effort (and performance) should be lower if we believe that little effort is needed for success or that high effort will be fruitless. Just as people vary in the level of difficulty at which they expect gains in mastery, they vary in the level of difficulty at which they perform most effectively. Some of us find easy tasks challenging, others do not. However, provided difficulty levels are not extreme, all or most of us will expect to be able to improve our performance. We will therefore apply high effort in maximizing our improvement, which is an end in itself.

The above predictions contrast with those for ego involvement when levels of difficulty are normatively moderate. If we have high perceived ability, we should maintain high effort to establish that we are above average and perform effectively. But if we believe our ability is low, our performance will be impaired.

These predictions can be tested against the findings of studies where brief experimental tasks were presented as moderately normatively difficult or where tasks allowed a wide range of scores that could indicate either high or low capacity. In such cases, ego involvement will impair the performance of individuals with low perceived ability so that they perform worse than when they are task involved and more poorly than individuals with high perceived ability in task or ego involvement. But diminished performance is not expected for individuals with high perceived ability on the same type of short-term and clearly defined tasks. The studies reviewed employed manipulations that created ego involvement and more neutral settings that would allow task involvement.

Entin and Raynor (1973) compared students with high and low resultant achievement motivation in testlike and in neutral conditions. High-motive students performed better under ego than task involvement, whereas the reverse occurred for low-motive students. Similar findings were obtained by Raynor and Rubin (1971). Gjeseme (1974) obtained identical results with anagrams presented as a school test versus a type of problem students would be tested on one year later.

A number of researchers have compared the effects on performance of presentations of tasks as tests (usually of intelligence) with neutral, informal, or less evaluative conditions. Studies by Paul and Eriksen (1964), I. G. Sarason (1959), and S. B. Sarason, Mandler, and Craighill (1952) reported (a) poorer performance from anxious students in test than in neutral conditions; and (b) no difference for unanxious students. I. G. Sarason and Minard (1962) obtained this result for comprehension but not for three other tests. Using a digit-symbol task, I. G. Sarason and Palola (1960) also found lower performance from anxious students and higher performance from unanxious students in an intelligence test condition. (With very easily discriminable symbols, anxious students, as expected, scored higher than did others in the test condition.) Russell and I. G. Sarason (1965), however, found no effect of testlike instructions on anagram performance. Given the number of factors that could lead to a failure to demonstrate the expected effects (the test could appear easy or not be task-involving), the above studies seem to favor the hypothesis that impaired performance is most evident at moderate normative difficulty levels in individuals with low perceived ability in ego-involving conditions.

Also consistent with present predictions is Perez's (1973) finding that an intelligence test condition led to lower performance for students with low self-esteem than did a neutral presentation, whereas students whose self-esteem was high performed alike in both circumstances. Similarly, induction of self-awareness produced poorer performance from students with low self-esteem than did a task focus (Brockner, 1979; Brockner and Hulton, 1978). High-self-esteem students were not affected by conditions, and task focus produced similar performance in high- and in low-self-esteem students. The task focus also reduced anxiety in low-self-esteem students (Brockner, 1979), while the presence of observers lowered performance in low-perceived-ability (Shrauger, 1972) and in test-anxious students (Ganzer, 1968), but not in high-perceived-ability and low-anxious students.

There is, then, good evidence of the predicted effects of ego versus task involvement when difficulty is perceived as moderate, problems are clearly defined, and time periods are short. Ego involvement produces lower performance in individuals of low perceived ability and equal or higher performance in those of high perceived ability.

Significant Accomplishment: Task Versus Ego Orientation

The preceding predictions apply to experimental settings where tasks are of relatively short duration, task requirements are clearly specified, and there is little scope for initiative. Researchers are able to induce ego involvement by asserting, for instance, that performance in such experiments will forecast students' IQs. A high IQ might facilitate a means of entry to some desirable positions and enhance one's self-esteem, but it is a questionable approximation of a significant human accomplishment. No performance on an IQ test does much to edify or promote human welfare.

When individuals are ego involved, understanding, learning, or improvement in performance is a means to an end. This is unlikely to impair the performance of students who are confident of their ability on short-term, testlike tasks. Indeed, their concern with scoring as high as possible can lead to a choice of easy items that will increase test scores at the expense of gains in understanding (Harter, 1978). On the other hand, it is not likely that a high level of task involvement could be induced in most of the experimental situations discussed above. It is hardly surprising, then, that ego involvement did not produce inferior performance except for individuals who doubted their competence. The question is how much direct relevance these studies have to significant accomplishment in the world outside.

Accomplishments such as gains in understanding of a new topic or advances in scientific thought should be better sustained by task involvement, where this understanding or the exercise of skills is an end in itself. To accomplish such things individuals must be ready to detect problems or inconsistencies in their own ideas or in scientific thought: to find as well as solve problems. Task involvement appears likely to foster sensitivity to problems (Condry and Chambers, 1978) and to favor the selection of tasks that might require high effort rather than those that might quickly enhance one's image. As Asch put it, "In thinking one needs to be concerned with the problem, not with one's self" (1952, p. 304).

Task orientation is more likely to maintain the long-term involvement that such significant accomplishments demand (Campbell, 1960; Kuhn, 1974). Effort would be less consistent over long periods and sensitivity to contradictions would be reduced when, as in ego involvement, action or thought is a means to an end. This would be especially marked when, as in many projects, evaluations may occur only far in the future and much work must be done before it is possible to estimate the quality of one's accomplishment.

No relevant experimental work has dealt with tasks involving long periods of striving and problem-finding or the development of logical thought. Two studies of artistic creativity by Amabile (1979; 1983, Chapter 5) come closest; she found that evaluative conditions lowered artistic creativity in college students. Butler devised a series of studies which required divergent thinking of junior high school students. They differ from the experiments just reviewed in that students performed in their regular schoolrooms on three occasions and did not expect evaluation of their final performance. Students' performance was affected by the feedback they received. Socially comparative grades and praise ("very good") both increased ego involvement and reduced performance (Butler, 1987; 1988; Butler and Nisan, 1986). Task-oriented comments on what the students had accomplished and what could be improved increased task involvement and performance. The case for the negative role of ego involvement in significant intellectual accomplishment is also supported by evidence that children's understanding of prose passages, but not their memory for details, was diminished by the statement, "I'm going to test you . . . to see if you're learning well" (Grolnick and Ryan, 1987, p. 893).

Studies of individual differences in motivational orientation may explain the basis of significant accomplishment in the real world. The possible role of task orientation in fostering understanding and a sensitivity to the complexities of tasks is suggested by evidence that task, not ego, orientation is associated with the belief that academic success is fostered by trying to understand rather than memorize material (Chapter 6). Another study used the orientation scales to forecast junior high school students' use of reading strategies that would promote understanding (rather than mere recall of data): this was predicted by Task Orientation but not Ego Orientation or Perceived Ability (Nolen, 1988). (The scales were administered four to six weeks prior to the reading assignment.) The associations between motivational orientations and questionnaire measures of cognitive style found by Kroll (1988) also add to this picture. He found Ego Orientation negatively associated with Tolerance for Ambiguity and Thoughtfulness, whereas Task Orientation was positively associated with Tolerance for Ambiguity, Thoughtfulness, and Openmindedness. These results all support the proposition that task orientation is more likely to favor the posing of new and challenging problems and the development of knowledge.

Associations of the motivational orientation scales with divergent thinking scores are also consistent with Butler's experimental evidence (Nicholls et al., 1988a). A divergent thinking task was presented to a university composition class as a task for improving ideational fluency. The resulting scores correlated with Task Orientation ($r(48) = .42$, $p < .001$) but not Ego Orientation ($r(48) = .07$, n.s.). Students who are task-oriented seem to exhibit greater readiness to contemplate diverse ideas.

The possible role of task orientation in fostering the long-term commitment that significant accomplishment usually requires is suggested by a study of high school students' participation in organized sport and in recreational (informal) sport (Duda, 1985). Students who participated in both organized and recreational games were distinguished from those who participated only in organized activities by being higher in task orientation, but not in interpersonal competitiveness. Similar findings were obtained with college students who were involved in recreational sports: task orientation was associated with practicing in free time (Duda, 1988). It seems then that task orientation more than ego orientation leads one to exercise one's skills when there is no outside pressure to do so.

Creative achievement in science and the arts is fostered by task orientation rather than ego orientation or other extrinsic factors (Nicholls, 1972). This position was suggested by Crutchfield (1962), who also argued that creative people can resist social pressure because of their dedication to task requirements. After a review of biographies, McCurdy (1960) concluded that the childhood pattern of genius involves early pleasure in the world of ideas. He also contended that eminent creators are highly independent by virtue of reliance on and commitment to their own ideas. Roe (1952) reported a similar pattern in physical and biological scientists. Creative architects whom MacKinnon studied (1965) were inclined to strive where independent activity was called for and were guided by self-generated standards of excellence, whereas less creative architects were more prone to conform to professional standards. A similar pattern was also found with mathematicians (Helson, 1971; Helson and Crutchfield, 1970). Taylor and Ellison (1967) and Chambers (1964) reported self-initiated, task-oriented striving as a distinguishing characteristic of creative scientists. Thus creative individuals do appear to be more task-oriented than their less creative peers. (See also Amabile, 1983.)

Perhaps the most convincing study on the topic at hand is one about research psychologists conducted by Helmreich and coauthors (1980). Psychologists whose research was cited more frequently were found to be higher on the Mastery and Work scales (task orientation). The Competitiveness scale (ego orientation), however, was negatively associated with frequency of citations. When different combinations of Competitiveness and Mastery and work were examined, it was found that those low on Competitiveness and high on Work and Mastery were cited most frequently, implying that theirs was the work most esteemed by their peers.

The findings of Helmreich and colleagues (1980) are consistent with results obtained in other domains of accomplishment. College students high on Work and Mastery but low in Competitiveness had higher grade point averages than students with other combinations of motive scores. Similarly, businessmen who were high on Work and Mastery but low on Competitiveness had higher salaries than did those with other motive score patterns (Spence and Helmreich, 1983).

When Winning Isn't Everything

The research reviewed in chapter 6 is consistent with the proposition that a task orientation or task involvement will foster equality in feelings of accomplishment and in striving for mastery. This need not happen at the expense of quality of accomplishment. Indeed, understanding excellence as superiority over others can bring second-best results when it takes the form of an individual's goal. In a few studies, ego involvement did lead to performance that surpassed that found in more neutral, and presumably task-involving conditions. But it worked only for students who perceived themselves as more competent than others when they were working on rather trivial, cut-and-dried, brief tasks in experimental settings where evaluative pressures were clear. Even in such cases the superiority of ego involvement is not consistent. But when we look at the quality of accomplishments in the real world—even when this is defined in the conventional terms of a less than perfect society—the best that can be said for the ego or competitive orientation is that it is better than no orientation at all (Spence and Helmreich, 1983).

It does not follow that task involvement means a complete lack of consideration of the accomplishments of others. One can look to other people for the purpose of learning without an explicit concern about one's standing relative to them. (See Chapter 1 and Veroff, 1969.) In many fields of endeavor some form of social comparison is ubiquitous. Yet it does not necessarily have the properties of ego involvement. Scientific work that does not tell us something new is of little interest. For some scientists this can have the implication that they must best their fellow scientists. But the construction of new ideas and the discovery of new things can be intrinsically satisfying. The insight or knowledge produced by our work and its usefulness to others can be more important than what it says about our standing relative to our peers. And a recognition of the adequacy of other people's constructions and discoveries can be a source of pleasure instead of a threat to self-esteem.

It is not easy to find academic psychologists making a case (in print) for increasing the emphasis on interpersonal competition, presumably because no compelling data have come up to support this position. There seems to be no shortage of others, such as historian Barbara Tuchman (1980) and political writer Michael Novak, who bemoan the low quality of the accomplishments of our schools and claim that this is because we have, in Novak's words, failed to "add the invigorating element of competition" (Lapham, 1986, p. 43). The evidence reviewed here might make us wonder if such people have simply got their facts about motivation wrong. But the intentional view allows the possibility that what we see as facts might reveal what we value. One might find it unfortunate that such critics do not assume that quality would be most effectively fostered by a desire to understand as fully as possible, to write as well as possible, or to build as well as possible rather than simply to beat someone else at these activities. Is it not also disturbing that such social and educational critics appear unconcerned about the link between interpersonal competitiveness and inequality of motivation and of feelings of accomplishment? These are inevitable consequences of a preoccupation with interpersonal competition.

A preoccupation with winning may well be accompanied by a lack of concern about justice and fairness. There is evidence to suggest that high levels of participation in competitive sports reduce prosocial impulses and commitment to fair play (Kleiber and Roberts, 1988). When winning is everything, it is worth doing anything to win. Recent cases of falsification of data have made that clear.

The unfortunate consequences of a preoccupation with winning are easy to overlook if one is concerned with being number one or identifies with those who appear to be "on top." It is consistent with the intentional perspective that those with the view that excellence amounts to being better than someone else should also overlook the problems associated with a preoccupation with one's rank in a hierarchy of competence. The point I want to make is that debates about topics such as competition in education are, and should be, debates about what we should aspire to—what we should want—as much as they are debates about empirical questions, such as what leads to high academic achievement.

I should not end this chapter with the impression that motivational influences on success defined in terms of indices such as grades, income, or frequency of citation play the critical role in the case for task orientation rather than ego orientation. There is no reason to think that task orientation will always predict such criteria. "In an effort to advance their careers, commanders at all levels [of the U.S. Armed Services] habitually report to their superiors that units under their command are more fit for combat than they actually are. A decade ago . . . a lieutenant colonel—who was regarded as one of the Army's finest by his peers—was ordered to report his tank battalion . . . as more ready to fight than it actually was. He refused . . . The Army's response to this action . . . was to force the officer out of the service" (Hadley,

1987, p. 27). One can visualize societies where readiness to cheat or to seek the favor of autocratic authorities could play an over-whelmingly larger role in outcomes such as college grades, in-come, and scientific recognition than they appear to do in our society. This would not make cheating or fawning admirable. Nor would it make for accomplishments that expand knowledge or protect and enrich our lives. If winning the Akron Soap Box Derby is predicted by ingenuity at cheating, as it once was (Woodley, 1974), should psychologists recommend cheating?

Citation frequency, grade point average, and salary may not be perfect indices of accomplishment. But if they are not of some value, our worlds of research, school, and business must be in a sorry state. Evidence suggesting that success, as measured by such conventional indices, is best fostered by a task orientation might be taken as an indication that our research, school, and business systems are not completely corrupt. Critics like Novak and Tuchman who fail to distinguish interpersonal competitive-ness from the desire to accomplish significant things do nothing to conserve this state of affairs.

9

A Review of the Theories

Part of my purpose has been to integrate features of diverse theoretical approaches to achievement motivation. This attempt was based on the observation that different positions employed different conceptions of ability and was developed in the belief that the different approaches all embodied unique and valuable features. In this chapter I will comment on the theories that I kept in mind while formulating my own, to acknowledge my intellectual debts in the process of explaining why I felt that the other positions were not, as they stood, entirely adequate—at least not for my purposes. The reader should not, therefore, expect anything approaching an adequate overall review. The authors of the diverse positions had concerns different from those that guided my efforts and I have attended only to those aspects that were important to my ends.[1]

Theories of Task Choice

Comparison of the predictions of Chapter 7 with those of other theories of task choice is complicated because other theories do not explicitly distinguish normative difficulty and subjective probability of success. Atkinson, for example, holds that "degree of difficulty can be inferred from the subjective probability of success" (1957, p. 362). He also postulates that the incentive value of success increases as the subjective probability of success decreases. That is, we value success more if we are less certain to achieve it. He does not distinguish this from the claim that success is more valued on tasks that only a few others can do (that is, normatively difficult tasks). From my perspective one would expect Atkinson's position to apply to states of task involvement wherein individuals are unlikely to distinguish between task difficulty in the normative sense and their own subjective probabilities of success. Yet in fact his predictions of task choice are closer to my predictions of task choice for ego involvement: a state that is marked by a clear distinction between task difficulty and one's subjective probability of success.[2]

Given that distinction, it is difficult to see why individuals who doubt their competence (or have low resultant achievement motivation) should, as Atkinson's model predicts, avoid tasks where their subjective probability of success are moderate. If we do not distinguish our subjective probability of success at a task from the difficulty of the task, we would all presumably be moderately sure of being able to establish our competence when we had moderate expectations of success. This is not a condition anyone seeking to establish her competence would have any reason to avoid. But if our subjective (and actual) probabilities of success are moderate and we also realize that the task concerned is easy for all our peers, we will have reason to avoid that task. Much of the drama of achievement motivation derives from the fact that our subjective probabilities of success are often not the same as those of our fellows. This is something of which Atkinson is aware—as illustrated, for example, by an intriguing study of the effects of tracking as a function of individual differences in motivation (O'Connor, Atkinson, and Horner, 1966). Yet this insight is not incorporated into his mathematical model.

Atkinson's position resembles the present one in that action is presumed to be a function of expectations of success and failure and of the values of these outcomes for the individual. On the other hand, the logic of the intentional perspective is not used to derive predictions. For Atkinson, "the strength of motivation to perform some act is assumed to be a multiplicative function of the strength of the motive, the expectancy (subjective probability) that the act will have as a consequence the attainment of an incentive and the value of the incentive" (1957, pp. 360–361). These are premises as well as predictions. Atkinson's mathematical model is a statement of these assumptions in algebraic form; it is not derived from some larger frame of reference, a more general conception of action, or higher-order assumptions. Atkinson announced his model without ever making the case for the position that motivation to act is a *multiplicative* function of motive, expectancy, and incentive value. From the perspective of those who see mathematics as the ideal basis of scientific prediction, this would not be a problem. From an intentional perspective, it is.

Pauline Sears's (1940) earlier analysis of choice under ego-involving conditions is similar to mine in that it embodies an intentional or empathetic stance, clearly distinguishes between individual levels of expectation of success and task difficulty, and makes similar predictions. Could Atkinson's mathematical model have failed to incorporate the distinction between expectations of success and task difficulty because of its rejection of the empathetic stance? Over the years I have been intrigued that my students' initial reactions to Atkinson's predictions were almost invariably of this empathetic type. They would point out, for example, that it can make sense to choose a very hard task because then you can't look incompetent. After some years of responding, "you might like to explain it that way but Atkinson's model doesn't," and then passing on to the next topic, I have adopted their stance.

We should, however, recognize that Atkinson's model does summarize much data on task choice. Meyer and coauthors (1976) find this summary unimpressive because they hold that Atkinson's predictions are violated any time individuals with low resultant motivation (low perceived ability) do not prefer extremely high or low probabilities of success. If one interprets Atkinson as predicting that as resultant motivation decreases, the tendency to prefer high or low over moderate probabilities of success will increase, much of the existing relevant data (collected in ego-involving contexts, see Chapter 7) supports Atkinson's model. (See review by Heckhausen et al., 1985.)

Meyer and his coauthors (and Kukla, 1978) also have a point in that there are times when the tendency to choose personally challenging tasks predominates across all levels of perceived ability. Their positions present another paradox: although these writers distinguish between subjective probability of success and task difficulty, their predictions resemble those developed here for task involvement. They fail to see that choice of a normatively easy task would be tantamount to an admission of low ability, and, for this reason, not a rational choice for anyone who was committed to establishing his competence in the differentiated sense. These theorists recognize that individuals differ in the level of task difficulty they find personally challenging. They appear to assume, however, that people may find personally challenging tasks attractive even if they recognize that such tasks are easy, rather than challenging, for most others. This would explain why, despite incorporating a differentiated conception of difficulty and ability into their positions, Meyer and his coauthors and Kukla offer predictions that resemble those for task rather than ego involvement.

Leaving aside questions of internal logic of theories of choice, we should not spend much time asking whether Atkinson's or Kukla's and Meyer's predictions are more accurate. We should ask instead in what circumstances are these different predictions more accurate. Then we will be in a better position to focus on the problem of discovering the circumstances that best promote a desire to tackle personally challenging tasks and, thereby, foster learning among students at all levels of perceived ability. These theories have not directed attention to this problem.

Theories of Performance

A major difference between my position and those of Atkinson (1957; Atkinson and Raynor, 1974) and Kukla (1972) is that mine distinguishes and makes separate predictions for task and ego involvement. The importance of this distinction is sustained by the evidence I have reviewed.

The present theory also distinguishes normative difficulty and expectation of success more sharply than Kukla's theory, which leads to inconsistent interpretation of data. At one point (1972) Kukla presents as consistent with his theory evidence that low-resultant-motive individuals perform better when half of their peers are predicted to fail than when the odds of success are clearly higher or lower (Atkinson, 1958). At another point, evidence that low-resultant-motive individuals perform better on a normatively easy than on a moderately difficult task is held to support his theory (Kukla, 1974). Such inconsistency is unlikely when a clear distinction is made between expectations of success and normative difficulty. Because Kukla uses a less differentiated (objective) conception of difficulty and ability, his predictions resemble my predictions for task involvement. There is no place in his formulation for the various impairments and enhancements of performance that occur in ego involvement.

The predictions of Atkinson's theory as modified by Revelle and Michaels (1976) are more compatible with the present predictions for ego involvement. It seems that in Revelle and Michaels' revision, as in the present theory, low-resultant-motive (or low-perceived-ability) individuals would be predicted to perform their worst at moderate normative-difficulty levels, and high-perceived-ability individuals would be expected to perform their worst at easy and at extremely difficult tasks. However, as Revelle and Michaels note (p. 400), their position does not predict higher performance in low- than in high-resultant-motive subjects after feedback indicating above-average performance (Weiner, 1966; Weiner and Schneider, 1971), whereas this theory does. Kukla (1972) argues that this effect is mediated by students' perceptions of low task difficulty as a consequence of the information that their performance is superior. It seems more plausible to assume that low-perceived-ability students accept the feedback indicating that they have outperformed their peers as evidence of their competence. In any event, Atkinson's position does not predict this phenomenon. More critical, however, is the failure to deal with task involvement, where performance (as predicted) is often as good as or better than in ego involvement.

It might be argued that task-involving situations are not achievement situations. The problem then would be to explain why individuals perform effectively and choose personally challenging tasks in such situations. This position would also have the anomalous implication that motivation that appears to make the most distinctive contribution to significant accomplishment is not a form of achievement motivation. As Spence and Helmreich (1983), Asch (1952), Covington and Beery (1976), and others have argued, there are good reasons for distinguishing striving the aim of which is superiority over others from striving where the task, understanding, or performing as well as possible are the prime concerns.

The concept of learned helplessness has been widely used to explain impaired performance. In one version of this position, Abramson, Seligman, and Teasdale (1978) differentiate personal from universal helplessness. The former occurs when the person believes that he (specifically) is unable to influence salient outcomes; the latter occurs when the inability to influence outcomes is also experienced by others. This position is seemingly based on a differentiated conception of ability. But Abramson and her colleagues are not consistent on this point. They see performance impairment as a function of perception of noncontingency between action and outcome. This implies that it does not matter whether the perception that one's actions are unlikely to influence outcomes is a result of one's incompetence or the difficulty of the task and suggests an undifferentiated conception of ability where task difficulty and subjective probability of success are not distinguished. As noted in Chapter 8, in ego involvement performance is most clearly impaired when peole believe that their difficulties in completing a task will indicate that they are incompetent. Yet when people are not ego-involved, perception of very high difficulty is more likely to lead to diminished performance.

Learned helplessness (perception of noncontingency of action and outcome) has been widely considered as an explanation for depression. But this cannot account for the fact that mania and depression can alternate. Indeed, as far as I know, this problem has not been raised. The existence of bipolar affective disorders seems less problematical from my perspective. They can be seen as a more global expression of the level of aspiration behavior of people who doubt their competence (Chapter 7). When individuals are highly ego-involved—committed to establishing their capacity but lacking faith in it—they set unrealistically high goals. This could be an analogue of mania, with its high energy levels and expectations. When hope and commitment die, we have depression. But in each case the individuals' fundamental concern seems to be with their competence rather than with what they might do in the world. Perhaps the biological basis of bipolar affective disorders involves a predisposition toward ego involvement or inability to control it.

Albert Bandura separates the lack of a sense of efficacy from the belief in an unresponsive environment. This would seem to indicate that he employs a differentiated conception of ability: "Success with minimal effort fosters ability ascriptions but analogous attainments gained through heavy labor connote a lesser ability" (1981, p. 205). A less differentiated conception is employed when he suggests that "failures that are overcome by determined effort can instill robust percepts of self-efficacy through experience that one can eventually master even the most difficult obstacles" (p. 203). A less differentiated conception is also implied when he argues that self-efficacy will be enhanced by improved behavioral functioning (1977, p. 195). Bandura does not specify the circumstances under which these statements apply.

Bandura and Abramson deal with a variety of topics that are well beyond my scope and my comments do not bear on many aspects of their frameworks. But insofar as they are concerned with remediation of behavioral impairment, it seems important to distinguish task involvement from ego involvement (and work-avoidance) by these or any other names. People's goals as well as their expectations about the likely outcomes of their actions need to be considered.

The importance of variation in focus of attention, in conjunction with expectations about the consequences of actions, have been the subject of much recent work (Carver, 1979; Carver and Scheier, 1981). These writers show that expectations of failure to complete a task are more likely to occasion impaired performance when we are publicly self-conscious than when we are not. Kuhl (1981) makes a similar point and I have adopted it in my framework. One difference is that Carver and Scheier argue that success (in the sense of task-completion) rather than the establishment of one's competence is the goal of achievement behavior (1981, Chapter 10). The evidence is complex, so interested readers might refer to Carver and Scheier's supporting evidence and argument. However, they do not sustain their own position. For example, at one point the writers qualify their position with Atkinson's assumption that success is more valued on more "difficult" tasks (p. 260). This contradicts their position that success in the sense of mere task-completion is the goal of achievement activity. If it were, easy tasks would be more attractive. The assumption that success is more attractive when the task is more difficult does not follow from their position, but is a natural implication of the view they reject—that task-mastery is valued to the extent that it indicates competence. Moreover, Carver and Scheier accept the notion that task choices are influenced by the fact that moderately difficult tasks are most diagnostic of ability (Chapter 13). Again, they do not sustain their initial position. The value of their work is the unambiguous demonstration of the importance for action of variation in focus of attention. We should also note that introducing self-awareness in achievement situations produces effects that are similar to evaluative and interpersonally competitive conditions— conditions that other researchers have construed as arousing test anxiety or achievement motivation.

Action as a Means or an End

The theories discussed so far have not focused on whether action is experienced as a means to an end or an end in itself. This has been the concern of others (Deci and Ryan, 1985; Kruglanski, 1975; Lepper and Greene, 1978; Maehr, 1976). The distinction between action that is an end in itself and action that is a means to an end (or intrinsic versus extrinsic involvement) becomes especially important when one considers the questions of continuing commitment over long periods.

The ego-involving contexts in which many experiments on motivation and performance are conducted tend to make performance a means rather than an end. But the implications of this for action and accomplishment in the real world would not show up in most of these short-term experiments. Ego involvement is associated with diminished readiness to persist when individuals are not constrained to do so and is less likely than task involvement to promote significant accomplishment. Thus it seems useful for a theory of achievement motivation to consider the extent to which action is an end in itself (task involvement) rather than a means to an end (ego involvement). It is certainly important to do so if that theory is to be applied to issues of education and if equality of motivation for learning is a concern.

Attribution Theory

Weiner's approach to achievement motivation (1979; 1985) involves the analysis of commonsense reasoning about the causes of success and failure on skill tasks. Different explanations for success and failure are held to produce different emotions, expectations, and actions. Weiner has not adopted the commonsense, intentional approach to predictions of behavior, given individuals' goals and what they need to do to attain these goals. His approach, however, has been applied to many aspects of achievement motivation and social action.

In categorizing the causal factors we employ to explain success and failure Weiner (1985) implicitly assumes that we employ the differentiated conception of ability, in that ability, effort, and task difficulty are treated as distinct factors with clearly separate properties. In task involvement, however, ability, effort, and difficulty are less perfectly differentiated. Most attribution theory research has not allowed for this possibility, which could resolve problems with some aspects of attribution theory.

A question of early interest to attribution theorists, for example, was whether effort or ability was a more important predictor of achievement affect. If this question is considered from the point of view of the differentiated conception (which is implicit in attribution theory), it is difficult not to come to the conclusion that ability attributions are the important mediators of affect. High ability indicates that future success is likely (Weiner, Nierenberg, and Goldstein, 1976). Therefore, if success brings pride, attribution of high ability to oneself should maximize expectations of continued success and feelings of pleasure or pride. If the differentiated conception is employed, a belief that success reflected high effort should imply low ability, less chance of continued success, and hence less pride. Surely it is ability attributions that are the main mediators of achievement affect.

But let us suppose that, on the contrary, positive affect was maximized when success was attributed to high effort, and negative affect was maximized when failure was attributed to low effort. This would mean that we would always maximize our gains and minimize our losses by trying as hard as possible. As Kukla

(1978) notes, we often do not do this. But if we did, causal attributions could serve no purpose. To maximize our gains and minimize our losses we would only need to assure ourselves that we had tried hard. We would have no reason to consider the role of factors such as ability, difficulty, or luck because effort can be perceived directly. We must control for effort and task difficulty to infer our capacity, but we do not have to control anything to judge our effort. If effort attributions were the prime mediators of achievement affect, causal attributions would be irrelevant to achievement motivation.

I could not persuade myself that I never make causal attributions or that I always try hard. Therefore, as long as I persisted in thinking in terms of the differentiated conception of ability, I had to conclude that ability attributions must be the critical mediators of achievement affect. Evidence consistent with this thesis was found in an ego-involving situation where success and failure were manipulated (Nicholls, 1975) and with students' attributions for their recalled academic successes and failures (Nicholls, 1976b). Feelings about success and failure thus appeared to reflect the extent to which they were attributed to ability (see also McFarland and Ross, 1982). Other researchers (Weiner and Kukla, 1970) found effort to be more important. If both views are right, the paradox may be explained by the suggestion that, although we prefer to have high ability, we recognize that effort is virtuous (Covington and Omelich, 1979; Nicholls, 1976a; Sohn, 1977). Effort is socially approved and teachers may reward effort more than ability (Lanzetta and Hannah, 1969; Weiner, 1979).

This, however, does not seem to exhaust the issue. As I argued in Chapter 6, for task-involved people higher effort can lead to greater learning and greater competence. One's perception that success was due to high effort could then result in feelings of competence and positive affect. Evidence in support of this prediction is presented in Chapter 6. Because attribution theory does not distinguish various meanings of effort and ability or tell when different meanings will be activated, these data are anomalous for that theory.

To complicate matters, different attributions are associated not merely with degrees of emotion, but also with different emotions (Weiner, 1979). But given that the meanings of ability and effort can change, the associations between given attributions and specific affects might also change. Brown and Weiner (1982), for example, found that embarrassment diminished and guilt increased when effort was low. These results make sense in ego involvement, where (if performance is fixed) low effort (compared to that of others) would enhance perceived ability and thus minimize the embarrassment that would follow any demonstration of low ability. At the same time, low effort would produce the guilt associated with slacking off. Effort would be a two-edged sword (Covington and Omelich, 1979) in ego involvement. In task involvement, however, higher effort can lead to greater competence. In this case, therefore, effort should minimize both guilt and embarrassment. These predictions were supported with task-involving and ego-involving scenarios by Jagacinski and Nicholls (1984a). When students are ego-involved, they are faced with the choice of trying hard and experiencing greater embarrassment (if they fail) or applying less effort and experiencing more guilt. In task involvement, effort minimizes both guilt and embarrassment.

Again, from the perspective of education, task involvement is the more desirable psychological state as it increases the possibility of motivational equality. Attribution theory may be useful in clarifying such questions as how students come to judge themselves as high or low in capacity and what are the emotional consequences of such judgments in ego-involving contexts. But it appears of less value for predicting emotion and action in task involvement. It also has not thus far and is unlikely in the future to lead researchers to discover how individuals can focus on accomplishing things rather find out how their accomplishments reflect on their ability.

Conclusion

My position evolved, in part, out of the desire to combine some of the strengths of the different approaches to achievement motivation, to deal with their various problems, and address the problem of explaining and reducing inequality of motivation and sense of accomplishment while fostering accomplishment. In the latter respect, I believe that the present approach has some advantages in that it specifies the psychic conditions that favor inequality versus equality and address the question of quality of accomplishment. (See also Covington and Beery, 1976; Dweck, 1986; Dweck and Elliot, 1983;[3] Heckhausen et al., 1985; Maehr, 1983.) But much remains to be said and discovered about how to create social conditions favorable to quality and equality in schools.

In other respects also the present position does not do all it ought to. I have, for example, given little attention to the effects of a variety of influences that can undermine intrinsic involvement in tasks without inducing ego involvement (See, for example, Boggiano and Main, 1986; Deci and Ryan, 1985; Lepper and Greene, 1978.) My analysis is also rather static in that it does not recognize the extent to which perceptions of our chances of affecting outcomes depends in part on the actions we take (Skinner, 1985). Furthermore, I have not considered the possibility that expectations of success or failure might be manipulated by individuals to control their motivational orientations. Norem and Cantor (1986), for example, found that a small proportion of students will deliberately adopt low performance expectations to get themselves sufficiently aroused to work hard for tests.

But there is, to my way of thinking, a more serious deficiency with the position I have presented. Although I systematically employ the intentional perspective—attempting to put myself in the shoes of others—I have so far not begun to deal with what others might see as the meaning of their lives and the place of their accomplishments in those lives. As Brewster Smith might put it, "We should expect and demand more of our science" (1974, p. 2). Lay persons might also reasonably hope to learn from motivation theorists something about the nature and consequences of different views about "man's chief end in life."

In their technical approach, researchers have often reduced human values to the importance accorded achieving success or avoiding failure without even acknowledging the possibility of varieties of success or failure. In this light, the distinction between the forms of success defined by task, ego, and extrinsic involvement is a minor step forward. We still know nothing about, for example, the larger purposes of a task-involved individual. What place, for example, does Mary's satisfaction with learning mathematics have in her life? Does she think that the book of Nature is written in mathematics and that she is communicating with God? Does she dream of improving the world in some way with her mathematical knowledge? Does she hope this labor will bring her a handsome house and husband? As long as our theories of motivation ignore such questions, they will not fully earn the status of theories of human motivation.[4] I therefore describe a preliminary exploration of such questions in the context of school in Chapter 12.

III

Motivation, Education, and Society

10

Inequality

Equality of accomplishment cannot serve as the aim of education because it would mean unequal fulfillment of potential. Just as we cannot all grow to a height of seven feet, we do not all have the same intellectual potential. Equal attainment would mean that individuals with more potential than others could not develop their powers as fully as possible. Apart from the injustice involved to these individuals, this would make for a boring world. It would diminish the pool of accomplishments that might entertain, inform, clothe, and feed us all. A more adequate conception of educational equality requires the fulfillment of each individual's potential: maximum intellectual development and accomplishment for each individual. If we all develop our powers as fully as possible, no one's powers will be diminished.

We will probably never be able to say for certain whether someone has reached his or her potential. We can, however, tell when individuals are developing their potential and when they are not. Students cannot be developing it in school if they are intellectually passive or if they avoid intellectual activity. If some students are optimally motivated to learn but others are not, unequal development is occurring. If all students are optimally motivated (and, in this book, that means task-involved), we are on the way to the goal of equality in the fulfillment of potential. We might never be able to recognize when students have attained their potential. But this is of no concern if we can recognize sound progress toward this goal.

When construed in this way, the goal of equality must mean different educational provisions for different students—especially in the later years of schooling. Appropriate work will be needed for various levels of talent, because we cannot all profit from work at the same level of difficulty. Some variety will also derive from students' choices or interests. We cannot develop in all directions at once and choice of one direction will leave other talents uncultivated. Furthermore, those who are able and committed to the study of engineering (for example) should, if possible, receive tuition for learning this topic that others do not. It makes little sense from the perspective of society or of the individual to send to engineering school students with the poorest accomplishments in academic domains relevant to engineering. We should not have to cross bridges designed by such people. But they should encounter environments that favor the development of their own talents and interests—even if those talents are more humble. So long as the only consequence of talent and interest is a commensurable opportunity to exercise that talent, all is well.

Unequal rates of intellectual growth and commensurably different educational provisions are neither inherently fair nor unfair. Devices such as tracking or ability grouping within classes become unjust if they selectively contribute to diminished motivation for intellectual growth. In an atmosphere that fosters ego involvement, educational practices of this type would heighten the extent to which learning is experienced as a means to the end of establishing one's superiority over others. Motivation would thus be diminished and inequality increased. But differential provisions cannot be equated with ego involvement. One could hardly maintain task involvement simply by having all students work at the same level of difficulty. The consequent absence of optimum challenge would produce unequal and ineffective motivation, even in the absence of ego involvement. If students are to be preoccupied with understanding as well as possible and if schools are to foster this preoccupation, some forms of differential provision will be necessary. So inquiry about the merits and demerits of practices like tracking is likely to be less enlightening than one might hope. They are not inherently problematic but become so if, as is often the case, they induce students to seek the higher group, track, or test score to establish their superiority over others rather than to develop their knowledge.

Difficulties do not always stop with differential educational provisions for learning and ego-involving climates. The greater accomplishment that follows from greater potential can bring gains that are not intrinsically related to that accomplishment. If, for example, greater educational attainment (gained fairly) happens to enable a person to be more accomplished than others as a politician, it is hard to cry foul if she gains more political influence. We might all hope for the grace to admire and learn from accomplishments that surpass our own. But if a person's political influence is a consequence of her having been more accomplished at schoolwork and of holding a degree from Yale (even if fairly earned), rather than a consequence of her accomplishments in the field of politics, a sense of injustice is in order (Walzer, 1983).

Analogous forms of inequality occur within classrooms when greater academic accomplishment leads to privileges of a non-academic nature—school-given opportunities to dominate one's peers socially and to enjoy greater personal freedom. Those of lesser accomplishments are thereby humiliated and set back in their efforts to construct their own destinies and the destiny of their group. Unequal accomplishment we should expect and accept. Levels of humanity we should not.

There are then, at least two forms of inequality. The first is unequal development of the intellectual and aesthetic potentials with which schools are most directly concerned. This might be promoted by no more than a highly ego-involving atmosphere. The second form is inequality in the distribution of rights, privileges, and respect that is not an intrinsic consequence of different levels of competence or rates of development. Both forms of inequality can be found in schools.

Ego-Involving Properties of Schools

Many writers have documented teaching and grading practices that induce ego involvement (for example, Bloom, 1976; Brophy and Good, 1974; Covington and Beery, 1976; Good, 1980; Heckhausen and Krug, 1982; Levine, 1983; Marshall and Weinstein, 1984; Pepitone, 1980). Grading on the curve and making grades and other evaluations of competence salient and public are common practices that would have this effect. Emphasis on the importance of students' percentile ranks on standardized achievement tests would have a similar impact (Eccles, Midgley, and Adler, 1984).

During the process of teaching teachers can indicate how they think students stand relative to their peers and, at the same time, imply this standing is an indication of personal worth. Weinstein (1976), for example, observed teachers of first-grade students making statements such as "Joey's group has all of this to do because they are very smart and this is difficult" (p. 115). Students in lower reading groups waiting for the teacher to assign them work were also commonly admonished to follow the assignment instructions for the highest group because some day they would also do that work. (It is not surprising, then, that reading group membership predicts later reading attainment even when initial reading readiness is controlled; Weinstein, 1976.)

The impact of the school's emphasis on student standing relative to others can hardly be lessened by parental pressures on children to be in the top group and on the teacher to ensure that this occurs (Weinstein, 1976, p. 116). Parents might reflect on what they ask their school-age children when they come home after a test. One could ask "Did you figure out what happened on the ones you missed?" or "Do you understand the topic as well as your score suggests?" But how often does the conversation go something like this: "How did the test go?" "Not bad." "What was your score?" "Eighteen." "So what did Michael and Geoff get?" In such ways do we convey the importance of rank in class and strengthen an ego orientation in our children.

Newspaper editors and school corporations often use social comparison to enhance the value of their schools. This year, for example, a school corporation near where I live placed, in the local paper, a full-page advertisement full of graphs revealing how far above the national average their students' standardized test scores were. Other school corporations find other ways of making such news widely known.

McDermott and Hood (1982, p. 236) hold that "In America 'Who is smart?' and 'Who knows?' are crucial questions for us and much of our time in school is organized around managing our respective places vis-a-vis such questions . . . After extended observation . . . we are increasingly overwhelmed with the importance of those times when each child is asked to perform some difficult task with the consequence of being called either competent/incompetent or smart/dumb. A good part of any teacher's day can be understood in terms of occasioning such scenes and even worrying about . . . different children so as to not put them on a line in ways that either underchallenge or embarrass them." (See also Stebbins, 1977.) Children who doubt their competence can be observed spending energy and often considerable social skill to avoid being put on the line. Hood, McDermott, and Cole (1980) described the problems faced by a "learning disabled" boy in a team quiz game in his classroom. He must simultaneously try to stay off the hot seat and focus on the questions being asked. When finally obliged to face a question, he shrinks down in his chair and begins to cry. This has his peers and the teacher rooting for him and it gets him a simpler question that he can answer. He survives this particular battle, but, for him, the war goes on.

Holt (1964) describes the many strategies children develop to make the teacher ignore them or to transform their environment in other ways so as to avoid feeling stupid. When Holt asked a group of students how they felt when they couldn't answer a teacher's question, "a paralyzed silence fell on the room" (p. 62). A student who broke the silence by calling out "Gulp!" spoke for them all. "They said they were afraid of failing, afraid of being kept back, afraid of being called stupid, afraid of feeling themselves stupid. Stupid . . . almost the worst thing they can think of to call each other" (p. 63).

These observations are paralleled by the results of a survey by Pinter and Lev (1940) of fifth and sixth graders' worries. Of 53 items about which children might worry, "failing a test" was most highly ranked. Similarly, Jackson and Getzels (1959) found that adolescents frequently checked "inadequate," "ignorant," and "dull" along with "bored" and "restless" to describe their characteristic feelings in school. Somewhat more recently, Adams (1968) wrote that when adolescents were asked to identify personal problems, they frequently mentioned academic problems. Males identified school-related problems much more often than other problems, whereas females mentioned family and interpersonal problems almost as often as academic problems. West and Wood (1970) found that only 35 percent of fifth through twelfth graders agreed that school problems were their greatest worry.

However, 68 percent agreed that they "feel a great deal of pressure to do well in school" and 65 percent agreed that they "frequently worry about examinations." Such surveys seem to have gone out of fashion, but students' concerns about their competence in school probably have not. Many students must feel their lives are like the lives of soldiers: long periods of boredom punctuated by moments of terror.

Ego Involvement and Its Classroom Effects

One concern of a number of researchers has been the effect of competition and social comparison on students' levels of perceived ability (Rosenholtz and Simpson, 1984). In the early grades especially it seems that an emphasis on social comparison of classroom accomplishments increases the extent to which students' ratings of their ability reflect their standing, relative to others (Chapter 3). This means that, on the average, students' evaluations of their academic competence will be less positive in ego-involving classrooms.

Although I would be one of the first to decry an emphasis on social comparison of abilities, especially in the early grades, there seems nothing inherently wrong with merely knowing one's rank in a hierarchy of competence. Members of effectively cooperating groups might be well aware of each others' competencies. Indeed one might wonder what is wrong with a group or society if appreciably more than half its members think they are above average or feel the need to make this claim. From this perspective, the adoption of high perceived ability as an educational goal is hard to justify.

We should not, as Rosenholtz and Simpson do, confuse knowledge of one's ability relative to others with consistent self-evaluation in terms of that rank. The undesirable outcome of competitive classrooms is ego involvement rather than knowledge of one's rank. Ego involvement is not the form of motivation that most fosters intellectual development and the fulfillment of intellectual potential. Moreover, ego involvement is likely to increase motivational inequality. A considerable amount of research on intrinsic interest, task choice, and accomplishment (reviewed in Part II) supports these assertions.

Like individuals, classrooms can be distinguished in terms of their average levels of task and ego orientation. When (in a study of 30 fifth-grade classrooms) classroom averages (instead of individual students' scores) on the Motivational Orientation Scales were used, these scales remained internally consistent (Nicholls and Thorkildsen, 1987). Class levels of Task Orientation and Ego Orientation were not significantly associated. Task Orientation was associated with low Work Avoidance ($r = -.49$, $p < .01$) whereas Ego Orientation was associated with high Work Avoidance ($r = .33$, $p < .05$). Furthermore, Task Orientation was associated with the belief that academic success depends on interest, effort, and attempts to learn ($r = .54$, $p < .001$) whereas Ego Orientation was associated with believing that success depends on being smarter than others and trying to beat them ($r = .67$, $p < .001$). Finally, Task Orientation was associated with satisfaction with school learning ($r = .74$, $p < .001$) whereas Ego Orientation was not ($r = -.15$, n.s.). These results for classrooms, which are slightly stronger than those for individuals, support the conclusion derived from the evidence reviewed in Part II. They indicate that task-oriented classrooms more than ego-oriented classrooms are characterized by beliefs that would sustain a commitment to working at and understanding schoolwork and satisfaction with this activity.

A further line of evidence suggesting the negative properties of ego-involving classrooms concerns students' readiness or reluctance to ask for help in their work. Russell Ames (1983) proposed that in ego-involving conditions students would be more likely to see a request for assistance as an admission of incompetence. Those who doubt their competence would thus be less likely to seek assistance and in this way too impair their intellectual growth. In task-involving conditions, however, Ames predicted that when students were "stuck," more of them would see a request for assistance as a way of learning. Students with both high and low perceived ability should thus readily seek advice when they are unable to solve problems on their own. Ames's review of the literature supports his predictions.

The ego-involving property of many classrooms presumably helps account for the evidence that students with lower attainment or lower perceived ability are more inclined to be at a disadvantage in terms of motivation. Students with higher attainment exhibit higher levels or frequencies of attention to classroom tasks than do their less accomplished classmates (Bloom, 1976, Appendix 5D). If students with lower attainment attend less fully to their work they cannot be using their time in school to develop their powers as effectively as their higher-achieving classmates. Researchers also find positive (though often low) associations between intrinsic motivation for school learning and perceived competence (Connell and Ryan, 1984; Gottfried, 1985; Harter and Connell, 1984; Nicholls et al., 1985) and negative associations between intrinsic involvement and test anxiety (Gottfried, 1982).

These findings indicate that the less accomplished students and those who see themselves as low in ability are unlikely to find learning as meaningful or to learn as effectively as those who are more able or who believe they are more able. Students who are highly able and who perceive themselves as well above average in ability can still vary widely in levels of task orientation, ego orientation, and work avoidance. Furthermore, a work-avoiding orientation has the same negative correlates for highly able students as for less outstanding individuals (Thorkildsen, 1988). Nevertheless, on the average, those with lower perceived ability and lower attainment appear less favorably motivated than their more able classmates.

From the Workingmen's parties of the 1820s and 1830s to Andrew Carnegie to the present, Americans have endorsed competition while seeking to remove the handicaps that make the race to the top an unfair one (Nisbett, 1974). In or out of school, the race has not been run entirely according to the rules, but, as Nisbett suggests, fairness has been simulated well enough to make failure even more personal and painful than it is when the barriers are more obvious. Fair competition has advantages over systems where status is ascribed. It can, however, increase our preoccupation with how our ability compares with that of our peers and thereby compound inequality of motivation and diminish the quality of learning and accomplishment. Competition cannot be fair if competing with others itself produces inequalities in the motivation necessary to develop skills. So even if the faster runners and more intelligent scholars do not gain unfair shares of political power, wealth, or other privileges as a result of these accomplishments, a significant form of inequality might be promoted by ego involvement.

Privileges for Superior Students

A competitive, evaluative atmosphere and the consequent ego involvement would reduce the quality of learning and increase inequality of motivation within classrooms. In addition, these conditions can coexist with the second form of inequality: inequality of respect or autonomy that is not an intrinsic consequence of unequal academic accomplishment. This is when "fair" competition transmutes into unfair advantage. As well as being unjust in its own right, such inequality might further promote inequality of motivation.

Observers assert that elementary school teachers treat students with high ability and attainment differently from those with low ability and attainment (Brophy, 1983; Good and Marshall, 1984). It is significant that students also report such differences. For example, they expect teachers to give more approval and leadership opportunities to those of their classmates who are high in ability and attainment (de Groat and Thompson, 1949). A more recent series of studies (Weinstein and Middlestadt, 1979; Weinstein, Marshall, Brattesani, and Middlestadt, 1982) describes how students expect that their classmates with lower ability and attainment will be given less opportunity to respond to the teacher's questions, will less commonly be given enough time to finish their work, and will not always be asked to complete assignments. In short, students see teachers as conveying lower expectations of performance for lower ability students. Some of this might be construed as legitimate responses to individual differences in competence (Good and Marshall, 1984). But not giving enough time to answer questions, for example, can hardly be seen in this light. As well as selectively reducing learning opportunities, this treatment is likely to undermine a lower achieving student's motivation to learn.

The abler students are often seen by their peers as receiving still further advantages (Weinstein and Middlestadt, 1979; Weinstein et al., 1982). Children expect students with higher ability and attainment to be given more say in choice of projects, more chances to suggest and direct activities, and more freedom of action after assigned activities are completed. That is, they believe that the abler students will be treated in a manner that implies that they are more responsible and deserve more autonomy. Low achievers, on the other hand, are seen as more likely to be treated in the coercive manner that reduces their personal freedom and responsibility (and undermines task involvement). The students thus report injustice on two levels: treatment that maintains inequality of motivation, and greater privilege accorded to higher achievers.

One might expect students in classes with high levels of ego orientation to experience more differential treatment of this sort. Recent findings (Nicholls and Thorkildsen, 1987) confirm this expectation. The more ego-oriented a classroom, the more did students expect their teacher to be pleased when an able student (but not a low ability student) showed interest, worked hard, and gained understanding. By way of contrast, the more task-oriented a classroom, the more likely its students were to report that the teacher was pleased when both high and low ability students showed interest, effort, and understanding.

It is fair to speculate that when schools promote ego involvement and distribute privileges on the basis of ability and attainment, they may have yet another effect—one that has received much less attention from psychologists. They may serve as models of a competitive, meritocratic society where autonomy, influence, and other rewards reflect individual differences in accomplishment. They may promote the notion that competition is, if not the only way people can live, at least the best way. Acceptance of such a system would induce students who doubt their competence to accept their lowly place or, at least, to opt out and not challenge the system. Academic anxiety, unrealistic levels of aspiration, and academic alienation would be seen as necessary aspects of the process whereby students of low attainment come to accept their place in the "natural order." In turn, alienation, lack of effort, and pursuit of nonacademic goals might, in the eyes of students and teachers, further justify low status and restricted freedom and responsibility. The less competent teaching that can be associated with low academic status (Rosenbaum, 1976) might be seen as justifiable within this framework. So too would more coercive teaching methods and more emphasis on rote learning. Those who are able and committed would, on the other hand, be seen as deserving approval, status, and leadership roles.

Our society is not a monolithic competitive system and our schools vary in the extent to which they promote ego involvement. Furthermore, students (including alienated students) play a more active role in the development of their own motivational orientations than I have just suggested (Giroux, 1983; Willis, 1977). Yet in something like the above fashion an ego-involving school system might project a view of social reality that helps maintain some of the objectionable features of our society.

Grade-Related Changes

The ego-involving characteristics of schools generally become more marked as students progress through the grades—at least this seems to be the case up to about the tenth grade (Eccles et al., 1984). School tends to become more formal, competitive, and evaluative. In the higher grades standardized tests are more often used as a basis for assigning students to classes, and the calculation of cumulative grade point averages and class standings is more usual. Finally, as one progresses through the grades, teachers' assessments are less likely to reflect the students' effort or progress and more likely to reflect class rank on formally evaluated tests or assignments. In a similar fashion, the emphasis on winning in sport increases over the school years (Chaumeton and Duda, 1988).

All of this would make sense in the context of a meritocratic, competitive society which requires that many people acknowledge that they lack the talents associated with positions of high status and be ready to accept roles with little freedom, influence, and income. A case can be made that our society is, to at least some degree, like this (Bowles and Gintis, 1976). Too much alienation would be counterproductive for such a society, especially if it occurred in the early school years. In this social framework it is appropriate that ego involvement should not reach high levels in the elementary school years when students are still acquiring the "basic" skills that even occupations of low status require. The development of conceptions of ability seems to parallel the age-related increase in the ego-involving properties of schools. Most elementary school students' conceptions of ability represent effortful accomplishment as competence. This should help maintain industriousness over the elementary school years. Adolescents, on the other hand, distinguish capacity from effortful accomplishment and are less likely than elementary school students to value effortful over effortless accomplishment. Adolescents are also more likely than younger students to show decreased accomplishment in ego-involving contexts when they expect to perform incompetently (Chapter 4). And junior and senior high schools are generally more likely than elementary schools to promote ego involvement. So, with age, developmental changes in the meaning of ability, combined with parallel increases in the ego-involving properties of schools, should make for growing inequality of motivation for intellectual development. These changes would make it progressively more likely that students who doubt their competence would seek occupations that do not require much schooling.

These grade-related trends appear to vary with school subject. Mathematics instruction, for example, seems to become more evaluative than English instruction at junior and senior high school (Eccles et al., 1984). At the upper grade levels, mathematics classes often take on "an air of prestige and exclusivity" (Stake and Easley, 1978, sect. 12, p. 20). It may be no coincidence that it is also in the upper grades that students distinguish abstract reasoning ability from the size of their vocabulary and value abstract reasoning over verbal intelligence (Chapter 5). This distinction probably also underlies the pecking order of academic disciplines, because the more prestigious subjects such as mathematics and the physical sciences appear to demand more abstract reasoning. Students who doubt their abstract reasoning ability or who find the humanities more absorbing would find it hard to resist the claims to superiority of those who exalt subjects like mathematics. To resist them might seem like an attempt to resist Nature. In this way school values prepare students to accept and maintain a society that values mathematics and the "hard" sciences over the humanities and that trusts technocrats who trust mathematical models to determine what we should invest in and how we should live.

A Caveat

There *is* diversity at every level of the school system. Elementary school classes vary considerably in their levels of task and ego orientation (Nicholls and Thorkildsen, 1987). Similarly, students' descriptions of how teachers treat high and low ability students vary across classes (Brattesani, Weinstein, and Marshall, 1984; Weinstein et al., 1982). Other studies reveal similar variability (Brophy, 1983). Bossert (1979) observed an elementary school class where the teacher emphasized the standing of students relative to one another and where student friendships reflected this standing. High achievers spurned the low achievers. But within the same school some classes were almost devoid of such concerns. In certain high schools pressure to get and maintain a head start on others is palpable and special courses and extra attention provide prestige for top students. But even within such schools there are teachers who strive to minimize competitive pressures and nurture a passion for learning in all students. Other schools more actively, and apparently with some success, confront the stereotypes of social and intellectual status (Lightfoot, 1983). This cannot be easy. This variation across classrooms and schools discredits the claim that it is impossible to combat the competitive pressures of our society.

11

Quality and Equality

Ironically, a preoccupation with intellectual potential is the very condition that will ensure, overall, its less than full development. The more heat and fuss develops over testing programs to determine students' intellectual or academic potential, the more ego involvement is likely to predominate, leading to a reduction in both quality and equality of motivation for intellectual development and significant accomplishment.

Fortunately, intelligence or aptitude tests are not necessary for effective teaching. One should not confuse the process of estimating a student's intellectual potential with the process of teaching so as to develop that potential. Teaching constantly involves decisions about what material to present, what question to ask, what approach to advise, and what source to suggest to a student or group of students. The conventional estimates of student potential are of no value in making such decisions. Aptitude tests are irrelevant to the opportunistic business of teaching, where children's interests and knowledge about specific topics can change rapidly and where "Plans are forever going awry and unexpected opportunities for the attainment of educational goals are constantly emerging" (Jackson, 1968, p. 166).

Philip Jackson's study of a group of particularly successful elementary school teachers gives cause for hope. The criterion these teachers most commonly employed to evaluate their teaching was student interest or involvement in learning. This finding is encouraging, because when students are task-involved they are developing their potential, regardless of whether they are prodigies or severely retarded. Knowing that a child is a prodigy or retarded does not help in telling whether they are task-involved.

Constructivism and Motivation

The case for task involvement is consistent with the constructivist view of intellectual development. Piaget's concept of equilibration implies that intellectual development occurs when children sense inadequacies in their own knowledge. This sense of inadequacy is not, however, a sense of personal inadequacy. In this framework, disequilibrium implies "epistemic shock" (Coie, 1973), not personal shock. It is more a matter of "What's going on here?" than of "Wrong again" or "I must be stupid." A disequilibrium state is resolved by the construction of more adequate knowledge or new states of equilibrium. Techniques designed to induce disequilibrium or a sense of contradiction in the child's own knowledge have been found to stimulate the development of logical thought (Kuhn, 1972; Smedslund, 1961) and more mature problem solving (Coie, 1973). There is also some experimental support for the view that giving students the initiative to propose questions and methods for examining them fosters the development of logical thinking (Kuhn and Ho, 1980).

In the constructivist view (Elkind, 1976; Kohlberg and Mayer, 1972), sound intellectual development requires that children reorganize their own physical and social worlds to make them more meaningful. If learning is a means to an end, the development of understanding will suffer. It would, however, be a mistake to conclude that the constructivist perspective means that teachers should not play an active role. The teacher's role is to stimulate, guide, and encourage rather than to direct. This "involves the Socratic method and is exciting and challenging for both teacher and learner" (Elkind, 1976, p. 230).

Progressive Education

The case for task involvement as a working educational objective can be supported by empirical evidence. But given that the research questions we ask and the data we collect reflect our values, this case should not rest purely on an appeal to empirical data. If, for example, task involvement produced slower learning than ego or extrinsic involvement, there could still be grounds for favoring task involvement. Would not something be wrong if children believed that the world is round or that two plus two equals four simply because "the teacher says it is" or because they get higher grades by learning such facts more quickly than others?

The case for task involvement is consistent with the progressive approach to education. "Intellectual education in the progressive view is not merely a transmission of information and intellectual skills, it is the communication of patterns and methods of scientific reflection and inquiry" (Kohlberg and Mayer, 1972, p. 475). A "Scientific" orientation resists indoctrination and frees the individual from dependence on arbitrary external authority. It does not substitute idiosyncratic impulse or unexamined notions for the imperatives of arbitrary authority, but fosters an open-mindedness that is disciplined by observation and rational reflection and renewed by novel hypotheses. No discipline is more severe or more liberating. Progressives do not merely assert that intellectual development is effectively prompted by the concern to understand that is exemplified by a scientific approach to the world; they also hold that intellectual development ought to be fostered in this way (Dewey, 1963; Kohlberg and Mayer, 1972). Even if learning could be advanced more rapidly by encouraging dependence on external authority or the desire to beat others, it should not be.

In research, the most critical action taken by a scientist is the formulation of a researchable question. Problem finding precedes problem solving. The creative scientist is distinguished by a sensitivity to problems—an ability to see problems that others do not and to distinguish important problems from trivial ones. These problems or paradoxes are the sources of irritation that precipitate the construction of new scientific perspectives (Kuhn, 1970). The progressive approach to education is based on the notion that development is most liberating and secure when students play an active role in the formulation of the questions they study. If learning is to be meaningful, it must answer questions that are significant to the student.

The progressive commitment to encouraging student initiative goes beyond a desire to foster the development of the understanding of the type of logical and physical problems that Piaget presented to students. A person who plays no role in the selection of their tasks is like a slave. "It is in the formulation of the problem that individuality is expressed, that creativity is stimulated, and that nuances and subtleties are discovered. It is these aspects of inquiry that give birth to new social movements and political orientations, and that are central in the emergence of insight" (Thelen, 1960, p. 26). As Dewey put it, "There is, I think, no point in the philosophy of progressive education which is sounder than its emphasis upon the importance of the participation of the learner in the formation of the purposes which direct his activities in the learning process" (1963, p. 67).

The progressive approach should not be confused with a mere emphasis on problem solving. We need to think about who poses the problems that students and citizens address and whether these problems deserve to be addressed. The aptitude for asking useful questions is not just critical in science. It is at the core of a democratic society. When we reduce the concepts of education and inquiry to finding solutions for problems that textbooks or authorities pose, we become technocrats. When we stand ready to solve any problem we are presented with, we have relinquished moral and political responsibility. When we encourage such a readiness in students, we cultivate the sort of person who would adopt the Nuremberg defense.

Individual responsibility does not, however, imply a solitary education or existence. On the contrary, "more numerous and more varied points of [social] contact denote a greater diversity of stimuli to which an individual has to respond; they consequently put a premium on variation in . . . action. They secure a liberation of [individual] powers which remain suppressed as long as the inclinations to action are partial, as they must be in a group which in its exclusiveness shuts out many interests" (Dewey, 1966, p. 87). Negotiation of meanings and purposes—itself the mark of a democratic society—is, for progressives, the means of developing the individual initiative, independence of judgment, and social commitment on which democracy in turn depends.

Only this strength and commitment can ensure that we do not create a society that would "set up barriers to free intercourse and communication of experience . . . [A democratic] society must have a type of education which gives individuals a personal interest in social relationships and control, and the habits of mind which secure social changes without introducing disorder" (p. 99). Advocates of forms of cooperative learning that emphasize the involvement of students in negotiation of tasks, methods, and solutions to problems see their work as belonging in the progressive tradition (Kagan, 1985; Sharan et al., 1984).

Research findings sustain this emphasis on the role of social transaction in the stimulation of intellectual development. In discussions between social equals, even young children are responsive to logic. Those with more advanced conceptions of topics under discussion are more successful in getting their peers to see it their way (Miller and Brownell, 1975). It is not surprising that a series of laboratory studies shows that such discussions promote intellectual growth (Doise and Mugny, 1984). Even when students are on the same intellectual level, disagreements and attempts to resolve them can produce significant intellectual gains—gains that are sustained over time, that carry over to new problems, and involve forms of reasoning that cannot be merely imitated and are new to the children using them (Doise and Mugny, 1984). In this sense, social conflict is welcome. It can induce disequilibrium, provide clues that help resolve disequilibrium, and stimulate active attempts to construct more adequate knowledge of the physical and social world (Kohlberg and Mayer, 1972).

In the progressive view, moral education cannot be isolated from education of the intellect. Memorization of givens that excludes inquiry is inadequate as moral and as intellectual education. It follows too that conventional academic achievement tests do not adequately evaluate educational programs. Indeed, there is evidence that the very use of conventional multiple choice achievement tests will undermine the progressive agenda by constraining initiative and limiting inquiry (Frederiksen, 1984). This is not to make a case for low scores on conventional achievement tests. But strengths of one type are often gained at the expense of others, and our schools should also promote a commitment to learning for its own sake, independence in question asking and answering, and social responsibility combined with maturity and independence in social judgment.

Teaching and Intellectual Growth

Achieving these progressive goals involves avoiding, insofar as this is possible, practices that foster ego involvement or extrinsic involvement: specifically, coercive forms of classroom control, rewards that smack of bribery, interpersonal competition, and public evaluations that focus attention on the person rather than the task and emphasize comparison of students' abilities (Chapter 6).

More positively, task involvement and intellectual and moral growth are likely to be fostered by techniques that encourage students to initiate and evaluate their own academic activities. This can be achieved, in part, by presenting or having available materials that are intrinsically interesting and challenging to students. Task involvement will be heightened if students are given choice or some say in matters such as which tasks to work on and the order in which they complete assignments. Choice itself tends to increase commitment to chosen activities. And, to the extent that task involvement is fostered, students will choose tasks that are personally challenging rather than too easy or hard for them (Chapter 7). This in turn will increase their chances of gaining satisfaction from developing their skills, knowledge, or understanding. They will choose topics they do not fully understand or are puzzled by rather than topics that would merely enable them to look superior to their peers or to avoid effort. Choice of activities makes it also probable that at any given time students will not all be working on the same task. This will reduce the frequency of social comparison of abilities (Pepitone, 1980) and, thereby, ego involvement.

Cooperative learning methods transfer responsibility from teacher to students. At the same time, as several studies show, in a cooperative climate a fellow student's knowledge can be a source of interest, stimulation, and information rather than a threat to one's own sense of competence (Johnson, Johnson, and Scott, 1978; Smith, Johnson, and Johnson, 1981). In this way public discussion of ideas need not be ego-involving. Cooperation and task orientation can also be expected to be mutually facilitating because task orientation is associated with the belief that helping one another to learn will lead to success in school.

Student choice, cooperative learning, and participation in decisions about curriculum are all consistent with the democratic emphasis of progressive education. There are limits. Teachers must live with school rules; curriculum decisions are often out of their hands; not everything can be up for student negotiation or choice. But if restrictions are presented with rational justifications, they need not be experienced as restricting. For example, creativity and interest in painting were not affected when children were told that the rules for the use of paints were needed to keep the colors clear and materials clean for other classes. However, assertion of the same rules without such a rationale diminished both interest and creativity (Koestner et al., 1984). Teachers do not have to choose between authoritarian control and laissez-faire child-centeredness. It is clearly foolish to give infants total responsibility for their daily lives. We can only gradually give children responsibility for their lives. But when we must "lay down the law," this can be done in ways that are comprehensible to students. Like parenting (Radke-Yarrow, Zahn-Waxler, and Chapman, 1983), teaching that minimizes the use of coercion for social control is more apt to produce active, independent, and responsible individuals.

Interpretation of research that bears on such claims is not simple. For example, comparison of a fine example of progressive education with a thoroughly incompetent example of more conventional methods would hardly be enlightening. And if one approach is harder to execute than another, it might only show the benefits claimed for it when highly skilled teachers are involved. Nevertheless, if studies that employ different methods to assess classroom differences and motivational, intellectual, and moral outcomes still come together in their findings, we can be a little more confident. The relevant studies are fewer than is desirable and leave us with no shortage of new questions, but there is some convergence of results.

Not all aspects of teaching discussed in this section go together (Marx, 1985). Yet some studies compare classrooms that exemplify all or most of these characteristics with others that lack all or most of them. I will consider these studies first and then those that sample fewer segments of the ideal pie.

Progressive Schools and Classrooms. Bossert (1979) describes a fourth-grade classroom with most of the factors that would sustain task involvement. Children worked individually or in small groups on projects that they or the teacher initiated. Several extensive group projects, such as the painting of large murals for a children's hospital, were under way with little overt supervision by the teacher. When children completed other work or had free time, they worked on these projects or read books of their own choice. Groups of students formed and reformed around projects and reading interests. For example, when two girls brought Nancy Drew books to school for independent reading, interest in them spread and led to the formation of the Nancy Drew Mystery Book Club and then to all the girls' in the class wanting to read Nancy Drew books. The teacher specified core assignments, but each student could schedule the order in which this work was completed. The fact that students accepted considerable responsibility and assisted each other freely in their work made it possible for the teacher to allow students to work on many different tasks at the same time. She could then work with students who needed help on assignments while the others were actively engaged on projects, reading, or assignments. This teacher noted that it was difficult to grade students' achievements because of the number of different projects they were working on. She commented that earlier in her career, when she used work sheets, it was easy to evaluate each child, "But it wasn't much fun" (p. 44). Here is a teacher who is committed to learning rather than to evaluation in terms of social comparison—to the development of potential rather than its evaluation. Bossert's observations indicated that this teacher's students were much more task-oriented and intellectually active than the students of two other teachers: one who exercised more direct control over her students and another who was concerned with socially comparative grading and fostered competition among students.

Cobb and his associates developed a constructivist mathematics program marked by dialogue and collaborative problem solving that ran for one year in a second grade class (Cobb, Wood, and Yackel, 1988; Cobb, Yackel, and Wood, 1988). When topics were introduced, students worked cooperatively in pairs on them. The teacher then orchestrated whole class discussions of solutions. She did not attempt to lead students to preconceived solutions. Instead she sought to sustain dialogue among them. When, as frequently happened, students offered conflicting solutions, the teacher framed the situation as a problem for students to resolve by discussion. The mathematical activities were designed to give rise to the experience of conceptual problems or questions for second graders. The materials most teachers have available are not adapted to this purpose. In this case, previous cognitive models of children's arithmetical knowledge were used to construct learning materials that would be genuinely problematic for children. Revisions were also made continually during the year on the basis of analyses of students' experiences with the materials.

There were five other second-grade classes in this school to which students had been randomly assigned. The teachers in these other classes taught in the way they normally had. At the end of the school year the class with the constructivist program proved high relative to the others on measures of task orientation in mathematics, beliefs that success in mathematics depends on effort, attempts to understand, and collaboration with one's peers. This class was low on the desire for superiority over one's friends, desire to avoid work, and the belief that success in mathematics depends on superior ability. In short, the collaborative problem-solving atmosphere had the expected motivational consequences (Nicholls et al., 1988b).

Clinchy, Lief, and Young (1977) compared a small progressive state school with a conventional state school and observed dramatic effects of teaching on levels of knowledge as described by Perry (Chapter 5) and levels of moral reasoning as described by Kohlberg. In the progressive school students participated fully in decisions about the curriculum and school governance. Classes were conducted as discussions in which disagreement was encouraged and students were challenged to support their positions. The relationship between teachers and students was predominantly cooperative. In all these respects, the conventional school was different. Lectures were the usual mode of instruction and teachers constrained and directed students more overtly. In both schools sophomores were at approximately the same level in conceptions of knowledge and in moral reasoning: namely, at the lower end of the scale, in a frame of mind where right answers are presumed to exist in the absolute and to be known to authorities from whom one acquires them. At the conventional school seniors did not differ from the sophomores. Seniors at the progressive school were significantly more advanced (on both indices) than seniors at the other school and sophomores at their own school. Forty-two percent of the seniors in the progressive school, but none in the other school, construed knowledge as relativistic in the sense that one's understanding reflects one's interpretational stance, and that many stances are possible. In other words, only in the progressive school did an appreciable proportion of seniors see intellectual positions as something for which each person bears some responsibility—a higher percentage than is found among college freshmen.

A study describing a similar contrast between two types of elementary school (McCann and Bell, 1975) found appreciably more advanced levels of moral reasoning in a school that allowed students to progress at their own rate, promoted student discussion and responsibility for school rules, and encouraged choice and scheduling of learning assignments. (These school climates should not be confused with laissez-faire regimes. In the progressive school described by McCann and Bell, for example, although children could choose tasks, they were expected to choose a task rather than do nothing, and they were expected to complete the tasks they chose.)

Complementary findings were obtained by Minuchin and her colleagues (1969) in a comparison of fourth graders in four schools. In the most progressive school, children construed rules and regulations as designed to maintain the social order and prevent harm to others. In the more conventional schools, school authority was experienced more as a constraining force that was sometimes resented and feared. When students discussed moral dilemmas, those from the progressive school were more likely to focus on the effects of actions on others and less inclined to refer to adults in positions of authority.

The study just mentioned is unusual in the number of additional dimensions it covered. With regard to intellectual growth, a complex picture emerged. The students of the most progressive school scored lower on standardized achievement and group intelligence tests but not lower on an individually administered intelligence test. On that test they performed below others on the coding subtest (which demands only clerical speed and accuracy), but not on subtests requiring analytical thinking. No significant differences were found between schools on a number of individual problem-solving tasks. On problem-solving tasks that required cooperation, the performance at the most progressive school was rapid, more technically accurate, more lively, and included more students in the work. Finally, the students of the most progressive school were clearly most positively and actively identified with the school.

The low scores on standardized achievement tests of students in the most progressive school might simply reflect low competence in these skills. The skills required by these tests matched the rehearsal of specific skills presented in discrete units that predominated in the conventional schools but were uncharacteristic of the progressive one. Furthermore, progressive school students were not accustomed to working alone on standardized tests or other timed tests and worked more slowly. The progressive school did not consider such tests wise. So, in the terms of the conventional wisdom, these students would not have been test-wise.

An additional factor can reduce test scores of students who, like those in the progressive school, are highly involved in their schoolwork. In another comparison of schools, Elkind, Deblinger, and Adler (1970) observed that the children from a conventional school "appeared reluctant to return to the classroom and seemed to enjoy the testing" whereas "just the reverse appeared to be true" (p. 352) for students of a more progressive school. In an experimental check on this phenomenon the authors found markedly lower performance on divergent thinking tests when students anticipated returning to interesting activities at the end of the testing session than when uninteresting activities awaited them. But whether or not this explanation applies, it seems safe to conclude that, in education, gains in one area often involve losses in another.

A review of literature comparing "open" classrooms with conventional classrooms justifies similar conclusions (Horwitz, 1979; Peterson, 1979). Classes were considered open if they involved student choice of activities, flexible use of space, richness of learning materials, integration of curriculum areas, and individual and small-group instruction. On the average, conventional classes were slightly superior on standardized achievement tests, but open classes had a slight advantage on "creativity" and problem-solving tests. Attitudes to school were slightly more favorable, curiosity was slightly higher, and independence was clearly higher in open classes.

Other evidence also suggests that progressive approaches are not the most efficient way of fostering high standardized test scores. There is some consensus that gains on such tests can be fostered by direct instruction, in which teachers present material in small steps followed by active practice, give detailed instructions and explanations, ask many questions, check on understanding, provide systematic corrections, guide during initial practice, and monitor students closely (Rosenshine, 1979; Rosenshine and Stevens, 1986).

A recent German study following students through their fifth and sixth-grade mathematics classes supports Rosenshine and Stevens' claims (Helmke, Schneider, and Weinert, 1986a, 1986b). At the end of the fifth grade, more direct instruction yielded higher achievement scores and had no negative effects on attitudes. By the end of grade six (with students having the same teachers), direct instruction in mathematics yielded low intrinsic motivation and negative attitudes. This was the strongest of all the effects observed. Because this effect was not apparent in the first year of the study, the other studies of direct teaching, which were of shorter duration, could not have detected it. We can only wonder whether students who score higher than others on math tests but have less interest in the subject will more often give it up as soon as they get the chance.

Direct instruction seems preferable to the hours of solitary plodding through worksheets that students sometimes face. And it is easy to believe that, if intelligently applied, it can prepare students to score highly on standardized tests. But as Penelope Peterson comments, "the picture of direct instruction seems not only grim but unidimensional" (1979, p. 66).

Direct instruction is not education. This distinction is recognized by a young grammar school teacher in England whose students had a high rate of success on external examinations. "I do pretty well; my results are all right . . . we teach for results . . . Tests all the time, and scrub the teaching methods, forget about the educational side . . . We've got no time for any questions or anything that leads off the syllabus . . . when I get established [as a principal] I might start looking around and thinking more about the educational side. But you've got to establish yourself first, haven't you? Right?" (Jackson and Marsden, 1962, p. 37). As his concluding appeal to the interviewer seems to acknowledge, he is not compelled to sacrifice education to instruction. And neither—simply because direct instruction increases scores on standardized tests—are we.

The scarcity of clear examples of progressive schools and classrooms makes it difficult to find many studies of them. Comparisons of their methods with more conventional practices are also fraught with problems. Yet the diverse studies discussed above do suggest that progressive methods promote the virtues progressives value. And it might be recalled that this evidence converges with the results of the experimental and psychometric studies of task orientation reviewed in Part II.

An interesting example of progressive education is the subject of Gray and Chanoff's 1986 study. In this school students of all ages are expected to set and pursue their own learning goals without any required courses. If a teacher initiates a class, it continues as long as students continue attending. At other times students' interests determine the subject. Although students solicit evaluation and advice, there are no grades or substitutes for grades. Every person has one vote in the school government. Students are also involved in all aspects of running the school. Graduation is decided on the basis of a presentation and defense, before all school members, of a thesis the theme of which is that the presenter is ready to function responsibly and independently in society.

As Gray and Chanoff acknowledge, their study of the graduates cannot show how the effects of this school compare to those of others. Yet their findings offer no support for the assumption that for children to survive in our world adults must make them study x basic subjects and do y hours of homework a night. The graduates of this school "have become, or are clearly en route to becoming, productive members of our society, contributing to the economy in nearly the entire range of ways that people can contribute" (p. 209). Relatively few graduates felt that the fact that their school did not oblige them to take any specific subjects was a significant disadvantage when they attended college. Specific areas of ignorance were quickly made up and grades were sound. Almost all felt at a clear advantage in that they were highly motivated and in charge of their own education.

Cooperative Learning. One cooperative learning method—group investigation—engages students collaborating in small groups in the formulation of learning responsibilities, methods, and goals (Sharan, 1980). It thus exemplifies much of the progressive approach. Another cooperative method, wherein teachers present learning materials, set goals, and have student groups competing against each other, does not. In the second case, teachers assign points to individual students that are added up to determine the group's standing. These points depend on each individual's progress so that low as well as high ability students can gain high scores (Slavin, 1978). It is not clear whether learning gains from this second method (Slavin, 1983) reflect its cooperative aspects or result from the emphasis on individual progress rather than social comparison. The approach also emphasizes learning facts or discrete items of knowledge rather than higher-order understanding. In this respect, it differs from the former group-investigation method where students face more complex problems and have responsibility for deciding how to learn and present material.

A careful comparison of these two cooperative approaches and of conventional, whole-class teaching was made by Sharan and others (1984) for the teaching of English (as a second language) and literature over three to four months of a school-year in Israel. In English classes, the two cooperative methods produced similar results on conventional achievement tests and both were superior to whole-class teaching. In literature classes, the group-investigation method produced the lowest retention of simple information but the highest performance on tasks requiring more complex understanding and evaluation of literature. (Whole-class teaching produced the lowest scores on these tasks.) These results are consistent with the findings of more closely controlled laboratory examinations of the effects of negotiation of interpretations on intellectual growth (Doise and Mugny, 1984). Perhaps Sharan's effects would be even clearer if cooperative classroom methods had been evaluated with more costly individual interview measures—such as Doise and Mugny used—which make it much harder to confuse good recall with new constructions. It is also interesting to note that although it was the teachers who assigned the tasks under the second cooperative method, the students' own discussions tended to turn to higher-order questions that teachers had not set. The situation thus came closer to the group-investigation method than it would have if the technique had been implemented as originally specified.

The favorable effects of the group-investigation method seem especially noteworthy because the teachers resisted implementing it. The transfer of control and responsibility to students that the method requires proved threatening to teachers. At the opposite extreme, teachers using the conventional whole-class method (who received the same amount of assistance with that method as did teachers using cooperative methods) were clearly happier about the way they were teaching.

Another ingenious cooperative method is "jigsaw learning" (Aronson et al., 1978). Although students do not set the goals, cooperation is made necessary (in a noncoercive fashion) by the way learning is organized. Material for each lesson is presented in sections. Students in groups of about four each learn one section of the lesson. They prepare to teach their section to other students who, at the same time, are learning other sections. When each group has mastered its section, it breaks up. New groups are formed in which each member has learned and must teach a part of the whole lesson. Each student must also learn from the others what they have learned. Students must, therefore, depend on each other if they are to get the whole picture. Compared to traditional methods, the jigsaw method reduces derogation of classmates, improves attitudes to learning and, for ethnic minorities, produces higher achievement. It also fosters the ability to adopt the perspectives of others (Aronson et al., 1978; Zeigler, 1981).

This and other work on cooperative learning (Johnson and

Johnson, 1985; Sharan, 1980) helps to confirm the soundness of the belief of task-oriented elementary and high school students in the value of helping one another learn (Chapter 6).

Classroom Components. In the remainder of this section I consider a number of studies that look only at certain aspects of classroom regimes. Regarding the amount of responsibility students are given for the evaluation of their learning, Maehr and Stallings (1972) and Salili and colleagues (1976) compared the effects of student evaluation of their own performance with normative evaluation by teachers. Teacher evaluation (where performance was assessed by the teacher and would contribute to grades) would be likely to induce ego involvement and make learning a means rather than an end in itself. Personal evaluation should make learning more an end in itself—children would be more likely to feel they are doing the work to learn it. In fact, personal evaluation did produce greater interest in further learning.

Another way to encourage student responsibility is student scheduling of classroom learning. Although in this approach teachers assign learning tasks (as in conventional classrooms), students are systematically encouraged to take responsibility for organizing their own learning schedules—for deciding what assignments they will work on first and when they will work on each topic. This should help make learning an end in itself. In the more typical system, where work is assigned by the teacher, interest is likely to be undermined because the teacher's instructions are a plausible reason for learning. Wang and Stiles (1976) found that assignments were completed more frequently with self-scheduling than with teacher scheduling of schoolwork. Similarly, high school science students showed more care and involvement in laboratory work when encouraged to organize their own experiments than when given detailed instructions and direction (Rainey, 1965).

Studies of naturally occurring differences among classrooms produce comparable findings. The students of elementary school teachers who (according to their responses to a questionnaire) encourage student autonomy rather than exert direct control or emphasize social comparison have higher levels of task involvement and a higher sense of competence (Deci et al., 1981). Similarly, students display greater interest in science in high school science classrooms where they have greater control over learning (Pascarella et al., 1981). (See also reviews by Deci and Ryan, 1985; Maehr, 1976; Ryan, Connell, and Deci, 1985; Thomas, 1980).

We should also expect that task involvement will be maintained by teachers who evaluate students in terms of their individual progress. Rheinberg (1983; described by Heckhausen and Krug, 1982) developed a questionnaire measure to distinguish teachers who evaluate student performance in terms of each individual's learning history from those who emphasize comparison of student performance. Those who focus on individual progress strive to provide students with tasks that present each of them with a moderate challenge and offer feedback on the basis of improvement. Teachers who compare students with others generally assign the same tasks to all students and approve of those who perform better than others. The students of teachers who individualized instruction had less academic anxiety, were less likely to attribute failure to low ability, and felt they improved more. These effects were most marked with low-achieving students—those who would suffer the worst effects of ego involvement and stand to gain most in well-being and learning from task involvement. (Related research is reviewed by Heckhausen and Krug, 1982; and Heckhausen and others, 1985).

Finally, let us consider the feedback that focuses attention on what might be done to improve performance rather than on the self or one's rank. As noted in Chapter 6, feedback on divergent thinking tasks that focused on positive features of students' work and suggested directions for improvement increased subsequent interest and accomplishment in both high- and low-achieving students (Butler, 1987, 1988; Butler and Nisan, 1986). Furthermore, students receiving this feedback were inclined to explain their effort in terms of interest and a desire to improve (Butler, 1987). In Butler's studies this feedback produced more task involvement and higher performance than socially comparative grades or praise ("Very good"). These findings nicely support Dreikurs, Grunwald, and Pepper (1982) who urge us to avoid praise but to encourage students by pointing out strengths and directions for improvement on the grounds that this increases independence and interest in learning.

"Back Here in Outer Darkness"

Regardless of the desirability of task involvement and progressive education, there should be no illusion that this vision can easily be made manifest in our schools. As Dewey suggested, "the road to the new education is not an easier one to follow than the old road but a more strenuous and difficult one" (1963, p. 90).

They do exist, but it is difficult to find schools that exemplify the progressive spirit. In a series of case studies of the teaching of science and mathematics, for example, Stake and Easley (1978) found "the objective of understanding widely honored, conscientiously pursued, and regularly obstructed by teachers"(sect. 12, p. 3). Goodlad (1983) also found much talk about critical thinking and, in most cases, a formidable gap between such talk and performance. Science kits, for example, which teachers justified as enabling individualization of instruction, were used so that "Every student was expected to complete the same readings, worksheets, experiments and tests—and to come to essentially the same conclusions" (p. 215). Similarly, despite talk of the role of mathematics in the development of logical and critical thinking, mathematics usually appears "as a body of fixed facts and skills to be acquired" (Goodlad, p. 215). In a study of science laboratory activities in six high schools (Guthrie et al., 1984), the researchers "never observed students formulating questions or hypotheses, predicting results, or designing procedures. [These] . . . were always specified by the teacher or text" (p. 919). (See also Garbarino and Asp, 1981, Chapter 1.)

It is not always much different at the most advanced levels of formal education. David Bakan (1968) argues that early in their graduate education, psychologists learn that

> research consists of the testing of hypotheses . . . There is nothing intrinsically wrong with testing hypotheses. It is an important part of the total investigatory enterprise. What I do wish to point out, however, is that by the time the investigatory enterprise has reached the stage of testing hypotheses, most of the important work, if there has been any, has already been done. One is tempted to think that psychologists are often like children playing cowboys. When children play cowboys they emulate them in everything but their main work, which is taking care of cows. The main work of the scientist

is thinking and making discoveries of what was not thought of beforehand. Psychologists often attempt to "play scientist" by avoiding the main work. (pp. 44–45)

Why education should often be seen as depending upon competition, grades, and coercion and why it should involve the finding and memorizing of answers (or the testing of hypotheses) rather than inquiry and the construction of meaning raises issues well beyond the ken of a mere psychologist. I will grapple with some of these in the final chapter.

12

The Meaning of Life
in School

An essential implication of the progressive philosophy of education is that students should play an active role in the formation of the purposes that govern their learning. It follows that, for researchers who adopt a progressive view, inquiry into students' views about the purposes of education would be a matter of some urgency. Some writers have paid considerable attention to adolescents' values (McKinney and Moore, 1982) and vocational role development (Vondracek and Lerner, 1982). Some attention has been paid to the related topic of students' views about the function of education (Feather, 1975; Goodlad, 1983). Lively psychological research on this topic is, however, conspicuously absent. Yet there seems to be no shortage of expressed views about the aims of education.

Friedenberg (1963) observed that when high school students or parents discussed students who were dropping out, "they spoke only of the trouble dropouts were going to have getting and keeping jobs . . . and a satisfactory level of social status . . . Nobody suggested that they might be missing anything in school that was worthwhile for its own sake or that might enrich their later life aesthetically or conceptually" (p. 165). More recently, the Indiana Conference of Higher Education (1984) put out an eight-page newspaper supplement headed "Education: Your First Step toward a Good Job, Increased Pay, More Self-Confidence [and] Self-Discovery." Throughout, this publication emphasized the way that education can advance one's status and income. A number of observers (such as Giroux, 1984) see this emphasis as having increased in recent years, having been exemplified and fostered by the report of the National Commission on Excellence in Education (1983).

In contrast, Albert Einstein argued that "one should guard against preaching . . . success in the customary sense as the aim of life . . . The most important motive for work in the school and in life is the pleasure in work, pleasure in its result, and the knowledge of the value of the result to the community . . . Such a psychological foundation alone leads to a joyous desire for the highest possessions of men, knowledge and artist-like workmanship" (1956, pp. 34–35). Empirical research cannot show us whether or not we should adopt Einstein's position. It can, however, give us more basis for discussion of this matter. We (Nicholls, Patashnick, and Nolen, 1985) tried to shed some light by examining the correlates of high school students' views about the purposes of school.

Students' Views

Researchers at times create a dichotomy between vocational goals of education and civic, cultural, and intellectual goals. This dualism manifests itself in the form of separate scales to assess views about the vocational and the other purposes of school. Our preliminary interviews indicated that students all assume that school has a vocational role but hold various views about why one should have a job and what that job's ultimate functions should be. One could, for example, want to be a physician solely to make money or mainly to help people. Accordingly, we wrote questionnaire items asking, for example, whether school should prepare students for work that will gain them wealth and status or for work that is useful to others. We found that such items generally had the same patterns of correlates (factor loadings) as similar items that did not refer to occupations (like school should "teach us things that will help society"). It is not necessary to create a distinction between vocational goals and civic and intellectual goals to capture a diversity of views on the purposes of school. Furthermore, this dichotomy implies that civic, intellectual, and cultural goals cannot be pursued as part of one's work—an implication that might increase our acceptance of the alienating nature of modern work.

We constructed four scales to assess views about the functions of school. The first was termed Wealth and Status. High scores on this scale are gained by agreeing that an important thing school should do is, for example, "prepare us for jobs that will give us enough money to buy the best of everything," "prepare us to reach the top in our jobs," and "help us get into the best colleges." The purposes assessed by the remaining three scales were less overtly individualistic and materialistic and these latter three scales correlated with each other more highly than they did with Wealth and Status. The scale called Commitment to Society contained items indicating that school should "prepare us to do things that will help others," "teach us to do our duty to our country," "teach us to respect authority," and "prepare us for jobs making or doing things that are useful to others."[1] Understanding the World referred to understanding "nature and how it works," understanding "the issues facing our state and country," and being able to "think clearly (critically) about what we read and see on TV." The Achievement Motivation scale gave students options such as: school should "prepare us for jobs where we can keep learning new things," and "teach us to not give up when work gets hard." (See Appendix B.)

The main point of our study was that the views about the ultimate purposes of school assessed by our four scales would differ in the extent to which they represent school learning as an end in itself versus as a means to an end. Specifically, school learning (gaining knowledge, mastering schoolwork) can be seen as an integral part of the process of becoming a knowledgeable, responsible, and industrious citizen. Thus the view that school ought to help students become useful and productive members of society should be compatible with, and therefore correlate with, task involvement.

On the other hand, the view that school learning should enhance one's opportunities to gain wealth and occupational status appears to represent learning as a means to an end. Academic "success" might increase one's opportunities to gain wealth and occupational status. It is not through the process of learning at school that one enhances one's wealth and occupational rank, whereas students may well see themselves as becoming informed and industrious individuals during their school years. The wealth and status rationale for schooling thus appears more likely than the other rationales to be compatible with the experience of learning as a means to an end. It would tend not to be associated with task orientation but could be associated with academic alienation or a tendency to avoid schoolwork.

The results shown in Table 12.1—from the ninth and twelfth grades of an upper middle-class school where most students were college-bound (School A) and from a small-town high school (School B)—generally support the above suppositions. The Avoidance of Work scale (Chapter 6) was positively associated only with the view that school should increase one's wealth and status. By way of contrast, the views that school should make one socially useful, help one to understand the world, and make one motivated to achieve were associated with a slightly diminished tendency to avoid work. (The latter associations differed significantly from those between Avoidance of Work and Wealth and Status; $p < .05$.)

This pattern was more or less reversed for associations with Task Orientation. Task Orientation was higher in students who were more inclined to think that school should make one committed to society, motivated to achieve, and increase one's understanding of the world. Task Orientation was unrelated to the belief that school should increase one's wealth and status in School A but was positively related to it in School B. However, the associations of Task Orientation with Wealth and Status were significantly lower than its associations with the other three views about the purposes of school in all but one of the twelve comparisons.

The results for Ego Involvement occupied a middle ground. There were positive associations between all views about the purposes of school and Ego Involvement. However, Wealth and Status was most highly associated with Ego Involvement in every sample.[2]

A similar though slightly stronger pattern of results was obtained with a sample of academically gifted students attending an academic summer camp (Thorkildsen, 1988). These students were able enough to make the prospect of gaining high income and

Table 12.1 Correlations of Motivational Orientations with Desired Aims of Education

Aim	Avoidance of work				Ego orientation				Task orientation			
	School A grade		School B grade		School A grade		School B grade		School A grade		School B grade	
	9th	12th	9th	12th	9th	12th	9th	12th	9th	12th	9th	12th
Wealth and status	22[b]	23[b]	22[c]	29[c]	43[c]	35[c]	24[c]	40[c]	03	03	16[a]	29[a]
Social commitment	−14	−19[a]	−24[c]	−11	16[a]	24[b]	15[a]	17[a]	47[c]	46[c]	54[c]	47[a]
Understanding	−07	−15[a]	−11	−15[a]	22[b]	12	18[b]	18[a]	31[c]	38[c]	45[c]	43[a]
Achievement	−25[b]	−24[b]	−27[c]	−13	14	19[a]	21[b]	25[c]	42[c]	54[c]	55[c]	60[a]

Note. Decimal points omitted. Values are italicized when $p < .05$ for all four samples and when $p < .01$ for at least three of the four samples. For School A, N = 130 and 121 for 9th grade and 12th grade respectively; for School B, N = 185 and 151.

a. $p < .05$.   b. $p < .01$.   c. $p < .001$.

occupational status through academic success appear much more plausible than it would be for most students. Nevertheless, the view that school should help one gain wealth and status was associated with academic alienation and not associated with task orientation. A study of ninth- and twelfth-grade samples from a school in an industrial area where unemployment was high and over 95 percent of students were black yielded similar results. A difference with the last sample was that Wealth and Status items separated into two factors and were, therefore, treated as separate scales. The view that school should enhance one's chances of gaining wealth was more highly associated with Avoidance of Work than was the view that school should help one gain a high status job. As in the other samples, however, Task Orientation was most consistently associated with Commitment to Society, Understanding the World, and Achievement Motivation (Patashnick and Nicholls, 1988).

In all samples, greater satisfaction with school was associated with stronger support of the views that school should develop one's commitment to society, help one understand the world, and foster achievement motivation. The view that school should enhance one's income and status was, on the other hand, not related to satisfaction in school. These results might be taken as an indication of at least reasonable health on the part of these schools. (Would it not be disturbing to find that students who were more concerned than their peers that schools should help them understand the world and prepare them to make it a better place were less satisfied with school?)

Views about the purposes of school were, like motivational orientations (Chapter 6), associated with diverse beliefs about the causes of success in school. The view that school should help students increase their future wealth and status was linked to the beliefs that success depends on attempting to beat one's peers and having teachers expect you to do well. A different pattern was found for Commitment to Society, Understanding of the World, and Achievement Motivation scales. These views were associated with the beliefs about the causes of academic success that were also associated with Task Orientation: namely, that success is more likely if students work cooperatively, work hard, are interested in learning, and try to understand instead of just memorize material. In short, beliefs about what leads to success in school were meaningfully related to views about what school should be for.

Overdetermination

The associations between views about the purposes of school, motivational orientations, and beliefs about the causes of success are, though replicated several times, not generally large. Perhaps this is because our questionnaires cannot capture the complexities or nuances of diverse views. Nevertheless, our data do give some hint as to why it might be extremely difficult to develop a favorable motivational orientation in disaffected students. Task-oriented students do not differ from academically alienated students merely in interest in learning and satisfaction with school, but also in their views about what schools should do and what are the causes of success in school. And though the beliefs of the alienated students might seem unfortunate, they have a basis in social experience. Motivational orientations are overdetermined, and changing them might involve changing the students' ethical position on what the purpose of school should be as well as their view of the reality of life in school. Apart from the ethical questions such an attempt at motivational change would involve, it hardly looks like a simple task.

Paul Willis confirms this conclusion in his fine-grained analysis of the world view of a group of academically alienated, working-class high-school boys in an English industrial city (1977). These boys, who called themselves "the lads," "specialize in a caged resentment that always stops just short of outright confrontation . . . There is an aimless air of insubordination ready with spurious justification and impossible to nail down. If someone is sitting on the radiator it is because his trousers are wet from the rain, if someone is drifting across the classroom he is going to get some paper for written work, or if someone is leaving the class he is going to empty the rubbish 'like he usually does'" (pp. 12–13). "The lads" sum up their feelings of superiority by calling those who accept the authority of the school "ear'oles" or "lobes"— terms that disparage the passivity of "good" listeners and absorbers. The lads' clothes, smoking, drinking, and sexual exploits distinguish them from the world of "ear'oles" and school and indicate their identification with the machismo of the male working class. They perpetrate so many acts of insurrection that when one is called to the principal's office he must prepare by recollecting all the acts about which he might be interrogated (most of which are never directly linked to any one of them) and work out tales for all contingencies. The excitement, self-determination, and comradeship involved in their adventures confirms their scorn of what they see as the passive world of school learning.

As Willis relates it, the lads' alienation from school is also made coherent by their views about what school might or might not accomplish. Not surprisingly, there is no thought that the school might help them understand the world or become useful members of society. Furthermore, they actively reject the notion that school can be a means to increased economic or social status. With some justification, given the employment possibilities in their city, they claim that there is no real chance that school could be a means to wealth and status. The only jobs that diligence at school might get them are low-level, white-collar jobs which they see as fit only for "ear'oles" who do not know how to enjoy life. And they know well that (at their time and place—where unemployment was very low) they will be able to get a job as soon as they reach the age when they can leave school legally.

These youths disparage the appeals of careers advisers to "escape" from the sort of occupations their fathers have. When a visiting speaker appears to imply that house painting is an inferior occupation, one of them "wanted to get up and say to him, 'There's got to be some silly cunt who slops [paint] on a wall'" (p. 93). They reject formal qualifications in favor of practical savvy and ability to survive in the real world. This stance is supported by their ability to earn money in after-school jobs, their improvised and constantly evolving adventures, and their successful flouting of school conventions. Their initiative would, in their view, be lost if they capitulated to the teachers and became "ear'oles."

If nothing else, Willis's study suggests the unprofitability of searching for simple or isolated causes and consequences of different motivational orientations and views about the purposes of school. And—like our evidence of convergence of views about the purposes of school, motivational orientations, and beliefs about the causes of success—Willis's analysis suggests the difficulty of changing a student's orientation toward school learning. These orientations are part of a more or less coherent complex set of beliefs and associated values concerning the nature of school and society. Though these positions are not without blind spots and contradictions, students are active observers of school and society and make their own analyses of both. (See also Fine, 1981.)

Getting What We Want From Our Schools

Our data do not indicate the source of views about the purposes of education or the causal role they play in the associations we found. Nevertheless, if inquiry, interest in learning, and satisfaction with school are the results we seek, our data give little encouragement to those who emphasize the financial gains school learning might bring. Of the views about the purpose of school that we sampled, the view that school should enhance a student's chances of wealth and status was the most likely to be associated with academic alienation and the least likely to be associated with task orientation, satisfaction with school, and plans to attend college. Schools and neighborhoods that emphasize the role of school in the pursuit of wealth and status might fail to encourage commitment to inquiry, intellectual exploration, satisfaction with life in school, and interest in further education. There is some support for this conclusion in Lightfoot's (1983) observations of high schools.

The Task Force on Teaching as a Profession of the Carnegie Forum on Education and the Economy endorsed "the principle that 'investment in education is one of the best investments the country can make, because well-educated people are the best guarantee of a rising standard of living for everyone'" (Carnegie Forum, 1987, p. 17). A survey they commissioned determined that 95 percent of the population concurred. This survey also documents "a deep-seated apprehension about the country's ability to compete [economically] abroad" (p. 17).[3]

It is a considerable leap from concerns about a nation's economic standing to students' views about the role of school. Conceivably such public concern could spur students to accomplish things for the good of their country—a motivation compatible with task involvement. But the current concerns of university students about education and the economy have little of this flavor. Over the past ten years they have become more concerned that their studies should lead to a high income and less concerned to develop a philosophy of life and make a contribution to humanity (Astin, 1983). The principle of "investment in education" seems to express a desire for skills that will pay rather than a passion to make things of value.

The argument can also be made that an emphasis on school as a means to wealth and status will do little for economic productivity. The findings of our study of 570 high school students' thinking about what one must do to succeed in occupations (Patashnick and Nicholls, 1988) supports this position. Their beliefs about the causes of occupational success fell into two main dimensions. In the first, success depended on interest in one's work, on believing that it is valuable, and on a readiness to cooperate with others. The second dimension was marked by beliefs in the decisive role of extrinsic factors that might enhance one's status rather than one's product. These included knowing how to impress the "right" people, knowing the "right" people, coming from a wealthy family, being physically attractive, being lucky, and trying to beat others. The belief that occupational success depends on interest and cooperation was associated with the views that school should make one socially useful ($r = .51$, $p < .001$) and motivated to achieve ($r = .44$, $p < .001$; $R = .54$, $p < .001$). Emphasis on extrinsic factors as causes of occupational success was associated with the view that school should lead to wealth and status ($r = .26$) and with rejection of the view that school should make one socially useful ($r = -.15$, $p < .001$; $R = .35$, $p < .001$). The motivational orientation scales produced complementary results. Belief in the importance of interest and cooperation for occupational success was correlated with Task Orientation ($r = .38$, $p < .001$). Belief in the role of extrinsic factors was predicted by Work Avoidance ($r = .29$, $p < .001$) and Ego Orientation ($r = .19$, $p < .001$; $R = .31$, $p < .001$).

These data raise the prospect that the increasing emphasis among students on school as a means to wealth and status might have unfortunate effects on our economy. A nation of individuals who believe that success depends on knowing the right people rather than producing something of value is not likely to have much to sell. Roland Dore (1976) notes that the Industrial Revolution in England was not preceded by an expansion of schooling. He also notes that in countries that have only recently attempted to "modernize," education is considered crucial for economic growth and educational qualifications are often competed for as passports to status and the good life. However, this competition is not accompanied by a drive to start businesses or do other things that would promote their nation's economic growth or even maintain traditional economies. Instead, there is only an ample supply of people who want to leave their villages, to wear white shirts, and to receive a salary.

On another plane, how meaningful is life when wealth and status (in the usual sense) are its controlling ends? Max Weber's reflections, written at the turn of the century, seem made for our time. The "idea of duty in one's calling prowls about in our lives like the ghost of dead religious beliefs . . . the pursuit of wealth, stripped of its religious and ethical meaning, tends to become associated with purely mundane passions . . . [Of this] cultural development, it might well be truly said: 'Specialists without spirit, sensualists without heart; this nullity imagines that it has attained a level of civilization never before achieved'" (1958, p. 182).

Beyond Technique

The view that school should help one understand the world and make a contribution to the lives of others was associated with task orientation, satisfaction in school, and beliefs that cooperative work, interest, and attempts to understand lead to success. This is good news, in that it suggests that love and work can coexist— at least in the minds of adolescents.

If we are to take students' views about the purposes of school into account in the attempt to foster task involvement and inquiry, we might have to look again at what we teach as well as the way we do it. For example, when mathematics educators justify their subject, one can almost hear the voice of Galileo declaring that the book of nature is written in the language of mathematics. But the connection between nature and what is written in most school mathematics books is probably discerned only by God. If mathematics should help students to understand the world, we ought not to teach it as separate from science. We might also make the content and methods of science and mathematics more responsive to the questions and constructions children evolve as they deal with nature, school, and society (Cobb, 1986; 1988; Kamii, 1985; Steffe, et al., 1983).

Furthermore, if one justification for the study of science is that science can make the world a better place, we might spend more time fostering inquiry about what sort of world would be better and what sort of science would promote such a world. We might have to abandon the notion that science is value-free and look again at textbooks that embody this notion and teaching methods that seek merely to transmit the revealed truths. I noted earlier that it is very rare for students to have a role in formulating the questions they address in the classroom. Since science cannot "tell" us what are "good" questions, how can we justify teaching it by having students only answer the questions or work on tasks of textbook writers and curriculum designers? If science should improve the world but doesn't always do so, classroom teachers and students of science ought to take some responsibility for the questions they ask.

A genuine concern on the part of educators with the students' understanding of the purposes of education demands increased student participation in the negotiation of those purposes. It is not enough, however, to call for the reduction of coercive classroom control merely on the grounds that this will increase student involvement in learning. The change needs to be more fully justified, on the grounds that it enables students to construct a more meaningful world and strengthens their capacity to direct their own lives in concert with their fellows.

Encouraging as it is to find that students who think school should help them function as knowledgeable, active, and altruistic citizens are also positively oriented to learning and to school, we are yet to be inundated with schools where subject matter and teaching methods clearly promote these purposes rather than what Weber called mundane passions. The reasons for this recalcitrant reality deserve attention.

13

Changing Our Schools, Changing the World

Many obstacles to the establishment of task involvement, inquiry, and equality in the schools have been diagnosed. (Topics I do not address are discussed by Goodlad, 1983; Lazerson et al., 1985; S. B. Sarason, 1971.) I want to end this book by considering only three. The first, which has been the object of extensive discussion, is the permeability of school walls to influences from the world of work. The second obstacle is the world of academic psychology, to which one might expect to look for guidance. Yet as others have noted (Argyris, 1975; Feinberg, 1983; Rorty, 1983; S. B. Sarason, 1981; M. B. Smith, 1974), psychologists' analyses do not often promote participatory democracy and personal development. In this respect, the work of psychologists can be seen as reflecting rather than reflecting on our established modes of living. Finally, I consider the likelihood that good ideas about knowledge, education, and equality might also be difficult ideas that cannot be transmitted but must be constructed by each individual—a process that is not favored by those classrooms or work places that foster ego involvement or extrinsic involvement, nor by the approaches to education often proposed by psychologists.

Economic Determinism

Dewey's hope was that progressive education would transform society. For him, "the aim of education is to enable individuals to continue their education . . . the object and the reward of learning is continued capacity for growth" (1966, p. 100). Individual growth was intimately linked with democracy, which "is more than a form of government; it is primarily a mode of associated living, of conjoint communicated experience" (p. 81). Such a society "counts individual variations as precious since it finds in them the means of its own growth. Hence a democratic society must in consistency with its ideal, allow for intellectual freedom and the play of diverse gifts and interests in its educational measures" (p. 305). Occupations too should foster growth, be intrinsically meaningful and of social value. "Any individual has missed his calling . . . who does not find that the accomplishment of results of value to others is an accompaniment of a process of experience inherently worthwhile" (p. 122). Dewey saw a danger that education would sustain the status quo of inequality and individual subordination typical of industrial labor (p. 120). He hoped, however, that progressive education would gradually transform the adult society: "It would give those who engage in industrial callings desire and ability to share in social control, and ability to become masters of their industrial fate" (p. 321).

The progressive education movement is credited by some with contributing toward equality and democracy (Cremin, 1964). Others see the world of work that Dewey hoped to transform through education as thwarting the progressive vision (Bowles and Gintis, 1976). In this view, the capitalist goal of profit maximization maintains hierarchical, top-down systems of control that give workers freedom of choice only between work in organizations as they find them and unemployment. "The roots of repression and inequality lie [not in the school, but] in the structure and functioning of the capitalist economy" (p. 49) and this repression and inequality are reflected in the structure and functioning of the school system.

Other analysts (Giroux, 1983) claim these opposing viewpoints are incomplete. Although schools respond to the demands of the workplace, they do not mirror these demands. Students and teachers construct their own interpretations of economic reality and evolve their own purposes and strategies for living with and transforming this reality. Even though these purposes and strategies can ultimately trap their creators in alienating work (Willis, 1977), we should not overlook the creative participation of individuals and groups in resisting, modifying, and adapting to economic and social conditions. Closely related is the view of schools as the realm where struggles over ideology and resources take place: where demands for economic equality and participation contend with pressure for industrious and obedient workers (Carnoy and Levin, 1985). In all these views the autocratic workplace and the ideologies associated with it—whether expressed in the functioning of the state, informal groups, or individuals—are seen as obstacles to equality, intrinsic motivation, and democracy in schools.

The world of work is not the same everywhere. Even the dirtiest, least intellectually stimulating jobs can be organized so that workers have responsibility for their work. The Sunset Scavenger Company, which collects half the garbage of San Francisco, is such a case. According to one of the company's 1934 by laws, "they were an association of workers who intended to form and carry on a cooperative corporation where every member was a worker and actually engaged in the common work and where every member did his share of the work and expected every other member to work and do his utmost to increase the collective earnings" (S. E. Perry, 1978, p. 197). This cooperative, whose members own it, elect its officers, and select new members, has survived and grown. Its members earn more than most equivalent workers, have lower accident rates, and experience better working conditions. These men who call themselves scavengers are, says Perry, more likely than most to look the customer in the eye and, on their own initiative, to provide extra services. Garbage collection might never become an intellectually or aesthetically exciting activity, but the satisfaction it can provide depends on how people organize and construe it. The example of the Sunset Scavengers indicates that the domination of autocratic employers is not necessary for the efficient conduct of necessary but mundane work. These scavengers give some substance to what Michael Walzer 1983) calls "the lively hope named by the word *equality*: no more bowing and scraping, fawning and toadying; no more fearful trembling; no more high-and-mightiness" (p. xiii).

The fact that such cooperatives are rare in the United States cannot be read as an indication that they do not "work" in terms of traditional criteria of efficiency. In 1984 there were eleven plywood manufacturing cooperatives in Washington and Oregon with a total membership of about 2,000 (Gunn, 1984). Co-op members own their companies and elect their officers. Members generally earn more than the average for such jobs and have higher labor productivity in terms of output per hour, economy of material input use, and value of product. (Measures of 30 to 50 percent higher co-op productivity have withstood the test of tax-court challenges.) These co-ops have also used less capital per worker than have traditional firms (Gunn, 1984).

Important though such criteria are, they are not the only ones that justify co-ops to their members. The relatively high survival rate of co-ops in adverse economic conditions reflects their function of supporting the members (Gunn, 1984). And not surprisingly—given their financial participation and role in election of officers (these co-ops are representative democracies)—co-op members also participate more actively than most workers in the daily decisions about the process of production and are more committed to doing the best job they can (Greenberg, 1984).

The Hoedads Co-op, an economically successful reforestation cooperative in Oregon, stresses participatory as well as representative democracy. And (unlike the plywood co-ops) Hoedads members devote emotional and financial resources to political action that aims to make society in general more hospitable to cooperative enterprises (Gunn, 1984). In the same spirit, the Mondragon cooperatives of northern Spain have created their own supportive environment that is consistent with their participatory ethic. They have a cooperative bank to support their operation, with a division to assist in developing new enterprises and a research and development center and service cooperatives that provide managerial assistance (Levin, 1984).

There can be no legitimate defense of the status quo on the grounds that economic democracy cannot "work" (Carnoy and Shearer, 1980; Gunn, 1984; Jackall and Levin, 1984). But the scarcity of cooperative economic enterprises must, like the scarcity of progressive classrooms, indicate that they are not easily established. Part of the difficulty derives from the lack of a collective vision of ways for workers to manage their own activities (Gunn, 1984). This might both contribute to and reflect a lack of commitment to "associated living" and "conjoint communicated experience." If we want other things more than we want economic democracy, chances are that we will get the other things.

The Technical Orientation

Almost anything we can conceive about people is probably true, at some time and some place. People can resemble robots. They can memorize material that is placed before them. They can also construct things that are new and which transform cultures. To the extent that any one vision of humanity is adopted, it transforms people. By changing the way our fellows construe each other, the way they treat one another can also be transformed. Thus a psychologist's conception of humanity can be free of value implications only by escaping the notice of humans.

Jean Piaget presumably had something like this in mind when he observed "how peculiar it is that so many American and Soviet psychologists, citizens of great nations which intend to change the world, have produced learning theories that reduce knowledge to a passive copy of external reality . . . whereas human thought always transforms and transcends reality. Outstanding sectors of mathematics [for example] have no counterpart in physical reality [yet] result in new combinations which enrich reality" (Piaget 1970; p. 714). Here, Piaget the constructivist objects both to the political implications of the behaviorist tradition and to its lack of conceptual coherence. The behaviorists whose perspective he criticized have since been overshadowed by a "cognitive revolution," but the issue remains.

Resnick (1983), for example, acknowledges a debt to Piaget when she argues that we should place "the learner's active mental construction at the very heart of the instructional exchange. Instruction cannot simply put knowledge and skill into people's heads" (p. 30). Although from the perspective of its intellectual antecedents this "cognitive revolution" does involve a new emphasis on meaningful learning and has produced much of value, it provides little comfort to those who seek to establish inquiry or promote student initiative and responsibility in classrooms. The recognition of the active role the learner plays in constructing knowledge does not, in this case, lead to questions about how teachers might detect what children see as problems and how to use children's problems as a starting point in education. Instead, the concern is with "how to present new information to students, what kinds of responses to demand from students, how to sequence and schedule learning episodes, and what kinds of feedback to provide at what points in the learning sequence" (Resnick, 1983, p. 31). These questions will, in her view, be answered by researchers and the answers will be transmitted to teachers. And in the classroom the teacher is firmly in the saddle. This is a vision of a hierarchical, top-down system of control. The overarching purpose remains the efficient adaptation of the child to the external structure of knowledge, which is revealed to experts. The cognitive revolution has not produced a place for a dialectical process in which teachers might expect to be surprised by students' questions and reconstruct their own teaching as a result of students' activities. This revolution has produced what Resnick calls a psychology of instruction, which is not a psychology of inquiry or of education. The paucity of inquiry in the schoolrooms of the nation is mirrored by the paucity of research on inquiry in the halls of academe.

Many students of social procesess in classrooms have been bothered by inequality. The research on teacher expectations or Pygmalion effects can be seen as one expression of this concern, yet this research itself has often taken a form that sustains inequality. Instead of studying the distribution and effect of teachers' expectations that their students, gifted and mediocre, will become committed to learning for its own sake, the preoccupation of researchers has been what one would expect of ego-oriented individuals: teachers' expectations for students' achievement relative to that of their peers. And when motivational mediators of this type of expectancy effect have been considered, on the top of the list of mediators is students' perceived ability, or expected attainment (Jussim, 1986). Within this framework, someone has to be a loser because we can't all have high ability or score above grade level.

Researchers who are concerned with inequality in classrooms might adopt the attitude of the teachers who judge themselves by the level of their students' involvement in learning (Jackson, 1968). We should reduce the general preoccupation with ability and relative achievement. Yet much research on teacher expectancy effects reflects rather than reflects on the preoccupation with how students stand in the race to the top.

One might hope that research on motivation would provide help in the pursuit of quality and equality. I have referred to an appreciable number of workers whose ideas and data help us build a picture that might both explain inequality and increase quality and equality. Yet the perspective that is perhaps most influential among researchers (and that, in many ways, has had a liberating effect on research on achievement motivation), the attribution theory approach (Weiner, 1979, 1985), can be used to explain the problems of inequality (Ames and Ames, 1984; Nicholls, 1979b) but offers little to alleviate them.

Achievement behavior is, in the attribution theory view, a function of expectancies of success and of emotions that are themselves a function of causal attributions for success and failure. Suggestions for improvement of motivation focus on the modification of students' interpretations of failure and success so that they will have higher expectations of success. The attribution theorists' analysis of people's interpretations of success and failure implies that people clearly distinguish the concepts of effort, ability, difficulty, luck, and more. In the terms of the present framework, attribution theorists assume that people employ the conception of ability as capacity, which means that to succeed or be competent, one would have to perform better than others. Because the nature of success is never defined in attribution theory, the impression is given that the problems of poor motivation will be solved by raising students' expectations of success. But unless we create task involvement, this is a zero-sum game.

Despite widespread acceptance (inspired by but probably not a necessary implication of attribution theory) of the value of attempts to persuade dispirited students that their failures are due to lack of effort (Dweck, 1986; Foersterling, 1985), the evidence for the effectiveness of this particular strategy is questionable. The results obtained could be as easily attributed to effects of intermittent reinforcement (Dweck, 1975) or to attribution of success (rather than failure) to effort (Fowler and Peterson, 1981). Telling students they are hard workers increases their effort, but telling them that they are not working hard or need to work harder is about as useful as doing nothing (Miller, Brickman, and Bolen,

1975; Schunk, 1982). One would not expect students whose disaffection derives from a belief in their incompetence to respond favorably to being told that their difficulties derive from a lack of effort—especially not if their classroom environment is competitive. The question of the social context of attribution retraining is generally overlooked. At the same time, the notion that disaffected students should be persuaded to attribute their failures to lack of effort tends to justify social inequality by maintaining the notion that people end up at the bottom of the academic or socioeconomic pile because they don't work hard enough and that those at the top have earned their places.

Like most psychological perspectives on motivation, attribution theory embodies a technical orientation in human affairs. The failure to consider the various possible meanings of success is one expression of this tendency. (See Chapters 6 and 9.) The strategy of increasing expectations of success by persuading individuals to change their interpretations of failure is also a technical manipulation. It involves no negotiation of purposes between child and teacher or patient and therapist.

A technical orientation (by no means limited to attribution theory) might appear to its exponents as objective science untrammelled by political and ethical considerations. But approaches that obscure the fact that inequality of motivation is inevitable in a society preoccupied with "who is on top" are hardly value free. Unless the problems of inequality are brought in, discussion is reduced and the status quo maintained. Denying the relevance of the ultimate and immediate purposes of individuals and groups to questions of motivation also has value implications. Examination, discussion, and negotiation of the purposes of individuals and groups are marks of a democratic life. Nothing that diminishes these activities is value-free.

Encouragement of students' participation in the formation of the purposes that govern their schooling is, as I have observed, rare. This state of affairs mirrors the relative neglect of questions concerning students' ultimate purposes, how parents and teachers influence these purposes, and the role that students might play in forming the purposes that govern their education. Even researchers themselves neglect questions of purpose—issues of seemingly paramount importance to students of motivation. We academic psychologists can hardly complain that inequality and the undemocratic nature of school life is the result of the failure of teachers to heed our words of wisdom.

I hope it is clear that I am not claiming that the approaches I have discussed are useless. Instruction, as distinct from education, has legitimate roles to play. It also makes sense to think that people can have technical malfunctions that might require technical "adjustments." People can, for example, quite wrongly judge themselves as incompetent (Lepper, Ross, and Lau, 1986). Manipulations designed to increase a person's perceived ability or performance expectations have a wholly legitimate place. I have no objection to the notion that public taxes should support research on such manipulations. The problem is that if this is the only type of solution we propose for the problems of motivation in the schools, we will have done nothing to sustain those features of our society that would make the paying of taxes a constructive act.

Most psychologists would probably object to Richard Rorty's claim that "the only sort of policy makers who would be receptive to most of what presently passes for 'behavioral science' would be the rulers of the Gulag, or of Huxley's *Brave New World*" (1983, pp. 161–162). Yet it is hard to find approaches to the psychology of motivation and learning that would obviously be rejected by the rulers of the Gulag.

The Trouble with Human Nature

Teachers who have tried to generate inquiry in schoolrooms have probably encountered a problem I did when teaching junior high school students. Students often discount an occasion when inquiry occurs because it looks to them like play. These occasions may have significant intellectual consequences, but although students enjoy them, they often do not take them seriously; it is not real schoolwork. The dualism of work and play is hard to overcome. Students will also sometimes almost ask to be told what to do. As far as they are concerned, routine answer-finding activities are real work. Many things must have contributed to this perspective—including the fear of looking stupid that novel and unpredictable intellectual activities can heighten. But there might be a problem here that will never go away completely.

As I noted in Chapter 5, the early conceptions of intelligence and knowledge dispose students to see virtue in schooling where teachers provide both questions and answers. The information-acquisition, trivial-pursuit conception of intelligence represents intellectual development as the acquisition of facts. It ignores the place of problem finding and solving in schooling. Similarly, in the early dualist conceptions of knowledge described by William Perry (1970; 1981) one learns by acquiring correct knowledge. A store of it is "out there" (rather than being constructed) and known to authorities from whom one must gain it.

In the opinion of one college undergraduate, "a certain amount of theory is good but it should not be dominant in a course. I mean theory might be convenient for them, but it's nonetheless— the facts are what's there. And I think that *should* be, that should be the main thing" (Perry, 1968, p. 67). Another undergraduate observed that in his high-school history course "the teacher would be telling you exact facts and here [at Harvard] it's altogether different . . . I suppose it's more immature but I like it better when they give you something concrete, exactly what happened." (Perry, 1968, p. 76). Such positions are indeed "more immature" and if, as seems to be the case, these are early levels of a developmental sequence that cannot be bypassed, a conservative tendency on the part of students will always make implementation of a progressive educational philosophy difficult.

It is not until the higher conceptions of knowledge are attained that we find views such as "I still enjoy papers above all, because it's something beyond the book . . . It takes a certain amount of creativity . . . and imagination . . . no matter what the subject" (p. 126). "Whatever you do there's going to be much more to do, more to understand, you're going to make mistakes . . . but you have a sense of being able to cope with a specific or rather small fragment of the general picture and . . . getting the most out of it, but never, never giving up, always looking for something" (p. 160). "I came here expecting that Harvard would teach me one universal truth . . . Took me quite a while to figure out . . . that if I was going for a universal truth or something to believe in, it had to come from within me" (p. 138).

In the second set of positions the learner appears more active and expresses naive constructivist views, whereas the earlier positions correspond to theories of cultural transmission and traditional learning theories. If there is no bypassing of early conceptions, progressive educators may have to face the problem that students will not fully "realize what is good for them" until their education is well advanced. But if, as in the progressive view, education is a dialectical transaction, such tension is essential. It could be a more productive tension, more of a dialogue, if we understood more about the way students' conceptions of the processes of education evolve.

The developmental immaturity of students would get in the way of progressive classrooms. But teachers can also have dualist conceptions of knowledge. Such people can hardly be expected to discern what Dewey is trying to say. For teachers who see the world in dichotomous terms of "we-right-good vs. other-bad-wrong" (Perry, 1968, p. 9), Dewey's thoughts must be incomprehensible. Dewey is always the dialectitian; always revealing the inadequacies of dichotomies. It is in our failure to synthesize fact and theory, theory and practice, interest and effort, interest and discipline, play and work, freedom and social control, science and values, that Dewey finds the core of our problems. But such ideas will be incomprehensible to individuals for whom right answers exist in the absolute and are known to authorities whose role is to teach them, and for whom acquisition of knowledge is the accretion of right answers by diligence and obedience. (The preceding sentence is a paraphrase of the lowest conception of knowledge described by Perry, 1968, p. 9.) If people cannot fully want what they cannot fully construe, it is unlikely that teachers with undifferentiated conceptions of knowledge will want to foster task involvement, inquiry, or democracy in their classrooms.

It may also be that a commitment to social equality is, in part, a function of developmental maturity. To assess undergraduates' orientations toward status, Standring (1976) presented them with a list of occupations. He first asked them to indicate the prestige society accords these occupations, and then to determine the prestige they personally believed each occupation deserved. The second set provided an index of orientation to equality—the number of occupations accorded the same level of prestige. Employing

Rest's (1979) Defining Issues Test as a measure of developmental maturity, Standring found no correlation with perceptions of the prestige society accords different occupations. However, when he asked students about the level of prestige they thought different occupations *deserved*, the ones with higher moral maturity scores were more prone to accord the same prestige to all or most occupations. The correlation between moral maturity and number of occupations receiving the same rank was .45 ($p < .01$).

Despite the apparently close links between the conceptions of knowledge described by Perry and approaches to teaching, this potential association has not been the subject of empirical study. However, a number of studies have been conducted employing a measure similar to his measures of complexity of belief systems (Harvey, Hunt, and Schroder, 1961). This distinguishes four levels of complexity, the least complex termed concrete and the most complex, abstract. Abstract teachers (who are in the minority) teach in ways that are more likely to sustain task involvement and inquiry. Compared to their colleagues with less complex belief systems, abstract teachers are less coercive, more encouraging of student responsibility, more resourceful in presenting learning activities, more encouraging of student searching and theorizing, and more empathetic (Harvey, et al., 1968; Harvey et al., 1966; Hunt and Joyce, 1967; Koenigs, Fieldler, and deCharms, 1977; Murphy and Brown, 1970). In short, these teachers are more inclined to teach in the fashion that Dewey advocated. Teachers with more concrete conceptual systems teach the way one would expect individuals with dualist, right-wrong conceptions of knowledge to do it: as if knowledge was something that they, as authorities (with the assistance of authoritative texts and workbooks), must transmit, and the students, as recipients, must retain. This is a technical orientation that seems likely to find virtue in technical advice—what has been termed the "make-and-take" orientation of many teachers' in-service courses.

If it is their own level of cognitive complexity that limits some teachers' appreciation of methods that promote intrinsic motivation and student responsibility, one would expect that it would not be easy to increase the use of such methods. Evidence confirms that this is so. One short-term intervention, designed to stimulate the teachers to see the point of encouraging student initiative and take advantage of information about how other teachers do this, did succeed in transmitting such information to teachers. But it did not lead to changes in observed behavior in classrooms (Cohen, Emrich, and deCharms, 1976). Neither did an attempt to implement the jigsaw cooperative learning method with a group of teachers who had shown interest in it. When the previously reported positive results of this method (Aronson et al., 1978) failed to materialize, the researchers took a closer look at these teachers' classrooms. They concluded that the teachers seemed unable to give up the amount of direct control necessary to implement the method. It was as if the teachers felt they weren't doing their job when the students taught each other (Moskowitz et al., 1983; see also Sharan et al., 1984).

Richard deCharms (1976, 1984) observed that we might do well to practice what we preach if we hope to encourage teachers to foster the active involvement of students in their education. His efforts to promote this sort of teaching appeared more successful when there was more teacher-input to in-service courses. Attempts to tell teachers what to do or to get them to use previously developed methods of enhancing student initiative were not effective. This result parallels evidence that student learning is enhanced in schools where approaches to curriculum and discipline are agreed on and supported by the school staff and where teachers feel that their views are acknowledged and considered seriously by administrators (Rutter et al., 1979).

Attempts to "transmit" information about how to teach may be of questionable value, but attempts to improve education by increasing evaluative pressure on teachers are worse. Deci and colleagues (1982) found that more coercive teaching was produced by telling student teachers that they were responsible for seeing that their students performed up to standards. The same phenomenon has been observed among parents. Those who thought an observing researcher was evaluating their child's ability were coercive and restricting, whereas those who thought the researcher was interested in the child's learning promoted their child's initiatives (Renshaw and Gardner, 1987). Yet the ancient notion of coercive and concrete evaluations of teachers is once again gaining currency.

Concrete information about how and what to teach is likely to appeal to teachers at lower levels of knowledge and cognitive complexity. There is no shortage of it: one example is the publication "What Works" promoted by Education Secretary William Bennett. In calling for material for the second publication of this series, Bennett said, "we would like to have evidence of education methods and practices that work" (Report on Education Research, 1986, p. 1). But this is teacher training (instruction), not teacher education. Could anyone really expect to promote equality, intrinsically meaningful learning, and accomplishments that will enhance the lives of others by telling people the way things are, by training them to do things "our" way, and by giving them low grades if they do not see the light? But this is what we find ourselves doing.

In the end we are unlikely to solve the problems of education without resorting to education—that form of experience that enables us to extract meaning from experience and promotes the desire for more such experience, and for modes of living that stimulate conjoint communicated experience.

Appendixes
Notes
Bibliography
Index

Appendix A: Motivational Orientation Scales

1. High School Students

Introductory question: When do you feel you have had a really successful day in school? Response scale: Strongly agree, agree, neutral, disagree, strongly disagree. (Data from Nicholls, Patashnick, and Nolen, 1985.)

Stem for each item: I feel most successful if . . .

Task Orientation I (Alphas = .84, .88, .85, .85)
   something I learn makes me want to find out more
   I get a new idea about how things work
   I learn something interesting
   I solve a tricky problem by working hard
   I finally understand a really complicated idea
   something I learn really makes sense to me
   a class makes me think about things
Task Orientation II (Alphas = .80, .75, .82, .68)
   I keep busy
   I work hard all day
Ego Orientation (Alphas = .79, .86, .84, .85)
   I do the work better than other students
   I show people I'm good at something
   I show people I'm smart
   I score higher than other students
   I am the only one who can answer the teacher's questions

Avoid Inferiority (Alphas = .74, .86, .84, .85)
  I don't do anything stupid in class
  people don't think I'm dumb
Easy Superiority (Alphas = .78, .84, .76, .86)
  I score high on a test without studying
  I do well without trying
Work Avoidance (Alphas = .87, .88, .85, .86)
  I don't have to do any homework
  I don't have to work hard
  all the work is easy
  the teacher doesn't ask any hard questions
  I don't have any tough tests
Alienation (Alphas = .84, .87, .89, .82)
  I get out of some work
  I do almost no work and get away with it
  I put one over on a teacher
  I fool around and get away with it

Note: When the two Task Orientation scales are combined, Alphas = .85, .86, .86, and .83. Addition of Ego Orientation and Avoid Inferiority results in slight reductions in reliability. Work Avoidance and Alienation combine to form an overall Work Avoidance scale (Alphas = .90, .90, .91, .88). Reliabilities are given for each of four samples in the order shown in Table 7.1.

2. Fifth-Grade Students

Introductory questions: When do you feel most successful in school? When do you feel school has gone really well for you? Response scale: Strongly agree, agree, neutral, disagree, strongly disagree. (Data from Nicholls and Thorkildsen, 1987.)

Stem for each item: I feel most successful if . . .

Task Orientation (Alpha = .88)
  something I learn makes me want to find out more
  I get a new idea about how things work
  I learn something interesting
  I solve a problem by working hard
  what I learn really makes sense
  a lesson makes me think about things
  I keep busy
  I work hard all day

Ego Orientation (Alpha = .88)
  I do the work better than other students
  I score higher than other students
  I am the only one who can answer a question
  I get higher test scores than my friends
Work Avoidance (Alpha = .91)
  I don't have to do any homework
  I don't have to work hard
  all the work is easy
  the teacher doesn't ask any hard questions
  I don't have any tough tests
Academic Alienation (Alpha = .92)
  I get out of some school work
  I do almost no work and get away with it
  I put one over on a teacher
  I fool around and get away with it

3. Second-Grade Students

General question: When do you feel really pleased about math? Response scale: YES, yes, not sure, no, NO. (Data from Nicholls et al., 1988b.)

Stem for each item: I feel really pleased in math when . . .

Task Orientation I (Alpha = .75)
  I solve a problem by working hard
  the problems make me think hard
  what the teacher says makes me think
  I keep busy
  I work hard all the time
Task Orientation II (Alpha = .84)
  something I learn makes me want to find out more
  I find a new way to solve a problem
  something I figure out really makes sense
  something I figure out makes me want to keep doing more problems
Ego Orientation I (Alpha = .68)
  I know more than the others
  I am the only one who can answer a question
Ego Orientation II (Alpha = .62)
  I finish before my friends
  I get more answers right than my friends

Work Avoidance (Alpha = .76)
  I don't have to work hard
  all the work is easy
  the teacher doesn't ask hard questions

Note: For the Task Orientation scales combined, Alpha = .79. For the Ego Orientation scales combined, Alpha = .71.

Appendix B: Scales Assessing the Purposes of School

General question: In your opinion, what are the main things schools should do? Response scale: Strongly agree, agree, neutral, disagree, strongly disagree. (Data from Nicholls, Patashnick, and Nolen, 1985.)

Stem for each item: A very important thing school should do is . . .

A. Wealth and Status (Alphas = .86, .87, .86, .80)

1. *Wealth* (Alphas = .87, .92, .88, .83)
   prepare us for jobs that will give us money for luxuries
   prepare us for jobs that will give us plenty of free time
   prepare us for jobs that will give us enough money to buy the best of everything
   prepare us for jobs that will give us long vacations and the money to travel
2. *Status I* (Alphas = .77, .83, .78, .71)
   prepare us to reach the top in our jobs
   help us get into the best colleges
   teach us to compete with others so we can compete for the top jobs
   give us a drive to get higher and higher jobs
   give us the skills that will get us top jobs with high status
3. *Status II* (Alphas = .69, .80, .74, .63)
   recognize the talents of able students to ensure they move toward the top jobs

make sure that the smartest students are prepared to be leaders and get top jobs

find out who is smart enough for top jobs

B. Social Commitment (Alphas = .88, .91, .90, .91)

1. *Community Spirit* (Alphas = .83, .82, .82, .84)
   prepare us to be useful to others
   prepare us to be active in the community
   teach us to work cooperatively with others
   prepare us to do things that will help others
2. *Loyalty* (Alphas = .85, .87, .79, .86)
   teach us to do our duty to our country
   make us responsible law-abiding citizens
   make us loyal to our country
3. *Self-Sacrifice* (Alphas = .75, .79, .76, .79)
   prepare us to do things we have to do, even if we don't want to
   teach us to respect authority
   teach us to sacrifice pleasures and work to do the right thing
   teach us to work hard to support our business and government leaders
   teach us to follow orders even when we don't feel like it
4. *Useful Work* (Alphas = .78, .84, .82, .85)
   prepare us for jobs that will make the world better for everyone
   prepare us for jobs making or doing things that are useful to others
   teach us things that will help society
   prepare us for jobs that will make other peoples' lives more interesting or satisfying
   prepare us for jobs that improve other peoples' health or standard of living

C. Understanding (Alphas = .85, .90, .84, .88)

1. *Understanding Science* (Alphas = .78, .82, .74, .78)
   help us understand the effect of new inventions
   prepare us to understand the importance of new scientific discoveries
   help us understand nature and how it works
   help us understand technology and how it works
2. *Understanding the Media* (Alphas = .69, .89, .77, .80)
   help us think clearly (critically) about what we read and see on TV
   prepare us to evaluate critically what experts say
   make us critical readers of the news
3. *Understanding Politics* (Alphas = .75, .87, .77, .83)
   help us think clearly about what politicians say
   help us understand how what our country does affects the world
   help us understand enough to vote wisely in elections

help us understand the issues facing our state and country (foreign relations, environment, etc.)

D. Achievement Motivation (Alphas = .83, .90, .83, .83)

1. *Creative Work* (Alphas = .79,. 88, .73, .78)
   prepare us for jobs where we can keep learning new things
   prepare us for jobs where we can be imaginative
   teach us to be creative problem-solvers at work
   prepare us for challenging jobs
2. *Persistence* (Alphas = .81, .90, .79, .82)
   help us to keep working in spite of obstacles
   help us to always work hard to do our best
   teach us to not give up when work gets hard
   teach us to set high standards for our own work

Note: Alphas are for the four samples referred to in Table 12.1.

Notes

2. Luck and Skill

1. Students' initial responses commonly underrepresent their knowledge (Danner and Day, 1977; Nicholls and Miller, 1984b).

4. Ability and Effort

1. It is important that the student who puts in less effort should not be shown to work hard at the beginning of the time designated and thus finish before the other student. An earlier time of completion would indicate superior ability—an inference that quite young children are able to make (Heckhausen, 1984). This would prevent the testing of children's ability to differentiate the concepts of effort and ability.

2. The conception of ability as capacity might be seen as an instance of what Barenboim (1981) terms psychological comparisons in person perception, whereas the normative conception of ability appears as an instance of the earlier behavioral comparison process he describes.

3. Though legitimate and interesting in its own right, this interpretation precludes examination of the student's conception of ability because it rules out ability as a factor in performance. The explanation that the child does not cheat is intended to standardize the student's interpretations of stimuli: to reduce the chance of interpretations of stimuli that deviate from those we intend.

4. It is sometimes suggested that young children may not exhibit a concept of ability as capacity because they are constantly learning new things, whereas in adolescence the rate of acquisition of skills levels off.

This suggestion shows a misunderstanding of the concept, at least as it is defined and assessed here. First, the concept applies to a given performance situation rather than a long-term learning situation. It refers to present capacity rather than to inherited potential or long-term capacity to acquire knowledge or skill. Second, the concept refers to capacity relative to others, not to capacity to do anything or to improve at any task or range of tasks. The fact that one can improve at something does not invalidate or qualify the concept of present capacity. Children show a resilient faith in the power of effort to improve ability, whether or not they construe ability as capacity and regardless of their conceptions of intelligence. (See next Chapter.) But can we all improve at the same rate? The answer, for individuals at level 4 at least, is no, and this takes us back to the notion of capacity.

5. As I noted in Chapter 2, although one can obtain parallel age-related trends in meanings of concepts and in judgments or attributions involving these concepts, it is chancy to assume that one trend implies the other. It might make sense to think of causal attributions and attributions of amounts of ability, effort, or other factors as involving questions of function and to distinguish them from structural-developmental questions—questions about the meaning or intensive content of concepts (Nicholls, 1980b). Much might be gained by coordinating these two perspectives in the fashion of Selman and associates (1986).

6. In a more extensive study of fifth graders (unpublished) we found that students with the conception of ability as capacity ranked themselves as more able in school (Nicholls and Patashnick). They probably were, but here the important point is that this makes it unlikely that the more impaired performance of students with a more differentiated conception of ability would reflect lower perceived ability on their part.

5. Intelligence and Knowledge

1. This does not mean that there are no controversies about test-presentation strategies. For example, Wallach and Kogan (1965) created a stir by arguing that creative abilities need to be assessed in a play-like context rather than in the way intellectual abilities are normally assessed. But this dispute hinges on the question of what motivation is optimum for assessing creative ability, rather than on the principle that optimum motivation is necessary to reveal individual differences in current capacity.

2. One could not, given our purposes, simply ask students ques-

tions such as "What does it mean to be intelligent (or smart)? How can someone get more intelligent?" It would be very difficult to tell whether responses to these questions reflected conceptions of ability, conceptions of intelligence, or both. Subjects might also interpret a question of changeability as referring to changeability of biological potential, current skill level relative to others, or the possibility of learning new things even if one's standing doesn't change. The stimuli and questions we chose were intended to limit, as much as possible, the referents of childrens' responses to those of interest to us. This is not to say that other intellectual abilities do not deserve attention. It would be of interest, for example, to know how conceptions of social intelligence develop. Changes in conceptions of physical skills would also be of interest given the importance of physical skill in the eyes of many children and youths.

Dweck and Bempechat (1983) report a questionnaire measure of children's "theories of intelligence." This instrument presents students with the views of intelligence as an entity versus something that can be increased through effort. This method seems likely to confound conceptions of ability and intelligence. Students with the conception of ability as capacity still believe that capacity can be increased by learning or practice. They recognize, however, that at any time one's performance relative to others is limited by one's current capacity. Furthermore, some skills are seen as more readily changed than others and the ones grouped under "intelligence" vary with age. Thus the choice as proposed in the questionnaire might oversimplify students' conceptions. In any event, the absence of clear age-related trends in responses to this scale (Bempechat, 1985) indicates that it is not assessing anything like the conceptions of ability or intelligence discussed here. Nor does it resemble other indices of concepts of personal characteristics (Barenboim, 1981) which do show age-related change. None of this, however, rules out the possibility that any level of conception of either ability or intelligence might contain individual differences in beliefs about the changeability of different skills. Such differences would need to be distinguished from differences in perceived competence or beliefs about one's own chances of behaving intelligently.

3. The level 2 conception of intelligence also appears congruent with the second of three levels described by Leahy and Hunt (1983), where motivation is seen as a major difference between people who are "smart" and those who are not. Leahy and Hunt's interviews focused on students' understanding and use of the word "smart."

4. The differences between the concepts of intelligence and ability probably account for the fact that it proved more difficult to develop an adequate interview for conceptions of intelligence than for conceptions

of ability. It took several tries to get an interview on intelligence that produced transcripts that could be scored reliably (Nicholls et al., 1986).

5. I am grateful to Bernard Weiner for suggesting the line of reasoning of this paragraph.

6. The Task and the Self

1. Ultimately the value of any framework also depends on the competence with which it is employed. For us to act as if a chess-playing computer is trying to beat us is not enough to ensure a win. We must also have skill at chess. In the same way, the mere adoption of scientific stance that is relevant to one's goal will not ensure the accomplishment of that goal.

2. Effortful accomplishment will occasion a sense of competence provided that the effort does not reach a level that exhausts us (Harter, 1978). Note that this discussion of the relation between one's effort and feelings of competence refers to one attempt at a given task. If repeated attempts were made on a given task, competence would be indicated by reductions in time or effort needed for mastery. But such reductions are, presumably, themselves accomplished with effort.

3. Following Festinger (1954), a number of writers have implied certain achievement standards are inherent in tasks. Festinger makes his point with the example of jumping a stream—something one can or cannot do. But this concept of achievement standards begs the main question. It does not explain why one should want to jump the stream at one rather than another point of its course. Most rivers have a point near their source at which we might jump them and many more points where we have no chance. We need to know why one might seek to leap at a particular point. For instance, the need to escape from a bull or to avoid a physical education teacher's wrath might make the ability to leap a given stream at a given point highly desirable. But these needs are not inherent in the stream. The stream is mute on the matter of where we should be able to jump it or whether we should instead try to swim across it. We might choose to jump only at points that stretch our skills to the limit or only where most others have difficulty. But, again, these choices are not merely a function of the stream. Tasks and the standards whereby we judge performance are defined by people. This is not acknowledged in the concept of standards inherent in tasks.

4. When mastery motivation is defined as "the desire to solve cognitively challenging problems for the gratification in discovering the solution" (Harter, 1975, p. 186) the meaning matches that of task involve-

ment—provided "challenging" means personally challenging rather than normatively difficult. Various other meanings of mastery are inappropriate: for example, the connotations of dominance, as in "mastery over nature" and "Masters of the Universe." To a task-involved kayaker, the phrase "mastery of the river" would not be apt: his healthy respect for the river would make connotations of mastery inappropriate. The experience of running a river might, for task-involved individuals, be better characterized as being at one with the river or as transacting with it rather than mastering it. In education, mastery-learning programs also have connotations that are troublesome in this context. These programs embody the notion that knowledge is divisible into discrete units on which diligent work will produce mastery. The assumption is that the tasks and knowledge we might seek to master are "out there" in the world rather than constructed in the process of our attempts to make sense of our experience. (See Perry's levels of conception of knowledge discussed in Chapter 5.) Finally, mastery often refers to competent or adaptive performance (as opposed to displays of helplessness) without specifying the goal "behind" the performance.

5. The statement that individuals can use an undifferentiated conception of ability to evaluate their performance could be taken to imply that they will consciously evaluate their competence in terms of an undifferentiated conception. This meaning is not intended. An explicit or conscious concern about the adequacy of one's competence will tend to activate the conception of ability as capacity.

6. Although the interactions of type of involvement and level of effort were all significant, the differences between ability judgments in task involvement when effort was high and when it was low were not significant in all cases. This is perhaps not surprising, since we were asking how able an individual would feel in a given circumstance. Reflection on this question would tend to engage the differentiated conception.

7. It may or may not be true that anyone can get to be President, but we certainly can't all be President.

8. Consistent with other evidence (Spence and Helmreich, 1983; Veroff, 1977), males tended to score higher on Ego Orientation. They were also higher on Work Avoidance and lower on Task Orientation. These effects were not large. However, the main concern here and in later chapters is with correlates of these orientations. In this respect, males and females did not differ consistently.

9. The indices of intrinsic motivation used in these two studies differ from the Task Orientation scale used by Nicholls et al. (1985). Among other things, they assess a preference for difficult schoolwork as

part of intrinsic motivation. Students would probably interpret difficult as normatively difficult rather than personally challenging. A stronger preference for normatively difficult tasks would be expected among students of high rather than low perceived ability—even if they were all task-oriented. Thus items on an intrinsic motivation scale that refer to preference for difficult tasks could make for higher associations of such scales with perceived ability. This might explain why, with a sample of fifth and sixth graders, Meece and Blumenfeld (1987) found that perceived ability correlated .61 with Harter's Intrinsic vs. Extrinsic Motivation scale but only .22 with a version of our Task Orientation measure.

10. The intentional and ecological perspectives on social perception should not be confused with the view that attitudes and values influence one's explanations in a nonrational fashion. Much research has been done on the relationships between personality (or values) and attributions (Feather, 1985). But these relationships are not usually represented as indicative of conceptual coherence or rational connections between what is important to individuals, the data they collect, and the way they analyze those data. For further comments on the social and goal-directed nature of cognition, see Zukier (1986).

7. Choosing a Level of Challenge

1. Although consistent with the present position, the evidence on expectations of success contradicts a fundamental assumption of Atkinson's (1957) mathematical model: namely, that task "difficulty can be inferred from the subjective probability of success" (p. 362). To the contrary, individuals' subjective probabilities of success reflect their resultant motivation as well as the difficulty of the task they face. This result also threatens the implication of Atkinson's model that the differences between low- and high-resultant-motive individuals reflect differences in the values associated with success and failure rather than expectations of success and failure. Alternatively, in terms of Atkinson's position, the measure of resultant motivation lacks construct validity; it produces results that are not consistent with the description of this construct given by Atkinson. (A valid measure would not be correlated with expectations of success.)

2. Mehrabian's (1969) Resultant Achievement-Motivation scale has been used extensively. Many of its items elicit preferences for challenging skill tasks versus easy or nonskill tasks. Evidence that higher scorers on this scale choose more challenging tasks might, therefore, merely show that people do what they say they do. This is useful information but of

questionable relevance to achievement theory (Nicholls, Licht, and Pearl, 1982). Therefore studies of task choice using this scale are not considered.

3. In the method now commonly employed to estimate subjective probabilities of success, individuals who prefer tasks on which they have low or high success rates are assumed to prefer low or high probabilities. Deviations of individual preferences from group (rather than individual) performance means have also been employed to estimate preferred levels of probability of success (McClelland, 1958). This method appears to reflect the assumption (Atkinson, 1957) that "degree of difficulty can be inferred from the subjective probability of success" (p. 362). Because (as others have noted, Heckhausen, 1968) this method fails to deal with individual differences in expectation of success at any given difficulty level, I have not reviewed studies employing it.

4. Kukla and Scher (1986) claim that this prediction does not follow from Kukla's position. I relied on Kukla's Figure 3 (1978, p. 132) which, like the associated text, supports my interpretation.

8. Accomplishment

1. I do not mean to imply that all cases of impaired performance involve self-evaluation in terms of the conception of ability as capacity. Severe impairment can occur in young children who lack this conception (Chapter 4). Furthermore, when individuals are not ego involved, impairment can result from mere perception of the probability of failure. Miller (1986), for example, found females to show reduced performance when failure appeared most probable (in a difficult task) whereas the performance of males was reduced when failure would indicate low ability (at a moderate normative difficulty level). This could reflect a tendency, in at least some contexts, for females to be less prone to ego involvement (Miller, 1986; Spence and Helmreich, 1983; Veroff, 1977).

2. A number of researchers argue that when people face the prospect of appearing incompetent, they will reduce effort so that failure can be attributed to low effort—leaving one's perceived competence unthreatened (Covington and Omelich, 1979; Frankel and Snyder, 1978; Nicholls, 1984a). However, this self-handicapping phenomenon has not been convincingly demonstrated (Jagacinski and Nicholls, 1984b). This mechanism would be self-defeating if it were conscious: to decide to reduce effort to avoid recognizing oneself as incompetent is to acknowledge that one cannot establish one's competence by performing well. Although students see it as a strategy others might adopt, they do not see it as one they themselves would find useful (Jagacinski and Nicholls,

1984b). Furthermore, individuals in situations where low effort might avoid the implication of incompetence do not report reduced effort (Frankel and Snyder, 1978; Miller, 1985). It is more likely, from the present perspective, that a conscious withdrawal of effort will accompany (or be an expression of) the devaluing of tasks that should occur as individuals become convinced they are incompetent. Such a reduction of effort would, however, be irrational for people committed to establishing their competence at a task (except if success appeared virtually certain). This position is supported by the finding that questionnaire items indicating that one would feel successful if performing well with low effort loaded on both Avoidance of Work and Ego Orientation factors (Nicholls et al., 1988a).

3. It is unlikely that many individuals with the lowest level of perceived ability would enter college or survive there long enough to find themselves included in the studies that psychologists conduct. Such students probably play a negligible role in effects obtained with students simply identified as low in perceived ability.

4. These predictions of performance resemble those in Revelle and Michael's revision (1976) of Atkinson's theory. Like the original theory, the revision holds that task difficulty and subjective probability of success can be equated. Because these notions are not equivalent, the predictions of the theory are ambiguous. In this case I assume that Revelle and Michaels's predictions refer to normative task difficulty—the factor manipulated in relevant studies.

5. Kukla employed Mehrabian's (1969) Resultant Achievement Motivation Scale. High scores on this scale are gained by asserting a preference for challenging skill tasks. Thus the study can be said to show that those who prefer challenging tasks perform better on them, while those who do not prefer such tasks perform better on easy tasks. In this light resultant achievement motivation or perceived competence are marginally relevant to Kukla's results. With this caveat, the results are consistent with present predictions. This problem also occurs in various other studies of performance and preference for challenge that use other scales.

9. A Review of the Theories

1. It was not my intention to provide a comprehensive list of perspectives on achievement motivation (see Heckhausen, Schmalt, and Schneider, 1985; Schwarzer, 1986; Sorentino and Higgins, 1986).

2. Although Atkinson's model applies best to situations where

individuals are concerned about their competence relative to others, he introduces one of his volumes with the observation that "Achievement is a we thing, not a me thing, always the product of many heads and hands" (Atkinson, 1974, p. xi).

3. As Dweck and Elliot (1983) note, their predictions and mine are similar in a number of ways. But the logic behind them differs considerably. For example, they define learning and performance goals that resemble task and ego involvement. Performance goals are defined in terms of seeking favorable judgments of one's competence. Ego involvement, on the other hand, is defined by self-evaluation in terms of one's most differentiated conception of ability. The sort of competence that defines a performance goal is not specified or measured. This makes for some ambiguity about the criteria of success and failure (or self-evaluation) and in the derivations of predictions. (As noted, confusion has already resulted from the propensity to define difficulty and ability imprecisely and to employ different conceptions on different occasions without recognition of these fluctuations in meaning.)

To oppose a learning goal to a goal of establishing one's competence is to deny the prospect (which is part of the concept of task involvement) that one can gain a sense of competence through learning. In both task and ego involvement a sense of competence is the goal, but in task involvement the experience of learning brings with it enhanced feelings of competence. Feelings of competence are part of successful task-involved as well as ego-involved action. More and less differentiated conceptions of ability also play a key role in the generation of predictions of interest, task choice, and performance. They also link the developmental and general motivational frameworks. Conceptions of ability do not play these roles in Dweck's analysis.

A second point of difference concerns intelligence. For Dweck and Elliot students are said to differ in the "theories of intelligence" they espouse and bring to achievement situations. An entity theory represents intelligence as "a fixed, general, judgeable entity." An entity theory represents intelligence as "a fixed, general, judgeable entity." A second theory is that "intelligence is an ever-growing repertoire of skills and knowledge" (p. 654). Unlike more and less differentiated conceptions of ability in my position, these theories of intelligence do not serve as the basis for definition or description of goals (which is to say criteria of success and failure, or of self-evaluation). Nor are they used in the construction of predictions. Instead, they orient students toward different goals: the entity theory fosters performance goals and the "incremental" theory fosters learning goals. (To the extent that the theories of intelligence play this pivotal role, the perspective lacks applicability to activities in the performing arts and sport where intelligence plays a minor role.)

A number of readers have equated the incremental theory with undifferentiated conceptions of ability and the entity theory with the conception of ability as capacity. Neither the descriptions nor the measures are parallel. To date, we have no evidence that Dweck and Elliot's description of theories of intelligence captures the ways people construe intelligence and some evidence that it oversimplifies (Sternberg, et al., 1981). The measure designed to assess the two theories allows no options but these theories (Dweck and Bempechat, 1983). It does not show the age trends we have found for the conception of ability as capacity. The development of the conception of ability as capacity also takes a different course from that of the development of conceptions of fluid and crystallized intelligence (Chapter 5). The case for the two theories of intelligence is also clouded by the appeal to earlier evidence on age-related changes in ability attributions. One should not confuse conceptions of intelligence, conceptions of ability, and attributions (judgments) of ability (Chapters 4 and 5).

At the practical level, a significant difference is that Dweck advocates teaching students the incremental theory of intelligence (Dweck and Bempechat, 1983). Furthermore, Dweck (1986) advocates training students to attribute their failures to lack of effort—a strategy that does not emerge from my position.

4. For examinations of people's views about the place of their accomplishments in their lives, see Bellah et al. (1985), Sarason (1977), Weber (1958), and Willis (1977).

12. The Meaning of Life in School

1. Some of the Social Commitment items have an authoritarian ring. The finding that they elicited responses that were similar to the items without an authoritarian flavor is consistent with the notion that, in adolescence, the social good tends to be more closely bound up with ideas of duty and the maintenance of the established social order than it is at advanced levels of development (Kohlberg, 1969).

2. Stepwise regression analyses indicated that Wealth and Status made a unique contribution to prediction of Work Avoidance in each sample. Achievement Motivation also made a unique contribution to prediction of Work Avoidance in three samples and Understanding did in the fourth. Ego Orientation was predicted only by Wealth and Status in three samples and by Wealth and Status and Social Commitment in

the fourth. Task Orientation was predicted by Social Commitment and Achievement Motivation in School A and by Achievement Motivation in School B.

3. Critics who link the relatively low multiple choice achievement test scores of the present student population to the recent economic decline of the United States (National Commission on Excellence in Education, 1983), to which the students could not have contributed, inadvertently put in question the schooling of their own generation.

Bibliography

Abramson, L. Y., M. E. P. Seligman, and J. D. Teasdale. 1978. Learned helplessness in humans: Critique and reformulation. *Journal of Abnormal Psychology*, 87: 49–74.

Adams, J. F. 1968. An introduction to understanding adolescence. In J. F. Adams, ed., *Understanding adolescence*, pp. 1–12. Boston: Allyn and Bacon.

Allport, G. W. 1961. *Pattern and growth in personality*. New York: Holt, Rinehart, and Winston.

Alper, T. G. 1946. Task-orientation vs. ego-orientation in learning and retention. *American Journal of Psychology*, 59: 236–248.

Amabile, T. M. 1979. Effects of external evaluation on artistic creativity. *Journal of Personality and Social Psychology*, 37: 221–233.

—— 1983. *The social psychology of creativity*. New York: Springer-Verlag.

Ames, C. 1984a. Achievement attributions and self-instructions under competitive and individualistic goal structures. *Journal of Educational Psychology*, 76: 478–487.

—— 1984b. Competitive, cooperative, and individualistic goal structures: A cognitive-motivational analysis. In R. Ames and C. Ames, eds., *Research on motivation in education*, vol. 1, *Student motivation*, pp. 177–207. New York: Academic Press.

Ames, C., and R. Ames. 1981. Competitive versus individualistic goal structures: The salience of past performance information for causal attributions and affect. *Journal of Educational Psychology*, 73: 411–418.

—— 1984. Systems of student and teacher motivation: Toward a qualitative definition. *Journal of Educational Psychology*, 76: 535–556.

Ames, C., R. Ames, and D. W. Felker. 1977. Effects of competitive reward structure and valence of outcome on children's achievement attributions. *Journal of Educational Psychology*, 69: 1–8.

Ames, R. 1983. Help-seeking and achievement orientation: Perspectives from attribution theory. In B. DePaulo, A. Nadler, and J. Fisher, eds., *New directions in helping*, pp. 165–188. New York: Academic Press.

Ankeny, N. C. 1982. Using game theory, via poker to examine Reagan's fiscal '83 budget. *New York Times*, February 14.

Argyris, C. 1975. Dangers in applying results from experimental social psychology. *American Psychologist*, 30: 469–485.

Arkin, R. M., C. S. Detchon, and G. M. Maruyama. 1982. Roles of attribution, affect, and cognitive interference in test anxiety. *Journal of Personality and Social Psychology*, 43: 1111–24.

Arkin, R. M., T. A. Kolditz, and K. K. Kolditz. 1983. Attributions of the test anxious student: Self-assessment in the classroom. *Personality and Social Psychology Bulletin*, 9: 271–280.

Aronson, E., D. L. Bridgeman, and R. Geffner. 1978. The effects of a cooperative classroom on student behavior and attitudes. In D. Bar-Tal and L. Saxe, eds., *Social psychology of education: Theory and research*. Washington, D.C.: Hemisphere.

Asch, S. E. 1952. *Social psychology*. Englewood Cliffs, N.J.: Prentice-Hall.

Astin, A. 1983. A look at pluralism in the contemporary student population. *NASPA Journal*, 21, no. 3: 2–11.

Atkinson, J. W. 1957. Motivational determinants of risk-taking behavior. *Psychological Review*, 64: 359–372.

—— 1958. Toward an experimental analysis of human motives in terms of motives, expectancies, and incentives. In J. W. Atkinson, ed. *Motives in fantasy, action, and society*, pp. 288–305. New York: Van Nostrand.

—— 1969. Comments on papers by Crandall and Veroff. In C. P. Smith, ed., *Achievement-related motives in children*, pp. 200–212. New York: Russell Sage.

Atkinson, J. W., and N. T. Feather, eds. 1966. *A theory of achievement motivation*. New York: Wiley.

Atkinson, J. W., and J. O. Raynor, eds. 1974. *Motivation and achievement*, Washington, D.C.: V. H. Winston.

Ausubel, D. P., J. D. Novak, and H. Hanesian. 1978. *Educational psychology: A cognitive view*, 2d ed., New York: Holt, Rinehart, and Winston.

Bakan, D. 1968. *On method*. San Francisco: Jossey Bass.

Bandura, A. 1977. Self-efficacy: Toward a unifying theory of behavioral change. *Psychological Review*, 84: 191–215.

—— 1981. Self-referent thought: A developmental analysis of self-efficacy. In J. H. Flavell and L. Ross, eds. *Social cognitive development:*

Frontiers and possible futures, pp. 200–239. New York: Cambridge University Press.

Barenboim, C. 1981. The development of person perception in childhood and adolescence: From behavioral comparisons to psychological constructs to psychological comparisons. *Child Development*, 52: 129–144.

Bellah, R. H., R. Madsen, W. M. Sullivan, W. M. Swidler, and S. M. Tipton. 1985. *Habits of the heart: Individualism and commitment in American life*. Berkeley: University of California Press.

Bempechat, J. 1985. Children's theories of intelligence: Impact and development. Paper presented at the meeting of the Society for Research in Child Development, Toronto, April.

Berry, J. W. 1984. Towards a universal psychology of cognitive competence. *International Journal of Psychology*, 19: 335–361.

Bird, J. E. 1984. Development of children's understanding of the concepts "easy" and "hard" in judging task difficulty. Paper presented at the meeting of the American Educational Research Association, New Orleans, April.

Bloom, B. S. 1976. *Human characteristics and school learning*. New York: McGraw-Hill.

Blumenfeld, P. C., P. R. Pintrich, and V. L. Hamilton. 1986. Children's concepts of ability, effort, and conduct. *American Educational Research Journal*, 23: 95–104.

Boggiano, A. K., and D. S. Main. 1986. Enhancing children's interest in activities used as rewards: The bonus effect. *Journal of Personality and Social Psychology*, 51: 1116–26.

Boggiano, A. K., and D.N. Ruble. 1979. Competence and the overjustification effect. *Journal of Personality and Social Psychology*, 37: 1462–68.

Bossert, S. T. 1979. *Tasks and social relationships in classrooms: A study of instructional organization and its consequences*. New York: Cambridge University Press.

Bowles, S., and H. Gintis. 1976. *Schooling in capitalist America: Educational reform and the contradictions of economic life*. New York: Basic Books.

Brattesani, K. A., R. S. Weinstein, and H. H. Marshall. 1984. Student perceptions of differential teacher treatment as moderators of teacher expectation effects. *Journal of Educational Psychology*, 76: 236–247.

Bretherton, I., and M. Beeghly. 1982. Talking about internal states: The acquisition of an explicit theory of mind. *Developmental Psychology*, 18: 906–921.

Brockner, J. 1979. Self-esteem, self-consciousness, and task performance: Replications, extensions, and possible explanations. *Journal of Personality and Social Psychology*, 37: 447–461.

Brockner, J., and A. J. B. Hulton. 1978. How to reverse the vicious cycle of low self-esteem: The importance of attention focus. *Journal of Experimental Social Psychology*, 14: 564–578.

Brody, N. 1963. N-Achievement, test anxiety and subjective probability of success in risk taking behavior. *Journal of Abnormal and Social Psychology*, 66: 413–418.

Brophy, J. 1983. Research on the self-fulfilling prophecy and teacher expectations. *Journal of Educational Psychology*, 75: 631–661.

Brophy, J. E., and T. L. Good. 1974. *Teacher-student relationships: Causes and consequences.* New York: Holt, Rinehart, and Winston.

Brown, J., and B. Weiner. 1984. Affective consequences of ability versus effort ascriptions: Controversies, resolutions, and quandaries. *Journal of Educational Psychology*, 76: 146–158.

Bruner, J. S. 1972. Nature and uses of immaturity. *American Psychologist*, 27: 687–708.

Buckert, U., W.-U. Meyer, and H.-D. Schmalt. 1979. Effects of difficulty and diagnosity on choice among tasks in relation to achievement motivation and perceived ability. *Journal of Personality and Social Psychology*, 37: 1172–78.

Burton, D., and R. Martens. 1986. Pinned by their own goals: An exploratory investigation into why kids drop out of wrestling. *Journal of Sport Psychology*, 8: 183–197.

Butler, R. 1987. Task-involving and ego-involving properties of evaluation: The effects of different feedback conditions on motivational perceptions, interest and performance. *Journal of Educational Psychology*, 79: 474–482.

———— 1988. Enhancing and undermining intrinsic motivation: The effects of task-involving and ego-involving evaluation on interest and performance. *British Journal of Educational Psychology* (forthcoming).

Butler, R., and M. Nisan. 1986. Effects of no feedback, task-related comments, and grades on intrinsic motivation and performance. *Journal of Educational Psychology*, 78: 210–216.

Campbell, D. T. 1960. Blind variation and selective retention in creative thought as in other knowledge processes. *Psychological Review*, 67: 380–400.

Carnegie Forum on Education and the Economy. 1986. *Redesigning America's schools: The public speaks.* Report of a survey by Lou Harris and Associates for the Carnegie Forum on Education and the Economy.

Carnoy, M., and H. M. Levin. 1985. *Schooling and work in the democratic state.* Stanford, Calif.: Stanford University Press.

Carnoy, M., and D. Shearer. 1980. *Economic democracy: The challenge of the 1980s.* White Plains, N.Y.: M. E. Sharpe.

Carver, C. S. 1979. Cybernetic model of self-attention processes. *Journal of Personality and Social Psychology*, 37: 1251–81.

Carver, C. S., and M. F. Scheier. 1981. *Attention and self-regulation: A control-theory approach to human behavior.* New York: Springer-Verlag.

Casler, L. 1961. Maternal deprivation: A critical review of the literature. *Monographs of the Society for Research in Child Development*, 26 (2, Serial No. 80).

Chambers, J. A. 1964. Relating personality and biographical factors to scientific creativity. *Psychological Monographs*, 78, 7, no. 584, entire issue.

Chaumeton, N., and J. Duda. 1988. Is it how you play or whether you win? The effect of competitive level and situation on coaching behaviors. *Journal of Sport Behavior* (forthcoming).

Chen, M. J., V. Braithwaite, and T. H. Jong. 1982. Attributes of intelligent behavior: Perceived relevance and difficulty by Australian and Chinese students. *Journal of Cross-Cultural Psychology*, 13: 139–156.

Clark, B. 1982. Royal Robbins: From first ascents to first descents. *Canoe*, 10, no. 6: 8.

Clinchy, B., J. Lief, and P. Young. 1977. Epistemological and moral development in girls from a traditional and a progressive high school. *Journal of Educational Psychology*, 69: 337–343.

Clinkenbeard, P. R. 1984. *Effects of competitive and individualistic success on problem solving and motivation.* Ph.D. diss., Purdue University.

Cobb, P. 1986. Contexts, goals, beliefs, and learning mathematics. *For the Learning of Mathematics*, 6, no. 2: 2–9.

———— 1988. The tension between theories of learning and instruction in mathematics education. *Educational Psychologist* (forthcoming).

Cobb, P., T. Wood, and E. Yackel. 1988. A constructivist approach to second grade mathematics. In E. von Glasserfeld, ed., *Constructivism in mathematics education.* Holland: Reidel.

Cobb, P., E. Yackel, and T. Wood, 1988. Young children's emotional acts while doing mathematical problem solving. In D. B. McLeod and V. M. Adams, eds., *Affect and mathematical problem solving: A new perspective.* New York: Springer-Verlag.

Cohen, M. W., A. M. Emrich, and R. deCharms. 1976. Training teachers to enhance personal causation in students. *Interchange*, 7, no. 1: 34–38.

Coie, J. D. 1973. The motivation of exploration strategies in young children. *Genetic Psychology Monographs*, 87: 177–196.

Cole, M., and S. Scribner. 1974. *Culture and thought: A psychological introduction.* New York: Wiley.

Coleman, J. S. 1961. *The adolescent society: The social life of the teenager and its impact on education.* New York: Free Press.

Condry, J. D. and J. Chambers. 1978. Intrinsic motivation and the process of learning. In M. R. Lepper and D. Greene, eds., *The hidden costs of reward: New perspectives on the psychology of human motivation* (pp. 61–84). Hillsdale, N.J.: Erlbaum.

Connell, J. P., and R. M. Ryan. 1984. Motivation and internalization in the academic domain: The development of self-regulation. Paper presented at the meeting of the American Educational Research Association, New Orleans, April.

Cooper, A. C., W. C. Dunkelberg, and C. Y. Woo. 1988. Enterpreneur's perceived chances for success. *Journal of Business Venturing* (forthcoming).

Covington, M. V., and R. Beery. 1976. *Self-worth and school learning.* New York: Holt, Rinehart, and Winston.

Covington, M. V., and C. L. Omelich. 1979. Effort: The double-edged sword in school achievement. *Journal of Educational Psychology*, 71: 169–182.

Crandall, R. 1973. The measurement of self-esteem and related constructs. In J. P. Robinson and P. R. Shaver, eds., *Measures of social psychological attitudes*, pp. 45–168. Ann Arbor, Mich.: Institute for Social Research.

Cremin, L. A. 1961. *The transformation of the school: Progressivism in American education, 1876–1957.* New York: Knopf.

Crockenberg, S., and B. Bryant. 1978. Socialization: The "implicit curriculum" of learning environments. *Journal of Research and Development in Education*, 12: 69–77.

Crutchfield, R. S. 1962. Conformity and creative thinking. In H. E. Gruber, G. Terrell, and M. Wertheimer, eds., *Contemporary approaches to creative thinking*, pp. 120–140. New York: Prentice-Hall.

Csikszentmihalyi, M. 1977. *Beyond boredom and anxiety.* San Francisco: Jossey-Bass.

Damon, W. 1977. *The social world of the child.* San Francisco: Jossey-Bass.

Danner, F. W., and M. C. Day. 1977. Eliciting formal operations. *Child Development*, 48: 1600–6.

deCharms, R. 1968. *Personal causation: The internal affective determinants of behavior.* New York: Academic Press.

———— 1976. *Enhancing motivation: Change in the classroom.* New York: Irvington.

———— 1984. Motivation enhancement in educational settings. In R. Ames, and C. Ames, eds., *Research on motivation in education*, vol. 1, *Student motivation*, pp. 255–310. New York: Academic Press.

deCharms, R., and V. Carpenter. 1968. Measuring motivation in culturally disadvantaged school children. In H. J. Klausmeier and G. T. O'Hearn, eds., *Research and development toward the improvement of education*. Madison: Dembar Education Services.

deCharms, R., and P. N. Dave. 1965. Hope of success, fear of failure, subjective probability, and risk-taking behavior. *Journal of Personality and Social Psychology*, 1: 558–568.

Deci, E. L. 1975. *Intrinsic motivation*. New York: Plenum.

Deci, E. L., and R. M. Ryan. 1980. The empirical exploration of intrinsic motivational processes. *Advances in experimental social psychology*, 13: 39–80.

―――― 1985. *Intrinsic motivation and self-determination in human behavior*. New York: Plenum.

Deci, E. L., A. J. Schwartz, L. Sheinman, and R. M. Ryan. 1981. An instrument to assess adults' orientations toward control versus autonomy with children: Reflections on intrinsic motivation and perceived competence. *Journal of Educational Psychology*, 73: 642–650.

Deci, E. L., G. Betley, J. Kahle, L. Abrams, and J. Porac. When trying to win: Competition and intrinsic motivation. *Personality and Social Psychology Bulletin*, 7: 79–83.

Deci, E. L., N. H. Spiegel, R. M. Ryan, R. Koestner, and M. Kauffman. 1982. The effects of performance standards on controlling teachers. *Journal of Educational Psychology*, 74: 852–859.

de Groat, A. F., and G. G. Thompson. 1949. A study of the distribution of teacher approval and disapproval among sixth-grade pupils. *Journal of Experimental Education*, 18: 57–75.

Dennett, D. C. 1978. *Brainstorms: Philosophical essays on mind and psychology*. Montgomery, Vt.: Bradford.

Dewey, J. 1963. *Experience and education*. New York: Collier Books Edition (original ed., 1938).

―――― 1966. *Democracy and education*. New York: Free Press (original ed., 1916).

Diener, E., and T. K. Srull. 1979. Self-awareness, psychological perspective, and self-reinforcement in relation to personal and social standards. *Journal of Personality and Social Psychology*, 37: 413–423.

Doise, W., and G. Mugny. 1984. *The social development of the intellect*, trans. A. St. James-Emler, N. Emler, and D. Mackie. New York: Pergamon (original ed., 1981).

Dore, R. 1976. *The diploma disease: Education, qualification, and development*. Berkeley: University of California Press.

Dreikurs, R., B. B. Grunwald, and F. C. Pepper. 1982. *Maintaining sanity in the classroom: Classroom management techniques*, 2d ed. New York: Harper and Row.

Duda, J. L. 1985. The relationship between motivational perspective and participation and persistence in sport. Paper presented at the meeting of the Canadian Society for Psychomotor Learning and Sport Psychology, Montreal, October.

———— 1986. A cross-cultural analysis of achievement motivation in sport and the classroom. L. Vandervelden and J. Humphrey, eds., *Current selected research in the psychology and sociology of sport*, 115–132. New York: AMS Press.

———— 1988. The relationship between goal perspectives, persistence, and behavioral intensity among recreational sport participants. *Leisure Sciences* (forthcoming).

Dweck, C. S. 1975. The role of expectations and attributions in the alleviation of learned helplessness. *Journal of Personality and Social Psychology*, 31: 674–685.

———— 1985. Intrinsic motivation, perceived control, and self-evaluation maintenance: An achievement goal analysis. In C. Ames and R. Ames, eds., *Research on motivation in education*, vol. 2, *The classroom milieu*, pp. 289–305. New York: Academic Press.

Dweck, C. S. 1986. Motivational processes affecting learning. *American Psychologist*, 41: 1040–1048.

Dweck, C. S., and J. Bempechat. 1983. Children's theories of intelligence: Consequences for learning. In S. G. Paris, G. M. Olson, and H. W. Stevenson, eds., *Learning and motivation in the classroom*, pp. 239–256. Hillsdale, N.J.: Erlbaum.

Dweck, C. S. and E. Elliot. 1983. Achievement motivation. In M. Hetherington, ed., *Handbook of child psychology*, 4th ed., IV, 643–691. New York: Wiley.

Eby, F., and C. F. Arrowood. 1940. *The history and philosophy of education: Ancient and medieval*. Englewood Cliffs, N.J.: Prentice-Hall.

Eccles, J., C. Midgley, and T. F. Adler. 1984. Grade-related changes in the school environment: Effects on achievement motivation. In J. G. Nicholls, ed., *Advances in motivation and achievement*, vol. 3, *The development of achievement motivation*, pp. 283–331. Greenwich, Conn.: JAI Press.

Edelman, M. S., and D. R. Omark. 1973. Dominance hierarchies in young children. *Social Science Information*, 12: 103–110.

Einstein, A. 1956. *Out of my later years*, Secaucus, N.J.: Citadel Press.

Elkind, D. 1969. Conservation and concept formation. In D. Elkind and J. H. Flavell, eds., *Studies in cognitive development: Essays in honor of Jean Piaget*, pp. 171–189. New York: Oxford University Press.

———— 1971. Cognitive growth cycles in mental development. In J. K. Cole, ed., *Nebraska symposium on motivation*, pp. 1–31. Lincoln: University of Nebraska Press.

———— 1976. *Child development and education: A Piagetian perspective.* New York: Oxford University Press.

Elkind, D., J. Deblinger, and D. Adler. 1970. Motivation and creativity: The context effect. *American Educational Research Journal,* 7: 351–357.

Entin, E. E., and J. O. Raynor. 1973. Effects of contingent future orientation and achievement motivation on performance in two kinds of task. *Journal of Experimental Research in Personality,* 6: 314–320.

Erikson, E. 1963. *Childhood and society,* 2d ed. New York: Norton.

Eshel, Y., and Z. Klein. 1981. Development of academic self-concept of lower-class and middle-class primary school children. *Journal of Educational Psychology,* 73: 287–293.

Ewing, M. E. 1981. *Achievement orientations and sport behavior of males and females.* Ph.D. diss., University of Illinois.

Feather, N. T. 1965. The relationship of expectation of success to need achievement and test anxiety. *Journal of Personality and Social Psychology,* 1: 118–126.

———— 1975. *Values in education and society.* New York: Free Press.

———— 1985. Attitudes, values, and attributions: Explanations of unemployment. *Journal of Personality and Social Psychology,* 48: 876–889.

Feinberg, W. 1983. *Understanding education.* Cambridge: Cambridge University Press.

Festinger, L. 1954. A theory of social comparison processes. *Human Relations,* 7: 117–140.

Fine, M. 1981. Perspectives on inequity: Voices from urban schools. In L. Bickman, ed., *Applied social psychology annual IV,* pp. 217–246. Beverly Hills: Sage.

Finkelstein, N. W., and C. T. Ramey. 1977. Learning to control the environment in infancy. *Child Development,* 48: 806–814.

Flavell, J. H., and E. M. Markman. 1983. Preface. In J. H. Flavell and E. M. Markham, eds., *Handbook of child psychology,* 4th ed., vol. 3, *Cognitive development,* pp. viii–x. New York: Wiley.

Forsterling, F. 1985. Attribution retraining: A review. *Psychological Bulletin,* 98: 495–512.

Fowler, J. W., and P. L. Peterson. 1981. Increasing reading persistence and altering attributional style of learned helpless children. *Journal of Educational Psychology,* 73: 251–260.

Frankel, A., and M. L. Snyder. 1978. Poor performance following unsolvable problems: Learned helplessness or egotism? *Journal of Personality and Social Psychology,* 36: 1415–23.

Fredericksen, N. 1984. The real test bias: Influences of testing on teaching and learning. *American Psychologist,* 39: 193–202.

Freedman, D. G. 1975. The development of social hierarchies. In L. Levi, ed., *Society, stress, and disease*, vol. 2, *Childhood and adolescence*, pp. 303–312. London: Oxford University Press.

Frey, K. S., and D. N. Ruble. 1985. What children say when the teacher is not around: Conflicting goals in social comparison and performance assessment in the classroom. *Journal of Personality and Social Psychology*, 48: 550–562.

Friedenberg, E. Z. 1963. *Coming of age in America*. New York: Vintage Books.

Frieze, I. H., W. D. Francis, and B. H. Hanusa. 1983. Defining success in classroom settings. In J. M. Levine and M. C. Wang, eds., *Teacher and student perceptions: Implications for learning*, pp. 3–28. Hillsdale, N.J.: Erlbaum.

Fromm, E. 1941. *The fear of freedom*. London: Routledge and Kegan Paul.

Furth, H. G. 1981. *Piaget and knowledge: Theoretical foundations*, 2d ed. Chicago: University of Chicago Press.

Ganzer, V. J. 1968. Effects of audience presence and test anxiety on learning and retention in a serial learning situation. *Journal of Personality and Social Psychology*, 8: 194–199.

Garbarino, J., and C. E. Asp. 1981. *Successful schools and competent students*. Lexington, Mass.: Lexington Books.

Garcia, J. 1981. Tilting at the paper mills of academe. *American Psychologist*, 36: 149–158.

Gelman, R., and R. Baillargeon. 1983. A review of some Piagetian concepts. In J. H. Flavell and E. M. Markman, eds., *Handbook of child psychology*, 4th ed., vol. 3, *Cognitive development*, pp. 167–230. New York: Wiley.

Geppert, U., and U. Kuster. 1983. The emergence of 'wanting to do it oneself': A precursor of achievement motivation. *International Journal of Behavioral Development*, 6: 355–369.

Giroux, H. A. 1983. Theories of reproduction and resistance in the new sociology of education: A critical analysis. *Harvard Educational Review*, 53: 257–293.

——— 1984. Public philosophy and the crisis in education. *Harvard Educational Review*, 54: 186–194.

Gjesme, T. 1974. Goal distance in time and its effects on the relations between achievement motives and performance. *Journal of Research in Personality*, 8: 161–171.

Good, T. L. 1980. Teacher expectations, teacher behavior, student perceptions, and student behavior: A decade of research. Invited address presented at the meeting of the American Educational Research Association, Boston.

Good, T. L., and S. Marshall. 1984. Do students learn more in heterogeneous or homogeneous groups? In P. L. Peterson, L. C. Wilkinson, and M. Hallinan, eds., *The social context of instruction: Group organization and group process*, pp. 15–38. New York: Academic Press.

Goodlad, J. I. 1983. *A place called school: Prospects for the future*. New York: McGraw-Hill.

Goodnow, J. J. 1980. Everyday concepts of intelligence and its development. In N. Warren, ed., *Studies in cross-cultural psychology*, I, 191–219. New York: Academic Press.

Gottfried, A. E. 1982. Relationships between academic intrinsic motivation and anxiety in children and young adolescents. *Journal of School Psychology*, 20: 205–215.

——— 1985. Academic intrinsic motivation in elementary and junior high school students. *Journal of Educational Psychology*, 77: 631–645.

Gray, P., and D. Chanoff. 1986. Democratic schooling: What happens to young people who have charge of their own education? *American Journal of Education*, 94: 182–213.

Greenberg, E. S. 1984. Producer cooperatives and democratic theory: The case of the plywood firms. In R. Jackall and H. M. Levin, eds., *Worker cooperatives in America*, pp. 171–214. Berkeley: University of California Press.

Greenberg, P. J. 1932. Competition in children: An experimental study. *American Journal of Psychology*, 44: 221–248.

Greenwald, A. G. 1982. Ego task analysis: An integration of research on ego-involvement and self-awareness. In A. Hastorf and A. Isen, eds., *Cognitive social psychology*. New York: Elsevier/North Holland.

Grolnick, W. S., and R. M. Ryan. 1987. Autonomy in children's learning: An experimental and individual difference investigation. *Journal of Personality and Social Psychology*, 52: 890–898.

Gunn, C. E. 1984. *Workers' self-management in the United States*. Ithaca, N.Y.: Cornell University Press.

Guthrie, L. F., J. R. Mergendoller, C. D. Leventhal, D. P. Kauchak, and T. S. Rounds. 1984. *Opportunity systems in high school science*. San Francisco: Far West Laboratory for Educational Research and Development.

Hadley, A. T. 1987. Questions about the Stark. *New York Times*, June 10, p. 27.

Halford, G. S., and F. M. Boyle. 1985. Do young children understand conservation of number? *Child Development*, 56: 165–176.

Hamilton, J. O. 1974. Motivation and risk taking behavior: A test of Atkinson's theory. *Journal of Personality and Social Psychology*, 29: 856–864.

Harackiewicz, J. M., S. Abrahams, and R. Wageman. 1988. Performance evaluation and intrinsic motivation: The effects of evaluative focus, rewards, and achievement motivation. *Journal of Personality and Social Psychology* (forthcoming).

Harackiewicz, J. M., G. Manderlink, and C. Sansone. 1984. Rewarding pinball wizardry: Effects of evaluation and cue value on intrinsic interest. *Journal of Personality and Social Psychology*, 47: 287–300.

Harari, O., and M. V. Covington. 1981. Reactions to achievement behavior from a teacher and student perspective: A developmental analysis. *American Educational Research Journal*, 18: 15–28.

Harlow, H. F. 1950. Learning and satiation of response in intrinsically motivated complex puzzle performance by monkeys. *Journal of Comparative and Physiological Psychology*, 43: 289–294.

Harter, S. 1975. Developmental differences in the manifestation of mastery motivation on problem solving tasks. *Child Development*, 46: 370–378.

———— 1978. Pleasure derived from challenge and the effects of receiving grades on children's difficulty level choices. *Child Development*, 49: 788–789.

Harter, S., and J. P. Connell. 1984. A model of the relationships among children's academic achievement and their self-perceptions of competence, control and motivational orientation. In J. G. Nicholls, ed., *Advances in motivation and achievement*, vol. 3, *The development of achievement motivation*, pp. 219–250. Greenwich, Conn.: JAI Press.

Harvey, O. J., D. E. Hunt, and H. M. Schroder. 1961. *Conceptual systems and personality organization*. New York: Wiley.

Harvey, O. J., M. Prather, B. J. White, and J. K. Hoffmeister. 1968. Teachers' beliefs, classroom atmosphere, and student behavior. *American Educational Research Journal*, 5: 151–165.

Harvey, O. J., B. J. White, M. Prather, R. D. Alter, and J. K. Hoffmeister. 1966. "Teachers" belief systems and preschool atmospheres. *Journal of Educational Psychology*, 57: 373–381.

Hearnshaw, L. S. 1979. *Cyril Burt: Psychologist*. Ithaca, N.Y.: Cornell University Press.

Heckhausen, H. 1968. Achievement motive research: Current problems and some contributions toward a general theory of motivation. In W. J. Arnold, ed., *Nebraska symposium on motivation*, pp. 103–174. Lincoln: University of Nebraska Press.

———— 1982. The development of achievement motivation. In W. W. Hartup, ed., *Review of Child Development Research*, VI, 600–668. Chicago: University of Chicago Press.

———— 1984. Emergent achievement behavior: Some early developments.

In J. G. Nicholls, ed., *Advances in motivation and achievement*, vol. 3, *The development of achievement motivation*, pp. 1–32. Greenwich, Conn.: JAI Press.

Heckhausen, H., and S. Krug. 1982. Motive modification. In A. Stewart, ed., *Motivation and society: Essays in honor of David C. McClelland*, pp. 274–318. San Francisco: Jossey-Bass.

Heckhausen, H., H. D. Schmalt, and K. Schneider. 1985. *Achievement motivation in perspective*, trans. M. Woodruff and R. Wicklund. New York: Academic Press.

Helmke, A., W. Schneider, and F. E. Weinert. 1986a. Main results of the German IEA classroom environment study and implications for teaching. Paper presented at the meeting of the American Educational Research Association, San Francisco.

———— 1986b. Quality of instruction and classroom learning outcomes: The German contribution to the IEA classroom environment study. *Teaching and Teacher Education*, 62: 1–18.

Helmreich, R. L., and J. T. Spence. 1977. The secret of success. *Discovery: Research and Scholarship at the University of Texas at Austin*, 11, no. 2: 4–7.

———— 1978. The Work and Family Orientation Questionnaire: An objective instrument to assess components of achievement motivation and attitudes toward family and career. *JSAS Catalog of Selected Documents in Psychology*, 35 manuscript no. 1677.

Helmreich, R. L., J. T. Spence, W. E. Beane, G. W. Lucker, and K. A. Matthews. 1980. Making it in academic psychology: Demographic and personality correlates of attainment. *Journal of Personality and Social Psychology*, 39: 896–908.

Helson, R. 1971. Women mathematicians and the creative personality. *Journal of Consulting and Clinical Psychology*, 36: 210–220.

Helson, R., and R. S. Crutchfield. 1970. Mathematicians: The creative researcher and the average Ph.D. *Journal of Consulting and Clinical Psychology*, 34: 250–257.

Hoffman, C., W. Mischel, and K. Mazze. 1981. The role of purpose in the organization of information about behavior: Trait-based versus goal-based categories in person cognition. *Journal of Personality and Social Psychology*, 40: 211–225.

Holt, J. 1964. *How children fail*. New York: Dell.

Hood, L., R. McDermott, and M. Cole. 1980. "Let's try to make it a good day"—some not so simple ways. *Discourse Processes*, 3: 155–168.

Horn, J. L. 1968. Organization of abilities and the development of intelligence. *Psychological Review*, 75: 242–259.

Horwitz, R. A. 1979. Effects of the "open classroom." In H. J. Walberg, ed., *Educational environments and effects*, pp. 275–292. Berkeley, Calif.: McCutchan.

Hunt, D., and B. Joyce. 1967. Teacher trainee personality and initial teaching style. *American Educational Research Journal*, 4: 253–259.

Hunt, J. Mc V. 1963. Piaget's observations as a source of hypotheses concerning motivation. *Merrill-Palmer Quarterly*, 9: 263–275.

Huntford, R. 1985. *The last place on earth*. New York: Atheneum. (Originally published as *Scott and Amundsen*, 1983, Atheneum.)

Indiana Conference of Higher Education. 1984. Take the first step. (Statewide newspaper supplement.) West Lafayette, In.

Inhelder, B., and J. Piaget. 1958. *The growth of logical thinking: From childhood to adolescence*, trans. A. Parsons and S. Milgram. London: Routledge and Kegan Paul.

Inhelder, B., H. Sinclair, and M. Bovet. 1974. *Learning and the development of cognition*. Cambridge, Mass.: Harvard University Press.

Jackall, R. J. and H. M. Levin, eds. 1984. *Worker cooperatives in America*. Berkeley: University of California Press.

Jackson, B., and D. Marsden. 1962. *Education and the working class*. London: Routledge and Kegan Paul.

Jackson, P. W. 1968. *Life in classrooms*. New York: Holt, Rinehart, and Winston.

Jackson, P. W., and J. W. Getzels. 1959. Psychological health and classroom functioning: A study of dissatisfaction with school among adolescents. *Journal of Educational Psychology*, 50: 295–300.

Jagacinski, C. M., and J. G. Nicholls. 1984a. Conceptions of effort and ability and related affects in task-involvement and ego-involvement. *Journal of Educational Psychology*, 76: 909–919.

—— 1984b. Reducing effort to protect perceived ability: "They'd do it, but I wouldn't." Paper presented at the meeting of the American Educational Research Association, New Orleans, April.

Johnson, C. N., and H. M. Wellman. 1980. Children's developing understanding of mental verbs: Remember, know, and guess. *Child Development*, 51: 1095–1102.

Johnson, D. W., and R. T. Johnson. 1985. Motivational processes in cooperative, competitive, and individualistic learning situations. In R. Ames and C. Ames, eds., *Research on motivation in education*, vol. 2, *The classroom milieu*, pp. 249–286. New York: Academic Press.

Johnson, D. W., R. T. Johnson, and L. Scott. 1978. The effects of cooperative and individualized instruction on student attitudes and achievement. *Journal of Social Psychology*, 104: 207–216.

Jopt, J. U. 1974. *Extrinsiche motivation und leistungsverhalten.* Doctoral diss., Ruhr University Bochum, West Germany.

Jussim, L. 1986. Self-fulfilling prophecies: A theoretical and integrative review. *Psychological Review*, 93: 429–445.

Kagan, J. 1981. *The second year of life: The emergence of self-awareness.* Cambridge, Mass.: Harvard University Press.

Kagan, S. 1985. Coop coop: A flexible cooperative learning technique. In R. Slavin, S. Sharan, S. Kagan, R. Hertz-Lazarowitz, C. Webb, and R. Schmuck, eds., *Learning to cooperate, cooperating to learn*, pp. 437–452. New York: Plenum.

Kamii, C. 1985. *Young children reinvent arithematic: Implications of Piaget's theory.* New York: Teachers College Press.

Karabenick, S. A., and Z. I. Youssef. 1968. Performance as a function of achievement motive level and perceived difficulty. *Journal of Personality and Social Psychology*, 10: 414–419.

Kelley, H. 1973. The process of causal attribution. *American Psychologist*, 28: 107–128.

Kernis, M. H., M. Zuckerman, A. Cohen, and S. Spadafora. 1982. Persistence following failure: The interactive role of self-awareness and the attributional basis for negative expectancies. *Journal of Personality and Social Psychology*, 43: 1184–91.

Kleiber, D. A., and G. C. Roberts. 1988. High school play: Putting it to work in organized sport. In J. Block and N. King, eds., *School play.* New York: Garland.

Klein, G. S., and N. Schoenfeld. 1941. The influence of ego-involvement on confidence. *Journal of Abnormal and Social Psychology*, 36: 249–258.

Klinger, E. 1975. Consequences of commitment to and disengagement from incentives. *Psychological Review*, 82: 1–25.

Klinger, E., and F. W. McNelley. 1969. Fantasy need achievement and performance: A role analysis. *Psychological Review*, 76: 574–591.

Koch, S. 1956. Behavior as intrinsically regulated: Work notes toward a pre-theory of phenomena called "motivational." In M. R. Jones, ed., *Nebraska symposium on motivation*, pp. 42–87. Lincoln: University of Nebraska Press.

Koenigs, S., M. Fiedler, and R. deCharms. 1977. Teacher beliefs, classroom interaction and personal causation. *Journal of Applied Social Psychology*, 7: 95–114.

Koestner, R., M. Zuckerman, and J. Koestner. 1987. Praise, involvement, and intrinsic motivation. *Journal of Personality and Social Psychology*, 53: 383–390.

Koestner, R., R. M. Ryan, F. Bernieri, and K. Holt. 1984. Setting limits on children's behavior: The differential effects of controlling vs. informational styles on intrinsic motivation and creativity. *Journal of Personality*, 53: 233–248.

Kohlberg, L. 1969. Stage and sequence: The cognitive-developmental approach to socialization. In D. A. Goslin, ed., *Handbook of socialization theory and research*, pp. 347–480. Chicago: Rand McNally.

Kohlberg, L., and R. Mayer. 1972. Development as the aim of education. *Harvard Educational Review*, 42: 449–496.

Kohlberg, L., C. Levine, and A. Hewer. 1983. *Moral stages: A current formulation and a response to critics.* New York: S. Karger.

Kroll, M. 1988. Motivational orientations, views about the purpose of education, and intellectual styles. *Psychology in the Schools* (forthcoming).

Kruglanski, A. W. 1975. The endogenous-exogenous partition in attribution theory. *Psychological Review*, 82: 387–406.

Kuhl, J. 1981. Motivational and functional helplessness: The moderating effect of state versus action orientation. *Journal of Personality and Social Psychology*, 40: 155–170.

Kuhn D. 1972. Mechanisms of change in the development of cognitive structures. *Child Development*, 43: 833–844.

————— 1974. Inducing development experimentally: Comments on a research paradigm. *Developmental Psychology*, 10: 590–600.

Kuhn, D., and V. Ho. 1980. Self-directed activity in cognitive development. *Journal of Applied Developmental Psychology*, 1: 119–133.

Kuhn, T. S. 1970. *The structure of scientific revolutions*, 2d ed. Chicago: University of Chicago Press.

Kukla, A. 1972. Foundations of an attributional theory of performance. *Psychological Review*, 79: 454–470.

————— 1974. Performance as a function of resultant achievement motivation (perceived ability) and perceived difficulty. *Journal of Research in Personality*, 7: 374–383.

————— 1978. An attributional theory of choice. In L. Berkowitz, ed., *Advances in experimental social psychology*, vol. 11. New York: Academic Press.

Kukla, A., and H. Scher. 1986. Varieties of achievement motivation. *Psychological Review*, 93: 378–380.

Kun, A. 1977. Development of the magnitude-covariation and compensation schemata in ability and effort attributions of performance. *Child Development*, 48: 862–873.

Kurfiss, J. 1977. Sequentiality and structure in a cognitive model of college student development. *Developmental Psychology*, 13: 565–571.

Lanzetta, J. T., and T. E. Hannah. 1969. Reinforcing behavior of "naive" trainers. *Journal of Personality and Social Psychology*, 11: 245–252.

Langer, E. J. 1975. The illusion of control. *Journal of Personality and Social Psychology*, 32: 311–328.

Lapham, L. H. 1986. Is there virtue in profit? *Harper's*, December, 37–47.

Larsen, G. Y. 1977. Methodology in development psychology: An examination of research on Piagetian theory. *Child Development*, 48: 1160–66.

Lazerson, M., J. B. McLaughlin, B. McPherson, and S. K. Bailey. 1985. *An education of value: The purposes and practices of schools.* New York: Cambridge University Press.

Leahy, R. L., and T. M. Hunt. 1983. A cognitive developmental approach to the development of conceptions of intelligence. In R. L. Leahy, ed., *The child's construction of social inequality*, pp. 135–160. New York: Academic Press.

Lepper, M. R., and D. Greene. 1975. Turning play into work: Effects of adult surveillance and extrinsic rewards on children's intrinsic motivation. *Journal of Personality and Social Psychology*, 31: 479–486.

————, eds. 1978. *The hidden costs of reward: New perspectives on the psychology of human motivation.* Hillsdale, N.J.: Erlbaum.

Lepper, M. R., L. Ross, and R. R. Lau. 1986. Persistence of inaccurate beliefs about the self: Perseverance effects in the classroom. *Journal of Personality and Social Psychology*, 50: 482–491.

Leuba, C. 1933. An experimental study of rivalry in young children. *Journal of Comparative Psychology*, 10: 367–378.

Levin, H. M. 1984. Employment and productivity of producer cooperatives. In R. Jackall and H. M. Levin, eds., *Worker cooperatives in America*, pp. 16–31. Berkeley: University of California Press.

Levine, J. M. 1983. Social comparison and education. In J. M. Levine and M. C. Wang, eds., *Teacher and student perceptions: Implications for learning*, pp. 29–55. Hillsdale, N.J.: Erlbaum.

Lewis, M., and J. Brooks-Gunn. 1979. *Social cognition and the acquisition of self.* New York: Plenum.

Liebert, R. M., and L. W. Morris. 1967. Cognitive and emotional components of test anxiety: A distinction and some initial data. *Psychological Reports*, 20: 975–978.

Lightfoot, S. L. 1983. *The good high school: Portraits of character and culture.* New York: Basic Books.

MacKinnon, D. W. 1965. Personality and the realization of creative potential. *American Psychologist*, 20: 273–281.

Maehr, M. L. 1976. Continuing motivation: An analysis of a seldom considered educational outcome. *Review of Educational Research*, 46: 443–462.

—— 1983. On doing well in science: Why Johnny no longer excels; why Sarah never did. In S. G. Paris, G. M. Olson, and H. W. Stevenson, eds., *Learning and motivation in the classroom*, pp. 179–210. Hillsdale, N.J.: Erlbaum.

Maehr, M. L., and L. A. Braskamp. 1986. *The motivation factor: A theory of personal investment*. Lexington, Mass.: Lexington Books.

Maehr, M. L., and J. G. Nicholls. 1980. Culture and achievement motivation: A second look. In N. Warren, ed., *Studies in cross-cultural psychology*, pp. 221–267. New York: Academic Press.

Maehr, M. L., and W. M. Stallings. 1972. Freedom from eternal evaluation. *Child Development*, 43: 177–185.

Mahone, C. H. 1960. Fear of failure and unrealistic vocational aspiration. *Journal of Abnormal and Social Psychology*, 60: 253–261.

Marecek, J., and D. R. Mettee. 1972. Avoidance of continued success as a function of self-esteem, level of self-esteem certainty, and responsibility for success. *Journal of Personality and Social Psychology*, 22: 98–107.

Marshall, H. M., and R. S. Weinstein. 1984. Classroom factors affecting students' self-evaluations: An interactional model. *Review of Educational Research*, 54: 301–325.

Marx, R. W. 1985. Classroom organization and perceptions of student academic and social status. In I. E. Housego and P. P. Grimmett, eds., *Teaching and teacher education: Generating and utilizing valid knowledge for professional socialization*, pp. 75–109. Vancouver: University of British Columbia Press.

McArthur, L. Z., and R. M. Baron. 1983. Toward an ecological theory of social perception. *Psychological Review*, 90: 215–283.

McCann, J., and P. Bell. 1975. Educational environment and the development of moral concepts. *Journal of Moral Education*, 5: 63–70.

McClelland, D. C. 1958. Risk taking in children with high and low need for achievement. In J. W. Atkinson, ed., *Motives in fantasy, action, and society*, pp. 306–321. New York: Van Nostrand.

McCurdy, H. G. 1960. The childhood pattern of genius. *Horizon*, 2: 33–38.

McDermott, R. P., and L. Hood. 1982. Institutionalized psychology and the ethnography of schooling. In P. Gilmore and A. A. Glatthorn, eds., *Children in and out of school: Ethnography and education*, pp. 232–249. Washington, D.C.: Center for Applied Linguistics.

McFarland, C., and M. Ross. 1982. Impact of causal attributions on affective reactions to success and failure. *Journal of Personality and Social Psychology*, 43: 937–946.

McFarlin, D. B., and J. Blascovich. 1981. Effects of self-esteem and performance feedback on future affective preferences and cognitive expectations. *Journal of Personality and Social Psychology*, 40: 521–531.

McKinney, J. P., and D. Moore. 1982. Attitudes and values during adolescence. In B. B. Wolman, ed., *Handbook of developmental psychology*, pp. 549–558. Englewood Cliffs, N.J.: Prentice-Hall.

Meece, J. L., and P. C. Blumenfeld. 1987. Elementary school children's motivational orientation and patterns of engagement in classroom activities. Paper presented at the meeting of the American Educational Research Association, Washington, D.C., April.

Mehrabian, A. 1969. Measures of achieving tendency. *Educational and Psychological Measurement*, 29: 445–451.

Meyer, W.-U. 1987. Perceived ability and achievement-related behavior. In F. Halish and J. Kuhl, eds. *Motivation, intention and volition*, pp. 73–86. Berlin: Springer-Verlag.

Meyer, W.-U., V. Folkes, and B. Weiner. 1976. The perceived informational value and affective consequences of choice behavior and intermediate difficulty task selection. *Journal of Research in Personality*, 10: 410–423.

Miller, A. T. 1985. A developmental study of the cognitive basis of performance impairment after failure. *Journal of Personality and Social Psychology*, 49: 529–538.

―――― 1986. Performance impairment after failure: Mechanism and sex differences. *Journal of Educational Psychology*, 78: 486–491.

―――― 1988. Changes in academic self-concept in early school years. The role of conceptions of ability. *Journal of Social Behavior and Personality* (forthcoming).

Miller, A. T., and J. Klein. 1986. Individual differences in value of demonstrating ability and persistence after failure. Manuscript, Southwest Missouri State University.

Miller, J. G. 1984. Culture and the development of everyday social explanation. *Journal of Personality and Social Psychology*, 46: 961–978.

Miller, R. L., P. Brickman, and D. Bolen. 1975. Attribution versus persuasion as a means for modifying behavior. *Journal of Personality and Social Psychology*, 31: 430–441.

Miller, S. A., and C. A. Brownell. 1975. Peers, persuasion, and Piaget: Dyadic interaction between conservers and nonconservers.*Child Development*, 46: 992–997.

Minuchin, P., B. Biber, E. Shapiro, and H. Zimilies. 1969. *The psychological impact of school experience*. New York: Basic Books.

Mischel, W. 1977. On the future of personality measurement. *American Psychologist*, 32: 246–254.

Morris, L. W., M. A. Davis, and C. H. Hutchings. 1981. Cognitive and emotional components of anxiety. Literature review and a revised worry-emotionality scale. *Journal of Educational Psychology*, 73: 541–555.

Morris, W. N., and D. Nemcek. 1982. The development of social comparison motivation among preschoolers: Evidence of a stepwise progression. *Merrill-Palmer Quarterly*, 28: 413–425.

Morrison, H., and D. Kuhn. 1983. Cognitive aspects of preschoolers' peer imitation in a play situation. *Child Development*, 54: 1041–53.

Moskowitz, J. M., J. H. Malvin, G. A. Schaeffer, and E. Schaps. 1983. Evaluation of a cooperative learning strategy. *American Educational Research Journal*, 20: 687–696.

Mostache, H. S., and P. Bragonier. 1981. An observational study of social comparison in preschoolers. *Child Development*, 52: 376–378.

Moulton, R. W. 1965. Effects of success and failure on level of aspiration as related to achievement motives. *Journal of Personality and Social Psychology*, 1: 399–406.

Murphy, P. D., and M. M. Brown. 1970. Conceptual systems and teaching styles. *American Educational Research Journal*, 7: 529–540.

Murray, D. M., and J. Bisanz. 1987. *Children's concepts of intelligence: Relations between prior knowledge and subsequent judgments.* Manuscript, University of Alberta.

Nakamura, C. Y., and D. Finck. 1973. Effect of social or task orientation and evaluative situations on performance. *Child Development*, 44: 83–93.

National Commission on Excellence in Education. 1983. *A nation at risk: The imperative for educational reform.* Washington, D.C.: U.S. Government Printing Office.

Nicholls, J. G. 1972. Creativity in the person who will never produce anything original and useful: The concept of creativity as a normally distributed trait. *American Psychologist*, 27: 717–727.

——— 1975. Causal attributions and other achievement-related cognitions: Effects of task-outcomes, attainment value and sex. *Journal of Personality and Social Psychology*, 31: 379–389.

——— 1976a. Effort is virtuous, but it's better to have ability: Evaluative responses to perceptions of effort and ability. *Journal of Research in Personality*, 10: 306–315.

——— 1976b. When a scale measures more than its name denotes: The case of the test anxiety scale for children. *Journal of Consulting and Clinical Psychology*, 44: 976–985.

—— 1978. The development of the concepts of effort and ability, perception of own attainment, and the understanding that difficult tasks require more ability. *Child Development*, 49: 800–814.

—— 1979a. Development of perception of own attainment and causal attributions for success and failure in reading. *Journal of Educational Psychology*, 71: 94–99.

—— 1979b. Quality and equality in intellectual development: The role of motivation in education. *American Psychologist*, 34: 1071–84.

—— 1980a. A re-examination of boys' and girls' causal attributions for success and failure based on New Zealand data. In L. J. Fyans, ed., *Recent trends in achievement motivation theory and research*, pp. 266–288. New York: Plenum.

—— 1980b. The development of the concept of difficulty. *Merrill-Palmer Quarterly*, 26: 271–281.

—— 1980c. Motivation for intellectual development and performance: An integrative framework. Paper in "Motivation in education: State of the art"; symposium conducted at the meeting of the American Educational Research Association, Boston, April.

—— 1980d. An intentional theory of achievement motivation. Paper in "Attributional approaches to human motivation;" symposium presented at the Center for Interdisciplinary Research, University of Bielefeld, West Germany, July.

—— 1983. Conceptions of ability and achievement motivation: A theory and its applications for education. In S. G. Paris, G. M. Olson, and H. W. Stevenson, eds., *Learning and motivation in the classroom*. pp. 211–237. Hillsdale, N.J.: Erlbaum.

—— 1984a. Achievement motivation: Conceptions of ability, subjective experience, task choice, and performance. *Psychological Review*, 91: 328–346.

—— 1984b. Conceptions of ability and achievement motivation. In R. Ames and C. Ames, eds., *Research on motivation in education*, vol. 1, *Student motivation*, pp. 39–73. New York: Academic Press.

Nicholls, J. G., and A. T. Miller. 1983. The differentiation of the concepts of difficulty and ability. *Child Development*, 54: 951–959.

—— 1984a. Development and its discontents: The differentiation of the concept of ability. In J. G. Nicholls, ed., *Advances in motivation and achievement*, vol. 3, *The development of achievement motivation*, pp. 185–218. Greenwich, Conn.: JAI Press.

—— 1984b. Reasoning about the ability of self and others: A developmental study. *Child Development*, 55: 1990–99.

—— 1985. Differentiation of the concepts of luck and skill. *Developmental Psychology*, 21: 76–82.

Nicholls, J. G., and T. A. Thorkildsen. 1987. Achievement goals and beliefs: Individual and classroom differences. Paper presented at the meeting of the Society for Experimental Social Psychology, Charlottesville, October.

Nicholls, J. G., C. M. Jagacinski, and A. T. Miller. 1986. Conceptions of ability in children and adults. In R. Schwarzer, ed., *Self-related cognitions in anxiety and motivation*, pp. 265–284. Hillsdale, N.J.: Erlbaum.

Nicholls, J. G., B. G. Licht, and R. A. Pearl. 1982. Some dangers of using personality questionnaires to study personality. *Psychological Bulletin*, 92: 572–580.

Nicholls, J. G., M. Patashnick, and G. Mettetal. 1986. Conceptions of ability and intelligence. *Child Development*, 57: 636–645.

Nicholls, J. G., M. Patashnick, and S. B. Nolen. 1985. Adolescents' theories of education. *Journal of Educational Psychology*, 77: 683–692.

Nicholls, J. G., P. C. Cheung, J. Lauer, and M. Patashnick. 1988a. Individual differences in academic motivation: Perceived ability, goals, beliefs, and values. *Learning and individual differences* (forthcoming).

Nicholls, J. G., P. Cobb, T. Wood, E. Yackel, and M. Patashnick. 1988b. Goals and beliefs in mathematics: Individual differences and consequences of a constructivist program. Manuscript.

Nisbett, R., and L. Ross. 1980. *Human inference: Strategies and shortcomings of social judgment*. Englewood Cliffs, N.J.: Prentice-Hall.

Nisbett, S. M. 1974. Education and equality: Israel and the United States compared. *Society*, 11, no. 3: 56–66.

Nolen, S. B. 1988. Reasons for studying: Motivational orientations and study strategies. *Cognition and Instruction* (forthcoming).

Norem, J. K., and N. Cantor. 1986. Defensive pessimism: Harnessing anxiety as motivation. *Journal of Personality and Social Psychology*, 51: 1208–17.

O'Connor, P., J. W. Atkinson, and M. Horner. 1966. Motivational implications of ability grouping in schools. In J. W. Atkinson and N. T. Feather, eds., *A theory of achievement motivation*, pp. 231–248. New York: Wiley.

Pascarella, E. T., H. J. Walberg., L. K. Junker, and G. D. Haertel. 1981. Continuing motivation in science for early and late adolescents. *American Educational Research Journal*, 18: 439–452.

Patashnick, M., and J. G. Nicholls. 1988. Adolescents' theories of education and attributions for the expected causes of success in the world of work. Paper presented at the meeting of the American Educational Research Association, New Orleans, April.

Patten, R. L., and L. A. White. 1977. Independent effects of achievement motivation and overt attribution on achievement behavior. *Motivation and Emotion*, 1: 39–59.

Paul, G. L., and C. W. Erikson. 1964. Effects of test anxiety on "real-life" examinations. *Journal of Personality*, 32: 480–494.

Pepitone, E. A. 1980. *Children in cooperation and competition: Toward a developmental social psychology*. Lexington, Mass.: D. C. Heath.

Perez, R. C. 1973. The effect of experimentally induced failure, self-esteem, and sex on cognitive differentiation. *Journal of Abnormal Psychology*, 81: 74–79.

Perry, S. E. 1978. *San Francisco scavengers: Dirty work and pride of ownership*. Berkeley: University of California Press.

Perry, W. G., Jr. 1970. *Forms of intellectual and ethical development in the college years*. New York: Holt, Rinehart, and Winston.

———— 1981. Cognitive and ethical growth: The making of meaning. In A. W. Chickering, ed., *The modern American college*, pp. 76–116. San Francisco: Jossey-Bass.

Peterson, P. L. 1979. Direct instruction reconsidered. In P. L. Peterson and H. J. Walberg, eds., *Research on teaching: Concepts, findings, and implications*, pp. 57–69. Berkeley, Calif.: McCutchan.

Piaget, J. 1952. *The origins of intelligence in children*, trans. M. Cook. New York: International Universities Press.

———— 1970. Piaget's theory. In P. H. Mussen, ed., *Carmichael's manual of child psychology*, 3d ed., I, 703–732. New York: Wiley.

Pinter, R., and J. Lev. 1940. Worries of school children. *Pedagogical Seminary*, 56: 67–76.

Pintrich, P. R., and P. C. Blumenfeld. 1985. Classroom experience and children's self-perceptions of ability, effort, and conduct. *Journal of Educational Psychology*, 77: 646–657.

Radke-Yarrow, M., C. Zahn-Waxler, and M. Chapman. 1983. In E. M. Hetherington, ed., *Handbook of Child Psychology*, 4th ed., vol. 4, *Socialization, personality, and social development*, pp. 469–545. New York: Wiley.

Rainey, R. G. 1965. The effects of directed vs. non-directed laboratory work on high school chemistry achievement. *Journal of Research in Science Teaching*, 3: 286–292.

Rawls, J. 1971. *A theory of justice*. Cambridge, Mass.: Harvard University Press.

Raynor, J. O., and I. S. Rubin. 1971. Effects of achievement motivation and future orientation on level of performance. *Journal of Personality and Social Psychology*, 17: 36–41.

Raynor, J. O., and C. P. Smith. 1966. Achievement-related motives and risk-taking in games of skill and chance. *Journal of Personality*, 34: 176–198.

Renshaw, P. D., and R. Gardner. 1987. Parental goals and strategies in teaching contexts: An exploration of "activity theory" with mothers and fathers of preschool children. Paper presented at the meeting of the Society for Research in Child Development, Baltimore.

Report on Education Research 1986. Ed seeks research for "What works II." July 30, vol. 18, no. 16, pp. 1–2.

Resnick, L. B. 1983. Toward a cognitive theory of instruction. In S. G. Paris, G. M. Olson, and H. W. Stevenson, eds., *Learning and motivation in the classroom*, pp. 5–38. Hillsdale, N.J.: Erlbaum.

Rest, J. R. 1979. *Revised manual for the Defining Issues Test*. Minneapolis: Minnesota Moral Research Projects.

Revelle, W., and E. J. Michaels. 1976. The theory of achievement motivation revisited: The implications of inertial tendencies. *Psychological Review*, 83: 394–404.

Rheinberg, F. 1983. Achievement evaluation: A fundamental difference and its motivational consequences. *Studies in Educational Evaluation*, 9: 185–194.

Rholes, W. S., J. Blackwell, C. Jordan, and C. Walters. 1980. A developmental study of learned helplessness. *Developmental Psychology*, 16: 616–624.

Roberts, C. G. 1974. Effects of achievement and social environment on risk-taking. *Research Quarterly*, 45: 42–55.

——— 1984. Children's achievement motivation in sport. In J. G. Nicholls, ed., *Advances in motivation and achievement*, vol. 3, *The development of achievement motivation*, pp. 251–281. Greenwich, Conn.: JAI Press.

Roberts, G. C., D. A. Kleiber, and J. L. Duda. 1981. An analysis of motivation in children's sport: The role of perceived competence in participation. *Journal of Sport Psychology*, 3: 206–216.

Roe, A. 1952. *The making of a scientist*. New York: Dodd, Mead.

Rorty, R. 1979. *Philosophy and the mirror of nature*. Princeton, N.J.: Princeton University Press.

——— 1983. Method and morality. In N. Haan, R. N. Bellah, P. Rabinow, and W. M. Sullivan, eds., *Social science as moral enquiry*, pp. 155–176. New York: Columbia University Press.

Rosenbaum, J. E. 1976. *Making inequality: The hidden curriculum of high school tracking*. New York: Wiley.

Rosenholtz, S. J., and C. Simpson. 1984. The formation of ability conceptions: Developmental trend or social construction? *Review of Educational Research*, 54: 31–63.

Rosenshine, B. V. 1979. Content, time and direct instruction. In P. L. Peterson and H. J. Walberg, eds., *Research on teaching*, pp. 28–56. Berkeley, Calif.: McCutchan.

Rosenshine, B., and R. Stevens. 1986. Teaching functions. In M. C. Wittrock, ed., *Handbook of research on teaching*, 3d ed., pp. 376–391. New York: Macmillan.

Ruble, D. N., N. S. Feldman, and A. K. Boggiano. 1976. Social comparison between young children in achievement situations. *Developmental Psychology*, 12: 192–197.

Russell, D. G., and I. G. Sarason. 1965. Test anxiety, sex, and experimental conditions in relation to anagram solution. *Journal of Personality and Social Psychology*, 1, 493–496.

Rutter, M., B. Maughan, P. Mortimore, J. Ouston, and A. Smith. 1979. *Fifteen thousand hours: Secondary schools and their effects on children.* Cambridge, Mass.: Harvard University Press.

Ryan, R. M. 1982. Control and information in the intrapersonal sphere: An extension of cognitive evaluation theory. *Journal of Personality and Social Psychology*, 43: 450–461.

Ryan, R. M., J. P. Connell, and E. L. Deci. 1985. A motivational analysis of self-determination and self-regulation in education. In R. Ames and C. Ames, eds., *Research on motivation in education*, vol. 2, *The classroom milieu*, pp. 13–51. New York: Academic Press.

Safire, W. 1980. *On language*. New York: Time Books.

Salili, F., M. L. Maehr, R. L. Sorenson, and L. J. Fyans. 1976. A further consideration of the effects of evaluation on motivation. *American Educational Research Journal*, 13: 85–102.

Sansone, C. 1986. A question of competence: The effects of competence and task feedback on intrinsic interest. *Journal of Personality and Social Psychology*, 51: 918–931.

Sarason, I. G. 1958. The effects of anxiety, reassurance, and meaningfulness of material to be learned in verbal learning. *Journal of Experimental Psychology*, 56: 472–477.

——— 1959. Relationships of measures of anxiety and experimental instructions to word association test performance. *Journal of Abnormal and Social Psychology*, 59: 37–42.

——— 1961. The effects of anxiety and threat on solution of a difficult task. *Journal of Abnormal and Social Psychology*, 62: 165–168.

——— 1975. Anxiety and self-preoccupations. In I. G. Sarason and C. D. Spielberger, eds., *Stress and anxiety*, II, pp. 27–44. Washington, D.C.: Wiley-Hemisphere.

Sarason, I. G., and J. Minard. 1962. Test anxiety, experimental instructions and the Wechsler Adult Intelligence Scale. *Journal of Educational Psychology*, 53: 299–302.

Sarason, I. G., and E. G. Palola. 1960. The relationships of test and general anxiety, difficulty of task, and experimental instructions to performance. *Journal of Experimental Psychology*, 59: 185–191.

Sarason, S. B. 1971. *The culture of the school and the problem of change.* Boston: Allyn and Bacon.

——— 1977. *Work, aging, and social change: Professionals and the one-career imperative.* New York: Free Press.

——— 1981. *Psychology misdirected.* New York: Free Press.

Sarason, S. B., G. Mandler, and P. G. Craighill. 1952. The effect of differential instructions on anxiety and learning. *Journal of Abnormal and Social Psychology*, 47: 561–565.

Schalon, C. L. 1968. Effect of self-esteem upon performance following failure stress. *Journal of Consulting and Clinical Psychology*, 32: 497.

Scheier, M. F., and C. S. Carver. 1983. Self-directed attention and the comparison of self with standards. *Journal of Experimental Social Psychology*, 19: 205–222.

Schneider, K. 1973. *Motivation unter Erfolgsriskio.* Gotingen: Hogrefe.

——— 1984. Subjective uncertainty and achievement and exploratory behavior in preschool children. In J. G. Nicholls, ed., *Advances in motivation and achievement*, vol. 3, *The development of achievement motivation*, pp. 57–72. Greenwich, Conn.: JAI Press.

Schneider, K., K. Hanne, and B. Lehman. 1987. The development of children's achievement-related expectancies and subjective uncertainty. Manuscript.

Schunk, D. H. 1982. Effects of effort attributional feedback on children's perceived self-efficacy and achievement. *Journal of Educational Psychology*, 74: 548–556.

Schwarzer, R., ed. 1986. *Self-related cognitions in anxiety and motivation.* Hillsdale, N.J.: Erlbaum.

Sears, P. S. 1940. Levels of aspiration in academically successful and unsuccessful children. *Journal of Abnormal and Social Psychology*, 35: 498–536.

——— 1941. Level of aspiration in relation to some variables of personality: Clinical studies. *Journal of Social Psychology*, 14: 311–336.

Selman, R. L., W. Beardslee, L. H. Schultz, M. Krupa, and D. Podorefsky. 1986. Assessing adolescent interpersonal negotiation strategies: Toward the integration of structural and functional models. *Developmental Psychology*, 22: 450–459.

Semin, G. R. 1980. A gloss on attributional theory. *British Journal of Social and Clinical Psychology*, 19: 291–300.

Sharan, S. 1980. Cooperative learning in small groups: Recent methods and effects on achievement, attitudes, and ethnic relations. *Review of Educational Research*, 50: 241–271.

Sharan, S., P. Kussell, R. Hertz-Lazarowitz, Y. Bejarano, S. Raviv, and Y. Sharan. 1984. *Cooperative learning in the classroom: Research in desegregated schools*. Hillsdale, N.J.: Erlbaum.

Shrauger, J. S. 1972. Self-esteem and reactions to being observed by others. *Journal of Personality and Social Psychology*, 23: 192–200.

―――― 1975. Responses to evaluation as a function of initial self-perceptions. *Psychological Bulletin*, 82: 581–596.

Siegler, R. S., and D. D. Richards. 1982. The development of intelligence. In R. J. Sternberg, ed., *Handbook of human intelligence*, pp. 897–971. New York: Cambridge University Press.

Skinner, E. A. 1985. Action, control, judgments, and the structure of control experience. *Psychological Review*, 92: 39–58.

Slavin, R. E. 1978. Student teams and academic divisions. *Journal of Research and Development in Education*, 12: 39–49.

―――― 1983. When does cooperative learning increase student achievement? *Psychological Bulletin*, 94: 429–445.

Smedslund, J. 1961. The acquisition of conservation of substance and weight in children: I. Introduction. *Scandinavian Journal of Psychology*, 2: 11–20.

Smith, M. B. 1974. *Humanizing social psychology*, San Francisco: Jossey-Bass.

Smith, K., D. W. Johnson, and R. T. Johnson. 1981. Can conflict be constructive? Controversy versus concurrence-seeking in learning groups. *Journal of Educational Psychology*, 73: 651–663.

Sohn, D. 1977. Affect-generating powers of effort and ability self attributions of academic success and failure. *Journal of Educational Psychology*, 69: 500–505.

Sorrentino, R. M., and E. T. Higgins, eds. 1986. *Handbook of motivation and cognition: Foundations of social behavior*. New York: Guilford.

Spence, J. T., and R. L. Helmreich. 1983. Achievement related motives and behaviors. In J. T. Spence, ed., *Achievement and achievement motives: Psychological and sociological perspectives*, pp. 7–74. San Francisco: W. H. Freeman.

Stake, R., and J. Easley. 1978. *Case studies in science education*, vol. 2, *Design overview and general findings*. Washington, D.C.: National Science Foundation, Directorate for Science Education.

Standring, D. E. 1976. Values, value change, and attitudes to occupations as a function of moral judgment level. M.A. thesis, Victoria University of Wellington, New Zealand.

Stebbins, R. A. 1977. The meaning of academic performance: How teachers define a classroom situation. In P. Woods and M. Hammersley, eds., *School experience: Explorations in the sociology of education*, pp. 28–55. New York: St. Martin's Press.

Steffe, L. P., E. von Glasersfeld, J. Richards, and P. Cobb. 1983. *Children's counting types: Philosophy, theory and applications*. New York: Praeger.

Steiger, J. H. 1980. Tests for comparing elements of a correlation matrix. *Psychological Bulletin*, 87: 245–251.

Sternberg, R. J., B. E. Conway, J. L. Ketron, and M. Bernstein. 1981. Peoples' conceptions of intelligence. *Journal of Personality and Social Psychology*, 41: 37–55.

Stipek, D. J. 1981. Children's perceptions of their own and their classmates' ability. *Journal of Educational Psychology*, 73: 404–410.

——— 1984. Young children's performance expectations: Logical analysis or wishful thinking? In J. G. Nicholls, ed., *Advances in motivation and achievement*, vol. 3, *The development achievement motivation*, pp. 33–56. Greenwich, Conn.: JAI Press.

Stipek, D. J., and D. H. Daniels. 1987. Declining perceptions of competence: A consequence of changes in the child or in the educational environment. Paper presented at the meeting of the American Educational Research Association, Washington, D.C., April.

Stipek, D. J., and L. M. Tannatt. 1984. Children's judgments of their own and their peers' academic competence. *Journal of Educational Psychology*, 76: 75–84.

Stott, D. H. 1961. An empirical approach to motivation based on the behavior of a young child. *Journal of Child Psychology and Psychiatry*, 2: 97–117.

Strayer, F. F., and J. Strayer. 1976. An ethological analysis of social agonism and dominance relations among preschool children. *Child Development*, 47: 980–989.

Surber, C. F. 1980. The development of reversible operations in judgments of ability, effort, and performance. *Child Development*, 51: 1018–29.

Taylor, C. W., and R. L. Ellison. 1967. Biographical predictors of scientific performance. *Science*, 155: 1075–80.

Thelen, H. A. 1960. *Education and the human quest*. New York: Harper and Brothers.

Thomas, J. W. 1980. Agency and achievement: Self-management and self-regard. *Review of Educational Research*, 50: 213–240.

Thomas, L. 1982. The art of teaching science. *New York Times Magazine*, March 14, 89–93.

Thorkildsen, T. A. 1988. Theories of education among academically able adolescents. *Contemporary Educational Psychology* (forthcoming).

Toulmin, S. 1983. The construal of reality: Criticism in modern and post modern science. In W. J. T. Mitchell, ed., *The politics of interpretation*, pp. 99–117. Chicago: University of Chicago Press.

Trope, Y. 1979. Uncertainty-reducing properties of achievement tasks. *Journal of Personality and Social Psychology*, 37: 1505–18.

Trope, Y., and P. Brickman. 1975. Difficulty and diagnosticity as determinants of choice among tasks. *Journal of Personality and Social Psychology*, 31: 918–925.

Tuchman, B. 1980. The decline of quality. *New York Times Magazine*, November 2, 38–41, 104.

Turiel, E. 1983. *The development of social knowledge: Morality and convention*. Cambridge: Cambridge University Press.

Valian, V. 1977. Learning to work. In S. Ruddick and P. Daniels, eds., *Working it out*, pp. 163–178. New York: Pantheon.

Veroff, J. 1969. Social comparison and the development of achievement motivation. In C. P. Smith, ed., *Achievement-related motives in children*, pp. 46–101. New York: Russell Sage.

—————— 1977. Process vs. impact in men's and women's motivation. *Psychology of Women Quarterly*, 1: 283–293.

Vondracek, F. W., and R. M. Lerner. 1982. Vocational role development in adolescence. In B. B. Wolman, ed., *Handbook of developmental psychology*, pp. 602–614. Englewood Cliffs, N.J.: Prentice-Hall.

Wallach, M. A., and N. Kogan. 1965. *Modes of thinking in young children*. New York: Holt, Rinehart, and Winston.

Walzer, M. 1983. *Spheres of justice: A defense of pluralism and equality*. New York: Basic Books.

Wang, M. C., and B. Stiles. 1976. An investigation of children's concept of self-responsibility for their school learning. *American Educational Research Journal*, 13: 159–179.

Watson, J. D. 1968. *The double helix: A personal account of the discovery of the structure of DNA*. New York: Atheneum.

Weber, M. 1958. *The protestant ethic and the spirit of capitalism*, trans. Talcott Parsons. New York: Scribner.

Weiner, B. 1966. The role of success and failure in the learning of easy and complex tasks. *Journal of Personality and Social Psychology*, 3: 339–343.

—————— 1979. A theory of motivation for some classroom experiences. *Journal of Educational Psychology*, 71: 3–25.

—————— 1984. Principles for a theory of student motivation and their application within an attributional framework. In R. Ames and C. Ames, eds., *Research on motivation in education*, vol. 1, *Student motivation*, pp. 15–38. New York: Academic Press.

—————— 1985. An attributional theory of achievement motivation and emotion. *Psychological Review*, 92: 548–573.

Weiner, B., and S. J. Handel. 1985. A cognition-emotion-action sequence: Anticipated emotional consequences of causal attributions and reported communication strategy. *Developmental Psychology*, 21: 102–107.

Weiner, B., and A. Kukla. 1970. An attributional analysis of achievement motivation. *Journal of Personality and Social Psychology*, 15: 1–20.

Weiner, B., and K. Schneider. 1971. Drive versus cognitive theory: A reply to Boor and Harmon. *Journal of Personality and Social Psychology*, 18: 285–262.

Weiner, B., R. Nierenberg, and M. Goldstein. 1976. Social learning (locus of control) versus attributional (causal stability) interpretations of expectancy of success. *Journal of Personality*, 44: 52–68.

Weiner, Y. 1970. The effects of "task" and "ego-oriented" performance on two kinds of overcompensation inequity. *Organizational Behavior and Human Performance*, 5: 191–208.

Weinstein, R. 1976. Reading group membership in first grade: Teacher behaviors and pupil experience over time. *Journal of Educational Psychology*, 68: 103–116.

Weinstein, R. S., and S. E. Middlestadt. 1979. Student perceptions of teacher interactions with male high and low achievers. *Journal of Educational Psychology*, 71: 421–431.

Weinstein, R. S., H. H. Marshall, K. A. Brattesani, and S. E. Middlestadt. 1982. Students' perceptions of differential teacher treatment in open and traditional classrooms. *Journal of Educational Psychology*, 74: 678–692.

Weisz, J. R. 1984. Contingency judgments and achievement behavior: Deciding what is controllable and when to try. In J. G. Nicholls, ed., *Advances in motivation and achievement*, vol. 3, *The development of achievement motivation*, pp. 107–136. Greenwich, Conn.: JAI Press.

Weisz, J. R., K. O. Yeates, D. Robertson, and J. C. Beckman. 1982. Perceived contingency of skill and chance events: A developmental analysis. *Developmental Psychology*, 18: 898–905.

Wellman, H. M. 1985. The child's theory of mind: The development of conceptions of cognition. In S. R. Yussen, ed., *The growth of reflection in children*, pp. 169–206. New York: Academic Press.

West, G. K., and E. S. Wood. 1970. Academic pressures on public school students. *Educational Leadership*, 3: 585–589.

White, R. W. 1959. Motivation reconsidered. The concept of competence. *Psychological Review*, 66: 297–333.

—————— 1973. The concept of healthy personality: What do we really mean? *Counseling Psychologist*, 4, no. 2: 3–12.

Willis, P. 1977. *Learning to labor: How working class kids get working class jobs.* New York: Columbia University Press.

Wimmer, H., J. Wachter, and J. Perner. 1982. Cognitive autonomy of the development of moral evaluation of achievement. *Child Development*, 53: 668–676.

Wine, J. 1971. Test anxiety and direction of attention. *Psychological Bulletin*, 76: 92–104.

Woodley, R. 1974. Soap box derby. *Harper's*, August, 62–69.

Wordsworth, W. 1904. Intimations of immortality from recollections of early childhood. In *The complete poetical works of William Wordsworth: Cambridge edition*, pp. 353–356. Boston: Houghton Mifflin.

Ziegler, S. 1981. The effectiveness of cooperative learning teams for increasing cross-ethnic friendship: Additional evidence. *Human Organization*, 40: 264–268.

Zuckier, H. 1986. The paradigmatic and narrative modes in goal-guided inference. In R. M. Sorrentino and E. T. Higgins, eds., *Handbook of motivation and cognition: Foundations of social behavior*, pp. 465–502. New York: Guildford.

Index